Suakin, 1885

Suakin, 1885
The Campaign against Osman Digna in the Sudan

ILLUSTRATED

Suakin, 1885

E Gambier Parry

Suakim, '85

Norman Robert Stewart

The 5th (Royal Irish) Lancers during the Nile Expedition, 1884-85

Walter Temple Willcox

LEONAUR

Suakin, 1885
The Campaign against Osman Digna in the Sudan
Suakin, 1885
by E Gambier Parry
Suakim, '85
by Norman Robert Stewart
The 5th (Royal Irish) Lancers during the Nile Expedition, 1884-85
by Walter Temple Willcox

ILLUSTRATED

FIRST EDITION

Leonaur is an imprint of Oakpast Ltd
Copyright in this form © 2022 Oakpast Ltd

ISBN: 978-1-915234-52-0 (hardcover)
ISBN: 978-1-915234-53-7 (softcover)

http://www.leonaur.com

Publisher's Notes

The views expressed in this book are not necessarily those of the publisher.

Contents

Preface	7
The Voyage Out	9
Suakin	19
Landing	30
Night Attacks	40
Preparation	59
The Advance	76
Hasheen	85
The "Zariba"	102
Convoys	120
Tamai	134
Hospital	149
Suakim, '85 *Norman Robert Stewart*	155
The 5th (Royal Irish) Lancers during the Nile Expedition, 1884-85 *Walter Temple Willcox*	181

Preface

The following chapters were written to while away many hours of pain and suffering, and for the amusement of some few friends.

They contain a simple record of the events which made up a war of peculiar privations and dangers, due to the climate we toiled in and the foe we fought against.

Every statement made may be taken as fact, and the experiences are those of one who took part in the campaign—the author.

No literary merit is claimed for the story, such as it is, and the indulgence of critics is therefore asked on behalf of one who has carried a sword more often than a pen.

CHAPTER 1

The Voyage Out

In the dark days towards the end of January news reached England telling us the exertions of our soldiers on the Nile had been rendered fruitless by treachery at Khartoum. For several days the most conflicting accounts were received as to the real state of affairs. At one moment Gordon was said to have escaped the general massacre and to have retired towards the equator, at another that he was defending himself in a church; and then later on that he had fallen—

His front with wounds unnumbered riven,
His back to earth, his face to Heaven.

Few will ever forget those days; a dull sense of pain was felt by all as the cry was raised throughout the length and breadth of the land—Too late!

In spite of the months of toil, and all the hardships and privations connected with Lord Wolseley's advance up the Nile; in spite of the hazardous march from Korti to Metemmeh and the shedding of some of England's best blood, a fragment of the expedition had only sighted the walls of Khartoum to find that treachery had been beforehand, and that one of England's greatest heroes had fallen when the succour was almost within reach. But this was no time for inaction, the *raison d'être* of the Nile expedition was no more, the power of the *Mahdi* was enhanced, and the fall of Khartoum had brought thousands of recruits to his standards.

A perpetual succession of cabinet councils, the closing of the telegraph wires for all messages except those from the government to Lord Wolseley for two or three days, and then the decision was promulgated that a fresh expedition was to be despatched immediately to operate from Suakin.

There was no doubt about the feeling of the country at this time.

We had been too late, it was true, but we must strike afresh now, strike with an irresistible force, and quell once and for all the power of the fanatic and the false prophet in the Sûdan.

It was no time now for further vacillation. The people of England demanded action; prompt, energetic, decisive. The cost was not to be counted; cost what it might a blow in real earnest was to be struck this time, and the power of the *Mahdi* crushed out for ever.

For a period of a fortnight there was a hurry and a bustle in all the war departments. Hundreds of fresh hands were taken on at Woolwich, and a scene of activity took place in the yards there such as has not been witnessed since the days of the Crimea.

In a few days the details of the new expedition appeared in the press, a number of vessels were immediately chartered for conveying this force to the scene of operations; and orders were sent out to India and Egypt for the immediate purchase of a large number of camels, mules, and horses, for the use of the Transport. A week followed during which the various portions of the force were inspected by H.R.H. the Commander-in-Chief, and then every day a constant succession of transports left the shores of England, carrying a force more perfectly equipped in every detail than ever force was before.

On the evening of the 11th of February, I was on my way home from the club, where I had been talking to various friends about the all-absorbing topic of the day, walking along the streets thinking what lucky fellows they were who were sailing the following week, and wishing, like every other soldier, that I could get a place somehow or other. I had reached my door when my reveries were interrupted by a telegraph-boy saying "Is this for you, sir?"

Quite unsuspicious of what it contained, telegrams in these days being pretty well as plentiful as letters, I was somewhat astonished when I found the purport of the message was as follows:

> From the Adjutant-General.—Be so good as to hold yourself in readiness to proceed to Suakin at once, and report yourself here the first thing tomorrow morning.

Had it not been to save the feelings of my wife, and otherwise alarming the household, I should have relieved myself by a good cheer; as it was, however, I kept my feelings to myself, and commenced at once to put my affairs in order, and to make out a list of things I should require, and which were to be purchased the following day.

The next morning early found me in Pall Mall, reporting myself.

"Yes," said my interviewer, "you must proceed to Ireland at once, and fetch over some men from there in time to sail from Southampton on Tuesday next."

I must confess that, in spite of all my military ardour, this was rather a blow. To be ordered out was one thing, but to be started off to Ireland at two hours' notice, without a particle of kit belonging to me, was quite another pair of shoes. Putting on my pleasantest manner, therefore, and giving my assurance that I was perfectly ready to go anywhere I was ordered, I finished up by suggesting mildly that, being a married man with encumbrances, it was just a trifle inconvenient.

"Well," said Sir —— "we will see if we can manage it. Sit down a moment."

In a few minutes my destination was, I am thankful to say, changed for Aldershot, and I went down there the same afternoon to ask for a couple of days' leave.

Monday, 16th of February, found me again at Aldershot, and the next morning at an early hour, and in drenching rain, we marched to the station *en route* for Southampton. We were all on board Transport No. 7 by one o'clock, and by three o'clock that afternoon were clearing our decks of visitors and saying goodbye to many friends, while bands played and crowds cheered again and again on the wharf. It is always an impressive sight watching troops embark for active service, but one thing there is no doubt about-it is worse for those that are left behind on the shore than for those in the ship.

The next morning, we were out of sight of Old England, and getting into what seemed like dirty weather; and so it turned out, for in a few hours our ship was kicking her heels very freely, and many of us were feeling not quite the men we did twenty-four hours before. The Bay of Biscay kept up its old character, and we got severely knocked about. The men were in a miserable condition, and the troop decks were swamped with water and littered with every conceivable article to be found in a soldier's kit. I always find it very difficult to rise to the occasion at sea.

"A life on the ocean wave" seems a horrible fate. This time proved no exception to the rule, and like many others on board, I spent two days in my bunk on a little ship's biscuit.

Sunday afternoon brought us to "Gib.," which was looking very beautiful and very grand, as it always does. We were not long in getting on shore, and as we were to stop for four hours to take some gunners on board, we made up a party and drove down into the town to luncheon at the "Royal." "Gib." was looking its best; there had been plenty of rain, so wild flowers of all sorts abounded. After a luncheon, such as we had not eaten since leaving England, we took a walk round the North Front, and out to the neutral ground.

There are few more imposing views than the Old Rock presents from the neutral ground. There is a wonderful air of majesty and strength about the place, and England will lose one of her brightest jewels when Gibraltar ceases to be her property. It *is* a place to be proud of, and there are few inches of it that are not familiar to me, as I was there more than five years one time.

It was dark before we put to sea again, and as we rounded Europa Point a band was playing "Auld Lang Syne," and we could hear away in the darkness the sounds of cheering coming to us across the still waters of the Mediterranean. The next morning found us pitching and tossing about merrily in a heavy sea, with a magnificent view of the Sierra Nevada on our port quarter, the snow-clad peaks standing high up in the sky and gleaming brightly in the warm sunshine. It is almost always rough in this part of the Mediterranean, and a severe tossing is, as a rule, experienced until Cape Gata is rounded, when the wind and sea often drop suddenly. We were very unfortunate on this occasion as, by the afternoon, we were only doing four knots instead of thirteen or fourteen, our usual pace. The sea was dead ahead and broke clear over us from stem to stern.

The destruction of crockery must have been considerable, the noise was almost indescribable; it was as if we were a big tin box full of pieces of china which some big giant had picked up and shaken to his heart's content. Soon after this we ran into lovely weather, the sun shone bright and warm, and the sea danced past us with its waves of deep sapphire hue. It was now time to set to work, for we had much to do in the next fortnight. The men had all to be fitted with their khaki kit and served out with their cholera belts, goggles, spine-protectors, and veils. It certainly seemed as if the people at home had determined no pains should be spared to protect the soldier against the climate and the sun, although we on our side felt bound to confess that when we appeared in full battle array we resembled a number of perambulating Christmas-trees more than anything else.

We were also anxious to get the men to a little position drill, for many among them were young hands and had much to learn. Among my own men I found many who knew nothing whatever about a rifle, and many more who had never fired a shot; so, explaining to them that their own safety, to say nothing of my own, lay in their being able to use their rifles with effect, we started to work in real earnest and two parades a day of an hour and a half each was the order. But it was not to be all work and no play on board, for we were all intent upon having a merry voyage and enjoying ourselves while we could.

A list was opened for a series of athletic sports, and in a short time the entries showed that should have many an afternoon's occupation. The events were as follows:—Long jump standing, wheelbarrow race, tug of war, Chinese puzzle, and cock-fighting, and much amusement was derived every afternoon by carrying out the programme.

But we were going to have evening entertainments besides this, and many of us were hard at work getting up a concert. Wherever there are soldiers you may depend upon it you will have music-music of a sort certainly, and not quite of a "Monday pop" order, but still music which gives a great deal of pleasure, and a great deal of amusement, and is not altogether without a little sentiment and pathos sometimes.

By good luck we had among the officers two excellent pianists, and several performers on the *mandolin*, banjo, accordion, and penny whistle; we also had one of the best performers on the bones it was ever my lot to hear. To fall back on, we had also in the company a professional dancer and a professional clown, also a conjuror; so, we were a merry family all round. Our days were taken up, then, as follows, and pretty much like another. *Réveille* sounded at six, then came breakfast at eight, prayers at nine, when the whole company were marched aft and at the word "caps off" the clergyman began reading a psalm followed by a few prayers, and finishing with the one for us soldiers.

There was always something impressive to me in this service; it only lasted ten minutes, but everyone was very attentive and all seemed to join in it. Prayers over, there came the first parade at 9.30, then dinners at twelve o'clock, and parade again at 1.45. At 3.30 we were running off the heats in the various athletic events till five o'clock, when "retreat" sounded and hammocks were drawn; the men also had their evening meal, but we did not have our dinner till 6.30. At 7.45, the piano having been carried on deck, music followed, till "First Post" sounded at 8.30 p.m., "Last Post" half an hour later, and "Lights out!" at 9.15. So ended the ordinary day's routine at sea.

But I must go back a little. The next land we sighted was the Galita Islands, which are sadly in want of a lighthouse. These islands belong to Italy, and though the government would be glad to erect a lighthouse there, people refuse to live on these islands, as they are said to be haunted—at least so runs the story.

On the 26th of February we saw Cape Bonn, on the African coast, far away on our starboard beam, and about midday we passed quite close to Pantalaria, a very fine-looking place, and used by the Italians as a convict station.

At 9.30 p.m. on the same day, we passed Gozo, and at 10 p.m. we sighted Valetta lights. After this we saw no land till we reached Port Said at 4 a.m. on the 2nd of March. Meanwhile our concerts were in full swing. The officers began by giving one to the men, the programme consisting of two piano solos, a comic song or so, two vocal duets, and a reading. The following night the men returned the compliment by giving a concert to the officers, and most amusing it was. A private soldier took command of the piano, and, defying any interference on the part of the singer, continued to bang out an accompaniment sometimes at the top of the piano and sometimes at the bottom, but always alike utterly and hopelessly independent of time and key.

However, everyone appeared very well satisfied, and the pianist above all. There was one man, a sergeant in the A.H.C., who had a really beautiful voice, a high tenor and well trained. He only knew two songs by heart, but these were both very good, and he took the precaution to have as his accompanist the accordion-player. The refrain of the most effective of his songs was one pointing out the uncertainties of life, and finishing with the words—

What is coming, who can tell?

This was encored again and again. The only other song with a certain sadness in it was sung by a trumpeter boy not more than fifteen years of age. He stood up a little nervously before the audience and sang a song the name of which I never heard, but the verses finished with—

It's only a leaf in my Bible,
I picked from my poor mother's grave.

He used to sing this song very frequently, as the men seemed fond of it, but I always noticed there was a certain quietness when it was over, though not from want of appreciation. There were many other well-known songs, and one of the most popular was that old friend the chorus of which runs

Wrap me up in my old stable-jacket,
And say a poor buffer lies low,

And six stalwart comrades shall carry me
With steps solemn, silent, and slow.

It is always a mystery where the things come from, but soldiers never seem at a loss if anything is required, never mind what it may be. In this way, and to our utter astonishment, the professional clown appeared rigged up in a complete fancy kit, with a wig, a very large false nose and spectacles, and a "billycock" hat.

Some excellent step-dancing followed, and then hats off and "God save the Queen," which was never omitted.

Our musical talents were further turned to account, and a choir having been formed, we managed to chant the whole service on Sundays, both morning and evening, very creditably.

The dawn was just breaking as we dropped anchor at Port Said, and as we were to go through the disagreeable proceeding of coaling, everyone who could get ashore did so directly after breakfast. The town lies on a dead level scarcely two feet above the water, and as far as the eye can reach is one endless extent of sand as flat as a billiard-table. We found some good ship-chandlers, where we bought sundry provisions at a price, also one or two shops of the Bon Marché order, where one could obtain anything, from a tea-tray to a double-barrelled gun, or from a Bath bun to a complete suit of Chinese armour. Port Said has, however, been described over and over again, no doubt, so it is not worthwhile wasting many words on it here.

By 11.30 a.m. we were all on board, and shortly afterwards we started to wend our weary way along the canal to Suez. I say "weary way" because this is a very wearisome journey. The speed is limited to five miles an hour, and setting aside constant stoppages, the risk of running aground, and the compulsory halts for the night after 6 p.m., there is nothing to relieve the monotony of the surrounding scenery.

The canal is hemmed in by banks on each side, and as these are in many places high, a sense of breathlessness and suffocation is experienced. We were very unfortunate, as we had only reached the first Gare, some seven miles from Port Said, when the vessel in front of us went aground, and in spite of much tugging and hauling could not be got off again. There was nothing for it then but to make the best of it, so, having made fast to the banks, we took our men ashore in squads of twenty and practised them firing at some extemporised targets in the shape of old biscuit-boxes. This kept us employed till dark, when we returned on board hoping for better luck next day.

There are some curious anomalies regarding the navigation of the canal. If a ship goes aground those behind it must stop too, though there is often plenty of room to pass. If demurrage is claimed by the owners of the vessels thus delayed the sum realised goes to the Canal Company. Again, the company compel every vessel to take one of their pilots; but if a vessel happens to go aground the pilot is not to blame, and moreover the damage that may be done to the banks of the canal by his running the ship ashore is at once claimed against the owners of the vessel. The cost of going through the canal is nine shillings per ton, and a further charge of nine shillings a head for everyone on board except the working hands.

Our ship, therefore, cost the sum of £1,823. This will give some idea of what it must cost the country to send this expedition through the canal. It must be a nice little item in the total expenditure when the number of ships and number of men are taken into consideration.

The first point of any interest after leaving Port Said is the Lake Menzalah, or ancient Serbonian Bog, where the great plague of the fifth century B.C., which afterwards desolated Athens, originated, and from which too almost all the plagues which swept over Asia Minor and across Europe in the Middle Ages are supposed to have had their origin. The shores of the lake, as well as its shallow waters, are almost always covered with thousands upon thousands of flamingos, standing all exactly in the same position and in lines fully three quarters of a mile in length.

Ten miles further on you pass the Gare of El Kantara, through which runs the direct road from Cairo to Jerusalem. There are a few reed and mud huts adjoining the ferry, and it was here we saw the first of our future friends—a camel. We dragged along slowly and lazily in the burning sunshine, for the weather had now become very hot, and we had quite given up work in the middle of the day, our parades being early and late. The rest of the time was employed studying maps and books on the Sûdan. We had each been served out with four or five maps of Suakin and its surroundings, also of the route to Berber.

These were all printed on white calico. We had also each a small English-Arabic Vocabulary, and *"Report on the Egyptian Provinces of the Sûdan, Red Sea, and Equator"* issued by the Intelligence Department. The Arabic Vocabulary was the cause of endless amusement, and shouts of laughter were to be heard over the catechisms that went on and the efforts at pronouncing some of the most unpronounceable words.

Just before sunset we arrived at Lake Timsah, and got a sight of

Ismailyeh. We did not stop here, but proceeded through the lake and into the canal again, where we anchored for the night between high banks and in a suffocating atmosphere. The next morning, by seven a.m., we were entering the Bitter Lakes, or Waters of Marah, and glad we were to get into this wide expanse of water, as we were able to quicken our pace a bit. We had a fine view of the mountains Gebel Geneffe, which run down the western side of the lakes, and about five miles inland. It must be twenty miles or through these lakes, and then you enter the last section of the canal again, and before long sight the Mountain of Deliverance, or Gebel Attaka, at the foot of which stands the town of Suez.

It is at the base of this mountain that the Israelites are supposed to have crossed the Red Sea. We were out of the canal by three p.m., and at anchor in Suez harbour before four o'clock (4th March). The port or harbour of Suez is connected with the town by a narrow isthmus about two miles in length, and along which runs the railway. A large open space adjoining the main wharf had been turned into a *depôt* for the camels, which had been collected from all parts of Egypt, and brought there to be branded with the Broad Arrow preparatory to being forwarded on to Suakin.

There were about two thousand or more of these animals, and a great number had been already sent on.

We had no time to go ashore, and only just managed to get our first letters from England before we were off again. While we were in harbour three other transports came in, and as we steamed out again about seven o'clock, the troops on board these cheered lustily, rockets were sent up, blue lights burnt, and trumpets and bugles sounded the "Advance" and the "Charge." Of course, we cheered back again till we were all as hoarse as crows.

We had been the first ship to leave England, and were very keen to be the first to arrive at Suakin; so, our disappointment may be imagined when we suddenly discovered that we were going dead slow, and that something was wrong with our boilers. By the next morning these were repaired, and though we had lost a good bit of our start, we were still ahead of the other transports. We all began to feel the heat very much and what little wind there was happened to be right behind us, so we regularly panted for breath in the middle of the day. Going down the Gulf of Suez, we had the coast in view the whole while. It is a fine, rugged outline, but the mountains looked utterly bare and barren, and there did not appear to be a particle of vegetation anywhere.

The next day was rough, but the wind still behind us. It always is more or less rough in the Red Sea, and there is almost sure to be a strong wind blowing either up or down it. I know this time the sea was quite high enough to make some of us feel very uncomfortable. We had lost sight of the coast since leaving the Gulf of Suez, but as the sun went down in a mist on the evening of the 6th of March, there stood up against it the sharp peak of some great mountain, and then we knew that the end of our journey was approaching, and that the next morning would see us saying goodbye to the comforts of board ship life, for we should be off Suakin.

Chapter 2

Suakin

(Lat. 19° 17' N., Long. 37° 20' E.)

There are three different passages through the reefs leading to Suakin. The northern passage is the shortest route for vessels coming from Suez, but it is the most dangerous of the three, and ninety miles in length. The southern passage is of course the most direct route for vessels from India, and is somewhat shorter, being only sixty miles long. The easiest and shortest in point of mere distance is the middle passage, thirty miles long, and running almost due east and west.

It was by this last-named passage that we entered, our captain being, like most other people, strange to the place. It was a very hot morning, and the air was thick with a hot haze, so that we did not sight the land until we were getting quite close to it. Then miles and miles of desert, and a lofty and rugged range of mountains in the distance suddenly came into view.

As we approached nearer, we could see, about four miles away on our right, two camps; these turned out to be the 49th (Berkshire) and 70th (East Surrey). On the left of the town of Suakin was another and much larger camp, where a part of the Indian contingent were lying. The whole country looked a burnt, parched-up wilderness, without a particle of vegetation except the dried-up bush of the desert. It certainly looked the hottest place I had ever seen, with a sky like one great sheet of burnished brass overhead, and with the sun scorching down on an arid waste of sand.

It was midday before we entered the long narrow channel leading into the harbour. The navigation of this channel is very hazardous, as it is nowhere more than 300 yards broad, and in some places much less than this. On both sides run the low coral reefs, and woe betide the ship that happens to run on them. This channel, which is fully three quarters of a mile in length, opens into a lagoon or bay, in which are two islands. One of these is known by us Quarantine Island, and has been used all through the war as a *depôt*, where stores were landed, and as a starting-point for the railway. Several piers and landing-stages have been erected here by the Royal Engineers, and vessels of 4000 tons are able to moor alongside these and discharge their cargoes. On the second island stands the old town of Suakin, and connected with the mainland by a causeway built by General Gordon some years ago.

The town proper, or old town, consists of a number of low, flat-topped houses of the ordinary Eastern type, built right up to the water's edge. The thoroughfares or streets are of deep sand, there being no necessity for roads, as wheel traffic is unknown here. On the mainland, and adjoining the causeway just referred to, is a suburb which has outgrown the town both in population and importance. Here there are several mosques and buildings of some pretensions, as well as a large open barrack occupied by a battalion of Egyptian troops. Beyond this again comes the native town, composed of a great number of huts made of a sort of coarse grass matting spread over a framework of stout sticks in several thicknesses. Outside all are the earthworks and defences, running completely round and enclosing the whole place; they have been all erected since 1881, as before this date the town was quite open.

These defences are exceedingly strong, and of considerable extent, and stretch over a distance of nearly two miles. The greater part of the lines are composed of strong earthworks, but in parts high walls of coral have been built. The principal forts and redoubts in these lines, commencing from the right or western side of the town, are Gerzireh Redoubt, close to the edge of the lagoons, and connected by a wet ditch with Yamin Redoubt on its left. The lines here turn sharply to the southward, the next strong points being Lausari Redoubt, Oorban Redoubt, Wastanieh Redoubt, and Forts Carysfort and Euryalus, the strongest points of the whole of the defences.

A little to the south-east of these two forts are Fort Commodore and Gedeedeh Redoubt, where the lines trend eastward till they reach the lagoons on the south side of the old town, passing through Fort Turk, and the Arab and Sphink Redoubts to the Left Redoubt. Outside these lines, and about three quarters of a mile distant, there is a complete chain of small, circular redoubts with the Right and Left Water Forts on the west, and Fort Foulah on the south.

There are two principal entrances in the lines on the right of Fort Carysfort, and at Yamin Redoubt this last being the one most used by us during the campaign.

There is a certain amount of trade carried on between Suakin and Suez, but this is much impeded by the heavy duties levied by the Egyptian Government.

Suakin has been formed by nature as the principal port of the Egyptian Sûdan and the Nile provinces, but has never risen to a position of any pretension, and even now its prosperity is only comparative. The place was formerly held directly subject to Turkey, but in 1865 it was sold and handed over to the Viceroy of Egypt. The inhabitants depend for their water supply on two or three wells about a mile from the town, and also on rainwater, which is collected during the wet season in a large sort of reservoir at the same place. The supply is at all times limited, and the quality of the water not particularly good, being strongly impregnated with salts.

Towards the close of the dry season, when the water becomes very scarce, it turns thick, and is dark brown in colour. During the early autumn the climate is almost deadly for Europeans, and the natives themselves suffer greatly from sickness, the most prevalent complaints among them being dysentery and enteric fever. The shallow lagoons and damp marshy ground all round the north-west side of the town add considerably to the unhealthiness of Suakin.

When the tide, which is only slight in the Red Sea, runs out, these lagoons are left exposed to the burning rays of the sun, and as they are full of filth and refuse of all sorts, the overpowering stench that arises from the foul black mud, festering and fermenting in the heat, simply defies description. The most unhealthy time of year is from August to the end of October, and during this period the battalion of Marines quartered here since May last had not unfrequently twenty *per cent* of their strength sick; and at one time the percentage rose as high as twenty-five. In September, the ratio of sick per month, that is, men who passed through hospital, was equal to fifty *per cent*. of the total strength.

During the ten months, counting from May last year to February this year, fourteen hundred men passed through this battalion; that is, a total of fourteen hundred men either died or were invalided during a short period of ten months. The weekly returns from which I have collected these statistics were prepared for the information of the officer commanding the battalion, who was in Suakin the whole time himself, and who kindly allowed me to look through them. The facts, therefore, are unimpeachable, and show a degree of suffering concerning which people at home knew nothing at the time, and know little now. The returns referred to were most carefully made out, and amongst other information contained in them, I noticed a calculation of the percentage of sickness as applied to the age of the men.

The cases were divided into three heads—men under 25 years of age, men between 25 and 35 years, and men between 35 and 45. I found that at least sixty-five *per cent.* of the total number of cases occurred among the men under 25 years of age, while the men between 35 and 45 escaped with comparative immunity. Of the fourteen hundred men who passed through the battalion, by far the greater number were lost during the unhealthy season, that is between August and the end of October, and I found that from the 15th of November to the 27th of February, there were only 333 fresh admissions into hospital, the strength of the battalion during this period averaging about 520 of all ranks.

The battalion was split up into various detachments, and the amount of sickness was materially influenced by the position of the detachment. In this way those who suffered least were those quartered at the Right Water Fort, some two miles out from the town; while the detachments at Fort Ansari and Island Redoubt, nearer the town, suffered most. The prevalent diseases were enteric fever, intermittent fever, simple continued fever (including typhoid), dysentery, diarrhoea, and debility, under which head were included affections from the sun.

Such, then, is the effect of the climate of Suakin on Europeans, and the above figures a fitting monument to what the British soldier is called upon to suffer for Queen and Country. I have no wish to be an alarmist, and long ere these pages appear in print, I pray that the English soldier may have left these shores, never to return. I mention nothing about the actual number of deaths, because, although a great number occurred at Suakin, by far the greater number took place at sea, between Suakin and Suez. There was often a difficulty in sending the worst cases away in time, as the vessels available were few, and in this way many valuable lives were lost that might have been saved.

There were, of course, many who recovered when they reached home, and numbers of these were not permanently lost to the service, but the after effects of climate are too well known to need a reference here. We had a sad experience after the Ashanti War, for I remember men being invalided and discharged two years after the regiment had returned home, entirely owing to the germs of disease gathered on the Gold Coast.

But let us turn from this somewhat depressing subject, and go back to Suakin itself and its surroundings. There is one thing I omitted in dealing with the climate of Suakin, and that is the rainy season. They generally count upon rain during November or December, but the heaviest rain does not last more than about two days, when it comes down in real earnest and true tropical fashion, and in a way quite foreign to all but those who have experienced it. This one great downpour is followed by showers, which occur now and then, but by no means frequently. The climate is not unhealthy during this season, as it is in so many places during the rains.

The temperature is highest during the month of August, and the highest point reached by the thermometer last year was 125° Fahr. in the shade; this was on the 20th of August. The official record of the temperature kept by the Royal Engineers on Quarantine Island gives the *mean* temperature during August last as follows: maximum 116.10°, and minimum 90.70°. On looking through these returns I found that in this month there were six days when the temperature was over 120° and thirteen on which it was over 116°, while there were only two on which the maximum temperature was below 100°, and on both these the thermometer stood at 99°.

After the middle of September, the temperature became slightly lower, but there did not appear to be very much difference between the two months. I shall refer to the temperature that we experienced during the campaign further on.

The population of Suakin is very "mixed." There are Arabs belonging to all the neighbouring tribes—Hadendowas, Amaras, Fadlabs, Beni Amers, Bisharems, and Shaharibs. There are also a number of Soumalis.

They are quite black in colour, and naked with the exception of a white cloth worn round the loins. The women, at least some of them, cover their faces with a thin white material, which they wear wound round them and over their heads. These are mostly the married women. They all wear gold ornaments in their noses and ears. Certainly, the operators who made the holes in their noses to support these ornaments had no qualms about the destruction of beauty, for if they had bored them with an augur they could not have been more roughly done. Some of the women I saw, and who were not troubled with any superfluous clothing, had their hair done in curious fashion; the commonest way, though, appeared to be to wear it in a great number of very thin, straight twists, about as thick as an ordinary pencil. These twists were about six inches in length, and each one preserved

An Amarar warrior

A Hadendowa warrior

in a thick plastering of grease.

The men's heads were much more curious, though; I noticed some who wore the hair frizzed till it stood out fully six or eight inches on either side of their heads. This extraordinary thick growth, half hair half wool, was then parted over each ear and round to the back of the head, the hair below the parting being brushed downwards and outwards, and that above the parting upwards. A long wooden pin or thin stick was run through the top part of this erection, and the effect was complete.

The Arab boys had their heads shaved with the exception of one tuft of hair, which was allowed to grow long, and this tuft was generally on the side and towards the back of the head, and gave them a very rakish appearance. Many of these little chaps are really nice-looking, with cheery faces and bright sparkling eyes. Their cheeks are almost always ornamented with three long slashes on each side, done with some sharp instrument when they are very young. I saw one or two little girls of twelve or fourteen years of age who were far prettier than I ever thought it was possible for blacks to be. They lose these good looks, though, almost entirely as they grow older.

The population of the place varies a good deal; but, counting Italians, Greeks, and Egyptian soldiery, there must be at the time I am writing little short of eight thousand people here.

One of the chief points of interest to us in Suakin was Osman Digna's house; not that there was anything particular about the house, either inside or out. It stood close to the water's edge up a small creek on the south side of the town. A stick cut from Osman Digna's garden was considered a great trophy.

Most people now know Osman Digna's history, but for those who do not it may be as well to give a short sketch of his antecedents. This person, then, was born at Rouen, and is the son of French parents, his family name being Vinet. He was called after his father, George and began his education at Rouen, but after a while was moved to Paris. A few years after this his parents went over to Alexandria in connection with some matter of business, and shortly afterwards his father died there. His mother then married a merchant of Alexandria, Osman Digna by name. This man took a great fancy to his step-son, young George Vinet, and brought him up as a Mohammedan, sending him to complete his education to the military school at Cairo, where he had for his companion Arabi.

Here he studied tactics and the operations of war under French officers. It was at this period that his father-in-law migrated to Suakin, where he set up as a general merchant and slave-dealer, and very shortly was doing a very lucrative business. At his father-in-law's death George Vinet continued to carry on the business under the same name, A few years passed, and when the war broke out in Egypt, in 1882, Osman Digna espoused the cause of his old friend and companion, Arabi, and became one of England's bitterest foes as the *Mahdi*'s lieutenant. In appearance Osman Digna is a fine-looking man, tall and well-proportioned, though rather fat. He wears a long black beard, and has lost his left arm. He never gets on a horse, and in the few engagements in which he has thought fit to risk his valuable life he has always been present on foot.

As for the *Mahdi*, the prime cause of all the misery and bloodshed of the past four years, he is, I believe, the son of a carpenter, and a native of Dongola. His proper name is Mohammed Ahmed, and he was born about thirty-seven years ago, and is much the same age as his lieutenant. In 1870 he went to live at the island of Abba, where he gained a great reputation for sanctity, and gradually collected a great number of holy men or dervishes around him. His subsequent actions are now a part of the history of the last five years of bloodshed, and call for no recapitulation here. How long he may be able to retain his position as the true prophet is a matter of doubt, but it is to be hoped that the poor deluded Arabs may be shown the folly of being carried away by the professions of a man whose sole aim is self-advancement, and who is ready to sacrifice everything, his religion included, for the attainment of this one end.

The Mohammedan religion appears to present peculiar attractions to the native tribes in Central Africa, and the false prophet is indebted for the number of his recruits to the enthusiasm of the converts to Mohammedanism, with whom the idea of the regeneration of Islam by force of arms is amazingly popular. The teachings of the *Mahdi* may be summed up as follows: universal law, religion, and equality; destruction of all who refuse to believe in his mission, whether they be Christians, Mohammedans, or pagans. The causes of the rebellion have been ascribed to the unjustness and venality of the Egyptian officials, the suppression of the slave-trade, and the military weakness of Egypt.

It was noon before we were safely piloted through the treacherous inner reefs, some of which run out only two or three feet below the surface. The channel had been buoyed out by the sailors, and an officer came off to bring our ship in. We eventually made fast to shore half-

A MOUNTED WARRIOR

way up the channel leading to the inner harbour, and right abreast of the English cemetery, which consists of a straight line of about thirty or forty graves, each with a cross at the head, some made of rough pieces of wood, and some of iron. Almost all are ornamented with a border of rough stones round them. This burial-ground is only about thirty yards from the water's edge, and is not at present enclosed in any way.

Since we have been here there have been men at work perpetually digging graves at the rate of two or three a day, so that there might always be several ready. Whenever it has been practicable, we have always brought in our dead and buried them here; the officers being for the most part buried in coffins, the men in their blankets. There are one or two of the common mimosa bushes among the graves, otherwise there is no vegetation of any sort, and nothing but the dry, hot sand of the desert.

We were all hoping we should be disembarked that afternoon; but orders were sent off to say that this was to be postponed till the following morning at daybreak. Some of us, therefore, determined to try and get a boat and go ashore, but it was with difficulty we did so, as boats are scarce at Suakin. It does not seem to have occurred to the native mind that a large fortune might be made plying this trade. I should be very sorry, however, to trust myself in one of their very narrow canoes, which are of the type one used to read of as a boy in Fenimore Cooper's novels—mere long logs of wood hollowed out and sharpened bow and stern. The dexterity with which they handle these frail craft is marvellous, and they go along at a great rate, with the water very often within an inch of coming over the side.

Our first object on landing was to find the post-office, and such a post-office it turned out to be-four walls and a flat roof, the floor of sand, the furniture a very rickety table, apparently made out of old biscuit-boxes. On this table and on the floor lay a pile of letters and newspapers a foot and a half high. We routed among these for some time without much result, so contented ourselves by handing to an Egyptian boy, who appeared to be in sole charge as the local postmaster-general, the letters we had brought ashore to post, feeling that they had a very poor chance of ever getting to their destination.

On our way back to the wharf we passed a row of about fifty Arabs, all sitting in the same position, with their backs against a white wall. This being my first introduction to black and withal naked people, the contrast of their black skins against the white wall struck me as very funny as they sat in a long row in solemn and perfect silence, staring at us as we passed.

It is a curious thing how many ways there seem to be of spelling the name of this place. One sees "Suakin," "Suakim," "Souakin," "Sawakin," and many others; but I believe, if one wished to be absolutely correct, the proper way is "Savagin," with the "g" pronounced hard, as in the word "begin." The Arabs have a legend about the place, and the story they tell you is as follows:—

> Many hundred years ago a prince came from the north bent on some warlike enterprise, and, according to the custom of that day, he carried with him his women. Among them were seven virgins, who, before he commenced his further advance, he placed for safety on the island on which the town of Suakin now stands. Many months after the prince returned to find his seven virgins the mothers of seven children. No explanation being forthcoming he christened the place 'Savagin' (*sava*, with, and *gin, a* fiend or devil), literally, 'the place of the devil.'

I can only assure my reader that we found the literal translation of "Savagin" to agree perfectly in our minds with the opinion we very shortly formed of the place.

CHAPTER 3

Landing

The dawn was just breaking on Sunday, the 8th of March, as the barges came alongside to put us ashore. It was a most lovely morning, and the air so clear and bright that one could distinguish every feature in the mountains, miles away inland. The sun was just showing itself above the horizon as we landed at one of the piers of Quarantine Island, and even at this early hour gave promise of the heat of the coming day. My company was sent on with a guide to show us where our camping ground was to be. We marched along the field railway for about a mile, leaving the town of Suakin behind us; and as we advanced H.M.S. *Dolphin* opened fire over our heads at some groups of the enemy five miles away on the desert. We could see the great shells pitch and throw the sand up into the air thirty or forty feet high.

The mounted infantry were also out skirmishing; and the first intimation we had that real work had begun was passing a man lying in a *dhoolie*, and wounded in both arms.

Turning to the left off the field railway, we marched along parallel with the earthworks of the town and about a mile from them, till at length we were halted on a bare piece of sandy desert-just a sample of the country for miles and miles, except that there was no scrub—and told that we were to start marking out our camp, and that tents would shortly be sent out to us. We accordingly piled arms and let the men take off their kits, as it was uncommonly hot.

We had provided each of our men with a piece of bread and a quarter of a pound of cheese; so this, with a suck from a water-bottle made an excellent breakfast. We had to wait a long while before our tents made their appearance, and it was ten o'clock before the first string of camels arrived with a part of them. We were all soon at work, though, and in a couple of hours we had transformed our bare patch of sand into a smart camp, all alive with the hum of many voices and the bustle of men getting everything ship-shape.

Our tents were certainly excellent, and were those known in India as "European privates." These tents are made of a thick white cotton fabric, and are double, so that, I think, no sun could ever get through them. The roof of the tent is supported by two stout bamboo poles standing about six feet apart, and there is a space of a foot or more between the two thicknesses composing it, both of which are again lined, the outer one with a deep maroon-coloured material, and the inner one with a pale yellow. A wooden bar connects the two poles, and forms a useful place for hanging things upon.

The walls of the tent are about four feet high, and are made in four pieces. There are thus four doorways to the tent, each having an awning over it, which is fastened to the roof and supported by two bamboo sticks.

This awning can be let down and the walls closed in at night if desired. As we had expected to find ourselves under double bell tents of the home pattern, we were agreeably surprised. We were four officers in a tent, so had plenty of room, the inside measuring about eighteen feet by twenty-three. The men were about twenty in a tent.

We arranged our tent in this way—a camp bed in each corner, with our kit-bags and spare baggage along the walls. We drew an ordinary deal barrack table out of store and put this on one side of the pole bar; on the other side was our mess-box, the top of which served for a sideboard. Our swords, belts, and water-bottles we hung on pole straps, and the floor we carpeted with the sacks in which the tent was packed on the march. We had each brought a camp-stool, so these completed our furniture and added materially to our comfort.

About noon some mules arrived, bringing our rations of *bouilli* beef and biscuit-also some ten-gallon tins of water. This was all very quickly served out and swallowed too. The *bouilli* beef is the ordinary tinned stuff, and always went by the name of "iron rations," to distinguish it from fresh-meat rations, which we got sometimes twice a week. The biscuit is very nasty, and quite uneatable unless stewed in some way, as it is as hard as steel. We always used to stew our beef and biscuit up together, putting in any fresh vegetables we could get-such as potatoes and onions, and occasionally some pumpkin. This concoction we called "soup;" and precious nasty soup it was too, even when swamped in Worcester sauce, or eaten with chutney or pickles, of which we had brought a plentiful supply. On days when we had no fresh vegetables served out, we had at first each a ration of lime-juice,

H.M.S. Dolphin

which was excellent stuff, to my thinking

In the afternoon I went into the town and had a look round, and much to my delight found one or two houses where all manner of tinned provisions were sold. These were kept by enterprising Englishmen, and a wonderful business they must have done with us soldiers. The best one was Ross's, but there were others which fell little short of this. It was here I discovered some really good white bread, which I promptly bought and carried back to camp in triumph. There was, however, not much use in buying this afterwards, as the ration bread served out to us was very good, though rather bitter, and we always had plenty of it.

By the time I got back to camp our horses had all come in, and were being picketed in rear of our tents. Some of them looked a bit tucked up after their voyage; but this was not to be wondered at, as they had had a roughish time of it. They all pulled round but two, both these having been very bad at sea.

I ought not to omit to mention that during the interval two men arrived in camp, of foreign and uncertain origin, bringing with them something which always appeals at once to the soldier's heart—a barrel, of beer! Having obtained leave to sell to the men, the amount being limited to a pint a man, they very soon came to the end of their barrel, no doubt with a handsome profit to themselves. The cask bore the homely and familiar name of "Bass," but the liquid that issued from the tap would have astonished any member of that excellent firm; it was dark in colour, as thick as pea-soup, and as sweet as treacle—which last, indeed, it rather resembled. But Thomas Atkins is not to be denied; beer is beer to him, and he is not over particular about the taste, more especially when the cask is labelled "Bass," and he is four thousand miles away from home and in the middle of the desert.

Having watered our horses and posted our guard and sentries, we had another turn at the "soup," and then lay down for the night in happy ignorance of any danger. We heard a few shots about eleven o'clock in the direction of the 70th camp, and in the morning were told they had had two men wounded and one killed.

This was the first of those memorable night attacks which were afterwards the cause of so much misery to us. I don't think any of us got much sleep after our hard day's work, for the heat was tremendous, and I lay all night with the perspiration pouring off me. The first part of the nights were generally very hot, as the wind which blew in from the sea during the day dropped altogether. Towards morning it became quite cold, and one was glad to get under a blanket.

The next morning, we were up before light, and out and about getting everything into its place. We generally had a cup of hot coffee or cocoa at half-past five or six o'clock, and then breakfast about eight, when there was more soup for those that liked it; but I am thankful to say we had brought plenty of sardines and potted meats with us, so there was an alternative.

At this time the force was composed as follows: The 70th (East Surrey), who were encamped about half a mile to our left front and close to the Right Water Fort; their camp, like ours, being completely isolated from the rest of the force. To our right front and about a mile away lay the 49th (Berkshire), and behind them were the Royal Marines and a battery of Horse Artillery. Further in rear still was the Headquarter camp, and between us and them lay the Medical Staff camp at "H Redoubt."

The Indian Brigade was on the south side of the town; our camp was all on the north-west side.

The Medical Staff were at this time under single bell tents, and suffered severely from the sun. I never saw fellows more sunburnt in so short a time, for they had only arrived the previous day; and some of them came over to us, complaining bitterly about it, as well they might. One of the newspaper reporters mentioned this in his telegram home, but the press censor struck it out as not the case. Seeing is believing, however, and there were the single bell tents right enough. Even at home in summertime a bell tent is almost unbearable, but under a tropical sun it must have been frightful, and never ought to have been allowed for a moment. They had a few double bell tents, but the sun came through these just as severely as through the single ones.

Our camping-ground was by no means well chosen; it was down in a hollow to begin with, and therefore damp. The sand, so close to the sea as we were, and on so low a level, is full of salt, and in the mornings the floor of the tent was always quite wet. The first night we hung our clothes up in the tent, and the next morning they were all wet through from the moisture rising from the ground. Only one of us was foolish enough to put his clothes on in this state, and suffered by getting a sharp touch of fever. After this we always, when we did undress—which was not often—put our clothes under our air pillows, and thus kept them dry.

Another unpleasant fact connected with our camp was, that it was quite close to the Arab burial-ground, and there were some hundreds of graves within sixty yards of our tents. As the Arabs do not bury their dead very far beneath the surface, but rather on the top of the ground, with a covering of stones over the bodies, the atmosphere at nights was unpleasantly loaded with the foulest odours. This, one would have thought, was hardly a healthy spot in a hot climate for even a temporary camp.

Of course, we all very soon had the skin burnt off our faces, not only by the direct heat of the sun, but by the refraction from the sand, which is almost as bad. One thing which nearly all of us suffered from was sore lips. Our lower lips would swell up to an enormous size and then break and fester. It was very painful, but when once cured we were not troubled again in this way. A good thick moustache was the best preventative, and I am sure a beard protected one's face a great deal. Some few of us shaved, but nearly all let their hair grow.

With all due deference to the remarks in "our only general's" (?) pocket-book, that it takes as long to clean a beard as to shave one off, I am inclined to think that a beard is by far the best thing on service. If cut once a week and kept short it is no trouble at all to keep clean. Another thing most of us did was to have our hair cut off quite short to the head, but I am not sure that this was a good thing. It was cooler and more easily kept clean, certainly; but in a hot climate a good crop of hair is a protection from the sun, hair being a non-conductor of heat.

Two battalions of the Guards arrived today (9th), and marched out to their camping-ground on the side of the field railway just beyond the 49th camp and in the direction of the West Redoubt. The camp of the Guards Brigade was at this time at right angles to the general run of the rest of the camp and in advance of it.

The next day there were more arrivals, and, in fact, all this week there was a constant stream of great transports coming into harbour full of either troops or stores. Gradually the whole of this side of Suakin was turned into one great town of white canvas, and unoccupied ground in the morning was ere night transformed into a scene of busy life. Long strings of camels were to be seen traversing the desert in all directions, bringing up supplies of all sorts to the camp from Quarantine Island. Fatigue parties were marching here and there, or toiling under the burning sun. Mounted orderlies galloped over the plain, and generals and staff officers visited the different detached camps and inspected the fresh arrivals.

Down at Quarantine Island there was indeed a busy scene. There men of all nationalities worked night and day like great swarms of bees, unloading the transports as they arrived in quick succession one after the other—at one time full of stores and equipment, at another of forage and fuel; at a third, perhaps full of camels from Berbera or India, when each camel had to be slung up from the hold and swung over the side.

At last Quarantine Island contained something of all sorts—tons of railway plant, camel-saddles in thousands, harness, gigantic cases full of clothing and equipment, mountains of compressed hay, camels, mules, horses, tents, ammunition, and a thousand other things, a list of which would fill a volume. We had to work and toil, to be sure, from daybreak to sunset, in the sweltering heat of that foul harbour, the air filled with dust and the sickening odours from the foetid swamps around, with the shouts of the Negros as they slaved in a state of nudity, and with the roar of steam and the scrunch and rattle of a hundred donkey-engines!

Those were days not easily to be forgotten; there were stirring times coming, and we all worked cheerily and merrily enough as looked forward to the day of the general advance, and the chance of a good fight with Osman Digna and his hardy followers.

The most disagreeable part of the work at Quarantine Island was unloading the camels. These long-suffering creatures are by no means sweet at any time, more especially after having been crowded up in the hold of a ship, where red mange has spread among them, and where fleas and ticks have multiplied innumerably. Our camels were from all parts. The finest to look at were those from India. They were much taller than either the Egyptian or the Berbera camels, some of them being nine feet to the top of the hump, and were able to carry heavier loads; but for all this they were nothing like so handy as the Berbera camels with their Aden drivers.

We could form these up in lines of twenty and march them abreast, but the Indian camels were generally marched four in a string, one behind the other, and thus it was difficult to close them up so as to occupy a small amount of ground. The camel is a curious sort of beast, and he gives one the impression of being in a chronic condition of low spirits. He grunts and moans in a doleful way when made to lie down or stand up, and at night gives vent to the most awful sounds, something between the roar of a bull and the grunt of a boar. As to his capabilities as a beast of burden, he is, no doubt, admirably suited to the ordinary requirements of desert travelling; but many of us thought we should have done better had we had more mules.

The Indian Brigade did the greater part of their own transport work with mules during the campaign, and of course we had many hundreds too, chiefly from Cyprus, and driven by natives from that island. Our ammunition column was composed almost entirely of mules. An average camel carries a load of four hundred pounds, and though an Indian camel can carry more than this, it is unadvisable ever to attempt to overload him.

We found three hundred pounds quite enough for the little Berbera animals, and also for the Egyptian, some of which last were too small and too young to be of any use, and never ought to have been bought even at a push. Loading a camel is not so easy a thing as it sounds, and though it depends mainly on balance, it depends also greatly upon the position of the load, and the lashing of the load in the *celita* to the saddle; unless great care is taken, a sore back will ensue, and the camel be rendered useless for some considerable length of time.

Many people labour under the idea that a camel can and will, with comparative comfort to himself, go for a considerable length of time without water. That he can do so I do not wish for one moment to deny, but that he does so only with a corresponding loss of power was apparent to us all at Suakin.

General Gordon has stated that in his experience camels have lived without water for as long a period as nine days; there is, however, no doubt that when in hard work and hot weather camels should, whenever it is possible, be watered twice a day. Seven to eight gallons a day is a fair allowance for them, but this may be greatly increased with advantage.

Many of our camels were driven with the ordinary nose-rope and nose-peg, but I think this unnecessarily cruel, and though it is a check on refractory animals, I see no reason why an ordinary running noseband should not be amply sufficient. Some of our camels were vicious, but not many of them; a few were kickers. The bite of a camel is very severe, and their kick, even with their soft feet, is quite sufficient to break a man's leg. When you see a camel open his mouth and give vent to a loud gurgling sound, a large red-coloured inflated bag as big as a good-sized melon appearing at the same time from his throat, my advice would be, to those who are strangers to camels, to stand off! A well-bred camel may be known by the fineness of his coat and the smallness of his hind feet.

The camels from India came accompanied by native drivers, and a certain number of transport officers from the Indian Transport Staff.

These drivers were a mixed lot, and for the most part understood their business well. They worked well enough under officers who could speak to them in good round Hindustani, but one would have to be a linguist indeed to speak to each different class of drivers in his own language. There were among them natives from all parts of India-Punjabees, Sidiboys, Bengalees, Scindees, Pathans, Hindoos, and sundry others.

The Aden drivers, Soumalis, with the camels from Berbera, were hardy fellows, and of course well used to the climate, caring as little for the sun as the Arabs themselves. You would see them going along with their camels during the hottest hours of the day with no covering to their shaven heads, and no garments except the white cloth round their waists.

It was curious to count up the number of different languages one heard spoken in and about Suakin at this time. Besides English, French, Portuguese, and Italian, there were amongst others the following: Turkish, Arabic, Somali, Greek, Armenian, Hindustani, Punjabi, Gujarati, Bengali, Mahrathi, and Pukhtu.

There was another native Indian corps—the Bhisti corps, water-carriers, composed mostly of Punjabee Mussulmans and Punjabee Hindoos. These were capital fellows to work, and did good service.

We often used to talk, as we looked round on all these vast preparations and this great concourse of men of all sorts and conditions, on the enormous outlay of money that was being spent without stint, on the toil and sickness and death around us, and we used to wonder then what it was all for. We knew that, being soldiers, we went where we were told, and did what we were told when we got there, but beyond this I do not believe there was a man in the whole of this magnificent force who could have given you any intelligible reason for which we were fighting, if indeed his ingenuity enabled him to give you any reason at all.

And yet there we were, a picked force, armed with every scientific means to effect our end—everything, from an air balloon, with its gas compressed and brought all the way from Chatham, to mule batteries of screw-guns, Gardners, and rockets, and to rifles of the most perfect pattern and greatest rapidity of fire. And all this to war against what? A foe worthy of our steel? Yes, undoubtedly yes. Armed? Yes; but with spears of the rudest make, with swords of the days of the Crusaders, with shields of crocodile skin, and with a certain number of Remington rifles which they scarce knew how to use.

A foe fighting with all the wild pluck and determination of their race, and supported by a fanaticism which turned them into men who courted death for two reasons—first, because it transferred them to a happier land; and secondly, because they preferred it a thousand times to a life which might show them their freedom gone, their land wrested from them, and their race decimated.

Chapter 4

Night Attacks

We received orders on the 11th of March that we were to shift our camp, and I was sent off to the Camel Depot to get a hundred camels and fifty Aden drivers.

The Camel Depot was inside the town lines, and was always the scene of much activity, as all camels, horses, and mules were taken there on being landed, and then turned over to the various departments and brigades on requisition or order, when they were numbered and branded, A more pestilential place it would be difficult to imagine, for all round it there was an expanse of open cesspools and stinking swamps. The native town was quite close round it, and the collection of filth from the huts was simply indescribable. There were some thousands of camels there that morning, and a perpetual stream of fresh arrivals was continually pouring in. There were camels of all sizes and shapes—camels from India, camels from Berbera, from Upper Egypt, from the Sûdan, and from any other part of the world where camels were to be bought and sold.

Some were strong-looking animals, and others weak and thin, while some had already given it up as a bad job and succumbed to the hardships and privations. Their drivers, too, of every hue and nationality, each wearing a tin medal bearing his number, were hustling these wretched animals about, whacking them with sticks, and getting them up to the picketing-lines. Their screams and hollos added to the general state of noise and confusion. Interpreters roared the orders in a variety of languages, and officers at their wits' end endeavoured by superhuman efforts to establish something approaching to order. Add to all this a scorching burning sun, deep sand, clouds of dust, and everyone running down with sweat and begrimed with dirt, and you may have a faint idea of what sort of place the *depôt* was.

I had a terrible job to thread my way through the line of camels to the *commandant's* tent, as the mare I was riding was simply terrified at the sight of a camel, and resorted to every trick she could think of to get rid of me and get out of the *depôt*; added to which she was quite unbroken. So, to say the least of it, it was hot work.

It took a long time before my hundred camels were picked out, and then I formed them up in line against a wall, and made them lie down while I went round and inspected them with the Soumali headman, who was to accompany me. It was with feelings the reverse of pleasant that I at length gave the order for them to follow me, as I could not help wondering, first, how I was to get the long string of animals through the maze and confusion in front of me, and second, how I was to retain possession of my mare (which by this time was nearly mad with fright) and keep my eye on the camels at the same time.

Like many other things, we achieved it at last, and as soon as I got outside the town, I halted to allow time for stragglers to come up.

The drivers now had a difference of opinion as to whether they were being led in the right direction, and, unfortunately, I laboured under two difficulties with them that day, as I could not speak a word of their language, and, moreover, was entirely unarmed. I had been on foot up to this, my horse being led by a couple of friendlies, who, I could see in the distance, had their work cut out for them; but I now again determined to mount, and see what could be done towards pushing along, as we had two miles to go to the Ordnance Store camp, to draw saddles and equipment for each animal, before they would be of any use in transporting our camp and baggage to our new ground.

It was midday before I got back to our camp, where I found all the tents struck.

We were soon hard at work loading up, which we found very disagreeable work and somewhat difficult, as we were quite inexperienced. Sometimes we had to load a camel three or four times over. First, one would get up before the load was adjusted; or perhaps, with another, the load was too heavy for him, and he would not rise at all. Then, with a third, a part of the saddle would give way, frighten the camel, and off he would go at a gallop, gradually kicking himself free, and smashing up saddle and load as he went. Then two men would have to go and catch him and bring him back, when a fresh saddle would be fitted, and a load beautifully balanced would be put upon him. Then he would get up when his head was let go, and, with an awkward lurch, round would go the load under his stomach.

Tommy Atkins would sit down on the sand then, and scratch his head and look at the animal in front of him with despairing eyes, as much as to say, "I wonder what your next little game will be."

By half-past six we had pitched our camp again on a fresh site, and on the extreme left flank of the front line. The position of the various regiments was at this time somewhat peculiar. There appeared to be no particular system about it, and we were told that military requirements had been allowed to sink before sanitary considerations in choosing the camping-grounds.

It appeared to us as if everyone had been allowed to take his choice, and regimental camps were scattered about pretty much like plums in a cake, and with just about as much foresight on the part of the chief cook.

The front line, two miles from Suakin town, was taken up by a chain of redoubts running from the Right and Left Water Forts on the left to the West Redoubt on the right. Both of these were signal-stations, and rendered quite impregnable by deep ditches and Gardner guns. The redoubts were circular-formed, and surrounded by a ditch ten or twelve feet broad, across which ran a plank which could be drawn inside at will. The line of the camps started from the Right Water Fort, where we were, and extended to a point about two miles away and half a mile in rear of the West Redoubt.

Two regiments of the 2nd Brigade, the 70th and 53rd, were on the left; then came an interval of a mile or more to the Guards Brigade, which ran at right angles to the front; the Coldstream, Grenadiers, and Scots Guards camps, being in line facing towards the Water Forts.

In rear of the Guards came the Sandbag Battery and the camp of the 49th. To their left rear was a battalion of Marines and a battery of Royal Horse Artillery. Further to the left was a part of the cavalry, the 19th Hussars, who left us shortly after this. Then half a mile to the right rear came the Headquarter camp; and further back still "H Redoubt," the camp of the Army Hospital Corps.

The Ordnance camp was a mile to the right rear and close to the water's edge, while the 5th Lancers and 20th Hussars were stationed in rear of the centre of the line and about three quarters of a mile from the town lines.

The Indian Brigade, both cavalry and infantry, were all encamped on the south-east side of the town, where there was also a long chain of redoubts and forts, the most important point being Fort Foulah, where there were some wells.

Thus, it will be seen that the camps were much scattered, and

19TH HUSSARS CROSSING THE DESERT

placed in such positions that not only were they unable to protect themselves, but were a source of danger to each other as well, for, with the exception of the front line, there was no direction in which the scattered units could fire without endangering comrades in one direction or the other.

The Arabs were quite alive to our condition, and, with their consummate craftiness, took advantage of the folly of our dispositions.

It seems almost incredible that a trained force, and some of the finest troops in the world, should have been liable night after night to be "rushed" by a few savages. Nothing goes further towards demoralizing troops than a sense of insecurity at night. Men are unable to get proper rest, and without sleep, especially in such an enervating climate as that of the Sûdan, a soldier cannot be depended on in daytime either to march or fight in the way he should. Added to this, a perpetual series of night attacks, carried on by a few determined and reckless individuals under cover of the darkness, tended so to shake the nerves of our men that the efficiency of the force was to a certain extent undermined.

I must mention that there was a line of pickets across the whole of the front, and these were stationed in the redoubts. The interval between these posts was, however, much too great, and in the intense darkness that prevailed at this time small parties of the enemy crept along on the ground and passed through the line without being detected by the sentries. They were then able to traverse the intervening space between the outposts and the camps, and choose their points of attack.

The unoccupied ground already referred to between the Guards camp and the two regiments of the 2nd Brigade gave them free ingress, and thus they were able to attack us in rear or on the flanks at will.

On the night of the 7th of March, the 70th had had their rearguard attacked, and had lost two men wounded. After this we had no peace at all at night, as directly it became dark the enemy would open fire on us from a distance which was not at all pleasant, or creep into our tents or up to our sentries and stab a man or two before we were aware of any danger.

The night of the 11th was one of the most disagreeable of all, as parties of the enemy attacked ever so many points at the same time.

We had just sat down to our soup at about seven o'clock, when heavy firing was opened by our pickets, in reply to the "*crack*," "*crack*," of the Remingtons which was going on in front.

As the night wore on, every now and then a single shot would break the stillness, and then would follow a volley or two, when all would be again quiet. The dismal cry of the sentries, "All's well!" would be taken up by one post after another, till it died away in the far distance. This shouting of the sentries was very trying, as it alone rendered sleep impossible. The men would call out at their very loudest, laying considerable stress on the "all's," and cutting short the "well." They seemed to call out far more than was absolutely necessary, and for the sake of company more than for anything else.

There was one great disadvantage besides in this calling, and that was that it enabled the Arabs to determine the exact position of each post. It was a relief to find that common sense came to our rescue for once, and the next morning an order was issued putting a stop to the practice, and also doubling each post, so that, by being two together, the men had more confidence, as one was able to patrol to the next post on the right or left, while the other kept a sharp look out.

About midnight the firing grew heavier, and as we stood in front of our tents, we could see the Sikhs in our rear hard at work, while firing was going on up at the Guards camp and also right away in rear at the Ordnance camp.

By 2 a.m. the whole of the front line of pickets were blazing away as fast as they could, and then there rose a cry that the pickets were coming in. Immediately bugles and trumpets sounded the "fall in" and the "double," and then there was the rush of many feet and the dull sound of many voices as men ran to the posts told off to them in case of attack.

The firing ceased for a time, and the pickets fell back on the main body, not without some loss. A patrol of two men and a corporal were set upon as they were retiring, and only one man escaped, the others being killed. They were marching back with their arms at the slope, when some of these daring fellows came up behind them, pulled them over backwards by their rifles, and immediately despatched them, only one of them, with a frightful wound in his face, escaping with his life.

No sooner had the pickets come in than a terrific fire was opened all along the line, and the many detached camps in our rear appeared to be having a merry time of it too, for their bullets came most uncomfortably near us.

To add to the weird appearance of the night the *Dolphin* threw the electric light far and wide across the country, making everything which came under its rays as bright as day. At one time a whole camp would suddenly be shown up distinctly, perhaps a mile or more off, and one could distinguish the men standing to their arms or firing away only too probably at some imaginary foe. Then in an instant our camp would be illuminated as if by sunlight, and every feature of the ground would be as distinct in our front as at twelve o'clock in the day.

This light, to our thinking, had its disadvantages as well as its advantages, and I am not at all sure that, under the existing circumstances, the former did not kick the beam. In the first place, the path of light thrown was not more than about thirty yards broad at a distance of two miles, and if by chance it happened to be directed on a party of the enemy, they were very soon put out of sight again as the light swept across the ground. They could also, by lying down when they saw the light approaching, completely evade observation, as they had a trick of covering themselves with sand in a moment and leaving nothing visible but their heads.

Sometimes the light was moved suddenly from point to point, and when this was done parties of the enemy were occasionally shown up and advantage taken of it immediately. The sailors working the light on board the *Dolphin* were, of course, unable to see when they hit off a point suspected by us on shore, and often and often after we had been peering through the darkness at what we took to be moving objects the light would cross us, and, before we had become accustomed to its brilliancy, would pass on and leave the darkness doubly dark.

The gravest fault connected with the light was that, from its position, it enabled the enemy to take note of our movements, as it showed up the various camps from time to time. I not unfrequently saw the light turned on to a suspected point of attack, and kept there for five minutes or more, when, of course, everything coming under its rays, the whole way from the ship was thrown up into light. In this way one could see solitary sentries or small pickets standing at their posts like so many statues.

I have no wish to derogate from the enormous advantages to be derived from this most useful scientific appliance, for I believe it to be invaluable. But I do wish to point out that its utility is proportionate to the position from which the light is thrown. Placed as we were, there was no alternative but to use the light from one of the ships in harbour. The *Dolphin* was lying right away to our rear, and two miles from our front line, so that the enemy, I am inclined to think, reaped more advantage from its use than we did, except in certain instances.

For the light to be used with the greatest effect it should be thrown from a point on either flank, thus sweeping the whole of the front of a position, and, so to speak, enfilading it. It should never be in rear of those for whose advantage it is being used, if it can possibly be avoided, as in throwing the light to the front it is bound to show up everything from the point where it is being worked. By working it from a flank the additional advantage is gained that the whole of the ground in front of a position is illuminated at once, instead of a space of thirty or forty yards, as it is then broadside on.

Modern science has not revealed to us at present a perfect mode by which we can be absolutely independent of steam power in generating an electric current of any strength; but when a thoroughly complete system of storing electricity has been invented, there is no doubt that apparatus for electric lighting will form a part of the equipment of every army, just as much as it does now every ship of war.

We stood to our arms for an hour or more, but the Arabs appeared to have drawn off, and contented themselves with firing a few shots at us at long range, resulting, so far as we were concerned, in one casualty only. Soon after this the day began to break, the firing ceased, and we were soon beginning another day of ceaseless toil.

Our killed were buried in front of the redoubts, where we found many traces of blood, but no dead. The Arabs always carried away their dead with them, so we were never able to arrive at what execution we had done. The firing had been very heavy off and on all night, and there is no doubt they must have had many casualties.

I was told afterwards that the Sikhs did some execution, and that a party of Arabs returned five times to try and fetch away one of their number who had fallen dead close to the tents.

The detachment in charge of the Camel Depot had also a rough time of it; they were up all night under a heavy fire, but, being behind the town lines, escaped without any casualties.

The most determined attack that night was made on the Ordnance Store camp, where there was some severe fighting.

This camp, as I have already said, was in rear of all the others, close to the water's edge, and adjoining two landing-stages or piers. Deep water close up to these piers enabled ships of considerable draft to come alongside and unload in the same way as at Quarantine Island, and all stores in the way of equipment and ammunition were landed here-clothing, arms, boots, helmets, blankets, harness of all sorts, pack-saddles, camel-saddles, carts of all sorts, sizes, and description; tents, storage-tanks for water, portable tanks and barrels, miles of telegraph wire, cases of stationery by the hundred, ammunition for all arms; and, in fact, anything and everything that could possibly be wanted by an army in the field.

It may be imagined, therefore, that many hundred thousand pounds' worth of stores were collected at this *depôt*, and it appeared that the enemy were fully alive to the importance of the place. In the creek behind the camp lay the *Dolphin* and the *Carysfort,* but the camp itself was almost entirely unprotected by any form of earthworks or *laager.*

I had occasion to go down to the Ordnance camp the next day, and received the following account of the fight from the senior Ordnance Store officer in command there, which I think it better to put as nearly as possible in his own words. His story of the fight ran as follows:

> When I first arrived at the Ordnance camp on the 8th of March, it consisted of four Indian double-poled tents and a *sepoys'* tent. Enormous quantities of camp equipment and stores of all sorts were pouring in in an endless stream from early dawn to late at night.
>
> The *depôt* was scarcely safe from attack, and very weakly defended by a *laager* of Maltese carts on the north and west sides only, the east and south sides being left open.
>
> It had been protected up till then by a nominal guard of one non-commissioned officer and twelve men at night-time, but I had this increased to one non-commissioned officer and twenty-four men of the 49th Berkshire Regiment, which at this time were finding the guard. It was generally believed that the enemy would never venture to penetrate so far in rear of our lines, especially as we were under the guns of the *Dolphin* and *Carysfort*; still, I never could see why they should not make a circuitous march, round by the sea-shore, as there was a wide stretch of open ground a mile and a half in extent between the right of our lines and the coast.
>
> My tent was pitched between two others on the north-west side of the *depôt,* the men's tents being on the east side.
>
> I slept alone in my tent, and felt in perfect safety until the night of the 11th of March, when, to our astonishment, we were suddenly attacked by the Arabs under Abdul Adab.

I usually let my candle burn out on the table, and kept all four doors of my tent open, but on this particular night, luckily for me, my candle blew out. I had slept soundly all the first part of the night, and until I was suddenly aroused by rapid firing and most frightful yells. I realised at once that we were attacked, and looking out of the door of my tent, saw distinctly some black forms moving about the yard on all-fours.

A few seconds afterwards, hearing somebody rushing towards my tent, and not being able to find my sword in the darkness, I ran out of another doorway and scrambled under the curtains into the next tent, where I narrowly escaped being shot by one of my own brother officers, who luckily though recognised my voice as he was going to fire.

As we came out of the tent a sentry ran towards us, calling out that we were surrounded. I then managed to get back to my tent, and found my revolver and sword, when I immediately joined the guard, who I opened out into skirmishing order. We then marched, or rather felt our way in the darkness, through the cases and bales of stores from end to end of the yard, every now and then coming across a wounded man as we went.

The electric light was then suddenly turned on us by the *Dolphin*—it had not been going before this—and the scene which presented itself to our eyes was one of awful horror. Two sentries had rushed in mortally wounded; one had dropped down dead, while the other was standing up, simply hacked to pieces, and bathed in his own blood, but without any sign of consciousness.

It was with a sense of relief that we heard the ships lowering their boats, and soon after they came alongside, and landed a party of blue-jackets and a doctor, who conveyed the wounded back on board.

By this time the enemy had made off, leaving their leader Abdul Adab dead on the ground. He had made across the yard to my tent, and was shot in the back by one of my men; but this only partially stopped him, for he hurried on and was eventually bayoneted by a man of the guard, who was himself cut down at the same moment.

His death evidently stopped the whole force outside coming down upon us.

There was a considerable force seen when the electric light

was turned on, hurrying away to the north-west, but the guns of the ships were unable to open on them for fear of the camp. Their idea was evidently to surround us, as, while one party attacked the guard in front, another party came round between us and the water, and entered the yard from that side. Their reserves were held in readiness to complete our destruction as soon as the first attack proved successful.

I am afraid the guard in the first instance was taken by surprise; the outlying sentries were pounced down upon before they could give the alarm, and most of the men of the guard were wounded as they came out of the guard-tent.

Had it not been for the determined bravery of the men, who one and all behaved splendidly, our losses must have been very great; as it was, we had three men killed and eight wounded.

Abdul Adab was a very fine-looking man, at least six feet two inches in height, and magnificently proportioned; he wore the ordinary white blouse, but had many ribbons across his chest, which we took to be decorations. He was afterwards recognised as Osman Digna's standard-bearer.

A report was current after this that Osman Digna had sent in word to say that if we would return the body of Abdul Adab, and not burn it, he on his part would undertake to forego all night attacks in future; but I am not able to vouch for the truth of the story. The body was not returned, but buried about a hundred yards in front of the Ordnance camp.

As to the losses sustained by the Arabs on this occasion, many traces were found of bodies being dragged away along the ground, and when the mounted infantry went out the following morning on their line of retreat, they came across many of their dead which had been dropped when the electric light had been turned on to them.

On the principle of shutting the stable-door after the horse had been stolen, means were at once taken to strengthen and defend the Ordnance camp. Earthworks were thrown up all round it, and strong parties of Egyptian troops were at work digging deep ditches and throwing up high parapets. These ditches soon filled with water, owing to the low level of the ground, and in a few days the stench there was frightful, and moreover was the cause of much sickness afterwards among the Ordnance Store Corps.

We were very hard at work all the next day getting our horses

Skirmish at a water hole

up from the Camel Depot. Most of them were English horses, and therefore unsuited to the climate, and they were, generally speaking, a seedy-looking lot. Many of them were unbroken, which fact did not lend to the pleasure of riding them in a hot climate. It would have been far better if we had had nothing but Arab horses for riding purposes, and mules for draft-work. Most of the horses we brought from England succumbed to the climate before very long. The mounted infantry were mounted on Arab horses, and had much the best of it over the rough ground. A part of our cavalry afterwards took over the horses from the Egyptian cavalry regiment at Suakin, who were also mounted on Arabs.

Night came again, and with the darkness the ball reopened and the bullets began to whistle over our heads. It was evident that we were to have no peace.

There was a large outlying picket of the 70th posted about four hundred yards to our front, and this kept firing away all night.

About one o'clock in the morning we suddenly heard a tremendous row going on just in our rear, and we thought at first that a party of the enemy had entered our horse-lines, but running out of the tent we found that the rear-guard of the 53rd were being attacked. It was always very difficult to make out from whence sounds came at night; the air was so clear that you could hear people shouting as if they were close to you, when in reality they were a mile or more off.

This attack on the rear-guard of the 53rd was a most audacious proceeding on the part of the enemy. The guard, fortunately for them, were lying down outside the guard-tent, while the double sentry patrolled up and down about fifteen yards in front, and behind a low-shelter trench. All at once party of some fifteen or twenty Arabs, who had crawled towards them in the darkness, jumped up, rushed up to the parapet, fired a volley or two into the guard, and then disappeared again immediately. The guard, who were under arms in a moment, fired in the direction of their retreat, but so far as could be gathered, without effect. The casualties among the guard were three men wounded, while a fourth had his rifle knocked out of his hand by a bullet which passed straight through the stock.

The night wore on, and our time was taken up going round our sentries and looking about, expecting every minute to be attacked; and again, we got no sleep. Firing was going on in every direction; and the bullets continued to hum and to whirr through the air, while many came through our tents.

We would not allow our men to fire, though they might have done so with perfect safety. We had begun during the day to throw up a shelter trench across the front of our camp, and we lined this with some of our men that night. It was three o'clock when we saw about a hundred yards to our front what we took to be something moving, and many of the men wanted to fire, but the order given in a low whisper was—

"Steady, men; wait till you can see the white of their eyes."

We were all lying on the ground, almost breathless with excitement, when we could see that, what some had thought to be bushes, were indeed a party of the enemy crawling stealthily towards us.

"Present," in a low tone, then a pause to allow for a steady aim, and then, "Fire!"

There was a cry and a shriek in front as the volley was thrown in, and then there was silence again. We gave them another, though, where we took them to be, and the next morning there was little doubt that some at least of our bullets had found their billets. So far as our camp was concerned, we were not troubled again that night, but we had no sleep.

I had to go down to Quarantine Island at daybreak to superintend the disembarkation of a shipload of camels from India, and was at work all day long at the job. I managed to secure a good breakfast though on board the vessel, the first I had had for some time.

The camels were packed pretty tight both on the upper and lower decks, and the smell of them was simply sickening. They were slung up from below by steam, and then dropped on an inclined plane and driven ashore. A native driver accompanied each three camels, and before the middle of the afternoon we had them all on the wharf and picketed inside the walls of the town for the night.

It was just growing dark as I got back to camp after a very hard day in the sun, and I would have given a good deal for a wash, but water was scarce, so I had to go without.

We began to take the firing at night now as a matter of course; and so, when the bullets began to fly about again, we took little or no notice of it, only passing a remark or two such as "They are beginning a little earlier tonight," or "No rest again, —— it!"

It was uncomfortable, though, letting alone the want of sleep. Lying all night long, either waiting for an expected attack, or peering into the darkness till every bush in front took the form of a man on the move, began to tell on our nerves. Then there was that sense of insecurity and the uncertainty of what might happen in the night, for none of us knew when we lay down at night whether we should be alive in the morning.

I was lying on my camp-bed with my sword on and my revolver ready to my hand. It must have been about half-past ten o'clock, and I may have been dozing. There had been no firing for an hour; and now that the sentries had been stopped calling "All's well!" the quiet of the camp was only broken by the neighing of a horse or the grunt or moan of a camel, when suddenly the stillness was interrupted by the most awful scream that it has ever been my lot to hear—a loud, long wail of agony, as of a man mortally wounded, crying out with his last breath. It was a sound that absolutely seemed to curdle the very blood in one's veins. Then came a rush through the camp as those men who had been in their tents turned out. A few random shots were fired without effect, and the enemy, if ever seen at all, had disappeared.

With the stealth of a wild beast, and with the wriggle of an eel, a party of Arabs must have entered the camp unnoticed by the sentries, and then rushing in through one door of a tent have stabbed and hacked with their long spears as they rushed through and out of the tent the other side. One poor fellow had been stuck with a spear right through the stomach, and with a last frightful and pitiful yell had expired at once.

How the Arabs managed to enter the camps we never discovered; but this sort of thing was repeated by them over and over again in the face of double sentries and guards and pickets all over the place.

We had a most uncomfortable night of it after this. Some of the enemy had got round in our rear, between the Water Forts and the cavalry camp, and had been sighted by a party of Indian infantry on the one side and the cavalry pickets on the other.

I had noticed, as I was coming home that night, that three circular redoubts had been thrown up on three sides of the cavalry camp, for what purpose has always been a complete mystery to me. What use they could possibly be nobody ever knew, as the cavalry camp was in rear of the centre of the front line of the encampment, and men firing from these redoubts at all must, in spite of every precaution, have fired into some camp or other either in front or to the right or left.

However, on the night in question, they were manned by the cavalry pickets. Whether any of the enemy really did get round in our rear I am unable to say; but there is no doubt that the men at this time fired at everything, and when they were not sure whether they saw anything or not they gave it the benefit of the doubt, and let fly.

In this way we very nearly suffered severely, and how we escaped being all killed is a mystery. Suffice it to say that we stood up there and watched the Indians fire volleys by squads clean into us, and we could count the number of men firing by the flashes, as they were not more than five hundred yards off. The firing from this side must have been infectious, for we very soon afterwards found ourselves under a crossfire from the cavalry redoubts on the other.

A pleasant variety of bullets were now cutting up the ground at our feet—the Indians, firing with Sniders, and the cavalry with Martini-Henry carbines. Our chief work was to prevent a stampede among our horses, but I am thankful to say the firing at length stopped before any serious damage was done, and we came out of action with our friends with the loss of a mule only. We, on our part, put the whole thing down to General Funk's account, as we saw nothing ourselves, and never fired a shot.

The main cause of danger was of course the utterly unsystematic arrangement of the camp, which could not have been too severely condemned, and it was generally considered that we ran more risks on account of our friends than we did on account of our enemies.

Our general arrived the next morning, so we all began to look forward to an advance being made very soon.

The whole force was now complete, and all the troops had arrived. Only one thing was not ready, and that was the water transport. We had plenty of transport animals, but nothing to carry water in; no tanks, or barrels, had as yet arrived from home, and it was impossible to move the force without the first requisite for an army operating in such a climate.

It was a most magnificent sight certainly, looking round the country from our camp in the early morning, for the Right Water Fort was the highest point between Suakin and the hills. Miles of tents were spread over the desert in every direction, like so many scattered hamlets. Long lines of camels and baggage animals traversed the plain, bringing up stores and munitions of all sorts, and mules were to be seen drawing water-carts up to the front with the supply of the precious fluid for the day. In the distance the white houses and squat towers of Suakin, with the harbour crowded with any number of gigantic transports, which seemed almost to dwarf the houses with their enormous proportions.

Behind the town one could see the low flat shores and surf-washed coral reefs of the Red Sea, trending away miles and miles to the southward till they were lost in the hot brazen mists of the horizon. On the other side, that is towards our front, there was nothing but the flat, hot, inhospitable desert, with its ragged patches of wild growth, and its clumps of mimosa thorn bushes scattered here and there, far and wide. Only one thing relieved the monotony of the scene in this direction—the mirage, which at this time of day was always most striking, as it converted parts of the desert into a series of beautiful lakes, with objects of fantastic form reflected on their smooth surfaces. A line of bush would be turned into a strong line of entrenchments, while a clump of mimosa often took the form of some outlying fort, or work of great strength.

Behind all came the magnificent range of mountains brilliant in a deep crimson colour, and standing up against the hot sky with a dark purple outline. There was a marvellous clearness in the atmosphere in the early morning, and every detail of the mountains could be seen as far off as forty miles or more. It was at this time of day, too, that the sailors stationed in the tops of the men-of-war in harbour very often sighted parties of the enemy retiring towards Hasheen after tormenting us all night. When they did it was not long before a "*boom*" was heard, and a great nine-inch shell went hurtling through the air, aimed with unerring precision at a range of nearly six miles. A dull echo of the shot and a column of dust thirty or forty feet high told us of their position, but we could never see whether the shots took effect or not, though there could not be much doubt about it.

We were hard at work all day branding camels, each animal having to be marked with the Broad Arrow and a distinguishing number. It was a tedious and tiresome job, but the camels bore it with their accustomed resignation, and we only had one accident during the several days we were at it—our farrier sergeant getting a kick from a vicious one full in the face. As fast as they were numbered, they were sent off on various fatigues, bringing up rations or firewood for the various regiments of the brigade. Every bit of firewood we used out there was brought hundreds of miles by sea, as there was none to be had in that part of the Sûdan.

The days seemed very long, and owing to the harassing night attacks both days and nights appeared to be mixed up. Want of sleep began to tell a bit on the men, but we had very little or no sickness, though we were toiling all day long, and watching and being shot at all night.

A curious order came out at this time, but I am unable to say how far it was ever carried out. Each man was to be provided with a cartridge or two, the bullet of which had been cut into four pieces, and these were to be used at night "pending the arrival of buckshot cartridges from England." The idea was good one, but we thought it somewhat of a slight on the men, as it was of course done to get over the danger of one camp firing into another. The men ought never to have been allowed to fire at all, or even to load their rifles. The bayonet was quite good enough, and several battalions out there gave up firing at night times altogether. We were firmly convinced ourselves that a great deal of the firing was due to shaky nerves, and many a bush got a hot peppering because of its imaginary likeness to a "Fuzzie."

I went out one morning in front of the redoubts to look at a point at which there had been some heavy firing the night before. It was a raised mound of sand where, when first we came out, a picket was always stationed. On the top of this mound stood a barrel filled with sand, behind which the sentry of the picket was posted. This barrel stood up against the sky line at night and in the darkness might have been taken for anything, and certainly resembled a crouching figure, as one of the staves had been broken and stuck out from the side like an arm.

This old barrel must have had a very hot time of it, for it was simply riddled with bullets; I counted thirty-eight shot-holes, and when I emptied it, among others, I found a shrapnel bullet, so all arms must have had a go at the barrel, and it was certainly very satisfactory to see how many of the shots had been successful.

We had now been four nights without sleep, and should have been very grateful to the Arabs if they would have kindly given us a night's rest and agreed to carry on the war according to ordinary principles. But not a bit of it; no sooner had we finished our evening meal than the firing began again, and another night was spent lying in the trenches, and watching till day dawned.

We only allowed half of our men to sleep in the tents, the other half sleeping behind the shelter trenches ready to repulse any attack in a moment. We had also at this time one or two "friendlies" of the Amarar tribe, who kept watch with our men during the night. The extraordinary keenness of eyesight possessed by these people we thought might have been of use to us, as they appeared to be able to see in the dark very nearly as well as they could in the daylight. Several times over they made signs to us that they could see figures moving across our front, and even became quite excited about it, and entreated us to shoot, but we could see nothing. It was very curious to watch them, but somehow, I never felt any trust in them.

These "friendlies" wore a scarlet serge blouse and carried spears and shields, and they were regularly in our pay. I am not at all sure, though, that these fellows did not strip off their red shirts and carry to Osman Digna's people a complete account of our strength and proposed movements, and many of us thought that the so-called "friendlies" in Suakin, who were suffered to walk about the place fully armed and to come and go as they liked, were the very fellows who made the night attacks on our camp. No native should ever have been allowed to carry arms unless he had been regularly enrolled among the natives in our pay.

It was no uncommon sight just before sunset to see groups of armed natives coming out of Suakin. Where they were going I for one never knew, but I should have been very sorry to have met them after dark. In the face of the acknowledged treachery of these people it was curious that no attempt was ever made to put a stop to this sort of thing; but we English are a confiding people.

Chapter 5

Preparation

We were getting tolerably accustomed to being out in the sun all day by this time. The weather was very hot and the sun shone down upon us with never a cloud in the sky to mitigate its rays. It set at night in a sky of the deepest crimson, and rose in the morning again to scorch us, to burn us, and almost sear us with its horrible power.

I often used to think of the old country at home, where the sunlight was a blessing, and then look round on this bare, bleak, desolate desert, where life was not, and where the sun was a curse, where pestilence and fever were hatched by it, and where men fled from it to escape, if it were possible, its pitiless power. And yet we toiled on beneath its rays; we rose in the morning and had done many an hour's hard work before the sun showed above the horizon of the Red Sea yonder. But we did not rise in order to get the work done before the heat of the day, but in order to crowd more working hours into the twenty-four.

It was wonderful to see how "Tommy" made himself at home. You would see him carrying on an energetic conversation with a native, and making up for his deficient knowledge of the language by talking at the top of his voice, and of course always addressing the native familiarly as "Johnnie." Then you would see him trying to make a pet of a camel, or riding one as if he had never ridden anything else. A hundred different duties fell to his lot, cooking, branding, fatigues innumerable, digging entrenchments in the very heat of the day, pitching tents, going on guard, watching all night under a heavy fire, and many other things besides. He got through them all, though, and was always to be heard chaffing and laughing, for he is a good fellow, Tommy Atkins, though he is bound to have a grumble and a growl sometimes, for "'tis his rights."

Among our most uncomfortable experiences were the sand storms, which came regularly almost every third day. The wind would rise and blow harder and harder with its hot breath till the air became filled with fine sand. There was no keeping it out of anything; the whole of the inside of a tent was covered with it almost immediately and everything buried. Everything one tried to eat was full of it, one's eyes and hair were full of it, it got into the water in the covered tins, and worked its way through one's clothes. If a tin of meat was opened it was filled with the fine dust at once, and all our food was full of grit and our bread spoiled.

Outside the tents the air was as thick as a London fog, and marching in it nearly blinded one; but we had to work on just the same, though it was very difficult to find our way from one point to another. The goggles we had been supplied with failed to keep it out, and the veils were of little use, only sifting the dust one swallowed a little finer, till eyes, nose, and throat were clogged with it. The temperature during these sand storms would generally be about 85°; so, the dust used to stick to us and plaster us, and there was little or no water to wash it off. As a rule, the wind dropped at about three o'clock in the afternoon, and the air became clear again.

It seemed to have struck somebody about this period that a better disposition of the camp could be made, and that probably the men might obtain a little rest at night if the camps were placed in such a position that they would be a support instead of a danger to one another.

Orders were accordingly given to close up, and we had a very busy time shifting all the camps into their new positions. The Guards were withdrawn and their camp pitched in the general alignment, their right-resting on Sand-Bag Battery. The 49th were shifted over to the right of the 53rd, and the Royal Marines next to them. This completed the front line, which thus ran from the Water Forts on the left to Sand-Bag Battery on the right. The headquarters of the 2nd Brigade were shifted in rear of the 53rd, while the Headquarter Staff were encamped between us and the Right Water Fort. The cavalry were moved up and encamped about one hundred and fifty yards in rear of the 70th, and next to them on their right were the Mounted Infantry. Then came the Artillery and Engineers and a Field Hospital, "H Redoubt" being now turned into one of the shore hospitals.

The whole of the Indian Brigade was withdrawn from the southwest side of the town and brought round and encamped in rear of our left, thus making a line of camps facing towards the south. This

9TH BENGAL CAVALRY

brigade was composed of the following regiments15th Sikhs, 17th Bengal Native Infantry, the 28th Bombay Native Infantry, the 9th Bengal Cavalry, and two companies of the Madras Sappers and Miners. Strength about 3,000.

The strength of the whole force under General Graham must have been between ten and eleven thousand men, not including the native camel drivers.

The Indian regiments seemed to be much better off than we were, and the officers appeared to live in luxury; they went in for table cloths and glasses, and gave a very excellent dinner. The natives helped them out considerably, as they are by nature servants and cooks. They know how to make you comfortable under adverse circumstances, and certainly appear to be able to make a very good curry out of very little, though where the ingredients come from in the desert, I don't know; like French cooking, however, it doesn't do to ask too many questions. We gave a dinner party one night, and borrowed an Indian cook for the occasion. Our bill of fare we thought was grand:—Soup *pot au feu*; *entrée*, curry and rice; *pièce de résistance,* more curry and more rice; *entremets*, sardines; sweets, preserved peaches. The whole washed down with a couple of bottles of dry Monopole.

A cup of coffee all round followed, and a glass of whiskey before turning in, when we felt prepared for any number of Osman Dignas. Whether it was the above magnificent banquet, or that the Arabs let us alone, I only know that we went to bed, certainly, in our clothes, soon after ten o'clock, and never woke till a little before four o'clock the next morning. There was a faint idea, though, that the changing of the camp may have had a little to do with it. The enemy may have thought something was up, as they watched our movements of the previous day; they certainly never fired a shot, and I suppose took a rest too, after their extraordinary feats of unexampled temerity.

The result was good all round, as we had our first sleep for five nights. There are limits to everybody's power of endurance, and the want of sleep after the exhaustion of the day was beginning to tell on some of us very much. With good food and plenty of water, men can stand hard work night and day; but with indifferent food, and no variety from the daily ration of *bouilli* beef, there is bound to be a certain loss of power in a climate like that of the Sûdan, even with the strongest.

Before leaving home there had been great talking about moving the army into the hills at once, and thus getting the troops into a good climate. Five minutes at Suakin would have shown any one the utter impossibility of this. People talk at home as if it was as easy to move an army from one point to another as it is to move chessmen; and as simple to feed the army when you get it there, as it is to feed a party of school children, or to carry out the arrangements for a picnic on the banks of the Thames. The general tone of the conversation was something as follows:—

> Well, of course the climate of Suakin is hot, but then you see as soon as you get there you will be moved at once to Sinkat, and stop there for the summer. The climate is a beautiful one, very bracing and very refreshing; in fact, you will be quite well off.

Now, setting aside the enormous and gigantic amount of labour entailed in moving even a small body of say three thousand men over a short distance of six miles, and maintaining them at any particular point, when every ounce of food and every drop of water has to be carried on camels—it may be imagined at what cost it would be possible to move an army twelve thousand strong "at once," to a point thirty-six miles off, through a trying country, covered with a thorny bush and huge black boulders, rendering progress more and more difficult at every step, and with the chance of being hourly attacked by a determined foe constantly on the watch to take advantage of any laxity in your movements.

The convoy of camels to carry stores for even a day's supply is prodigious, and the rate of progression so tedious, owing to the difficulty of preventing any straggling, that not more than a mile and a half an hour can be traversed with any certainty.

As far as the climate of Sinkat goes, it is of course far preferable to that of Suakin, and comparatively healthy; but the difference of temperature is one of degree only, as it is exceedingly hot in the summer months, though upwards of three thousand feet above the sea.

There was plenty of talk, too, about the ease with which a railway could be laid, and the wildest rumours were afloat about the rate at which the work would progress. Of course, the army would be moved to Sinkat, and of course nothing would be easier than for supplies to be run out every day from Suakin.: The contractors or agents employed by the government were not much behind the troops in their arrival at Suakin, and two or three days after we landed several transports entered the harbour with their cargo of five miles of railway plant complete in every detail; and before we had been there a week, the British navvy was to be seen laying the sleepers and fixing the metals.

The first part of the line was easy enough. The ground was firm and perfectly level, and so the work progressed with vigour; but it was a different matter when the sandy, bush-grown country beyond the camp was reached, and "drifts" had to be cut through the thorny mimosa. All this—the severest part of the work—fell to the lot of the army.

The line was ballasted by the soldiers, the sleepers were carried forward in carts by our transport animals, and the rails had to be dragged from the point up to which they were brought by the train, by teams of mules or horses. The contractor's work, and that performed by the navvies, was merely placing the sleepers at the proper intervals, and fixing the rails. For this the navvies received the princely remuneration of twelve shillings a day, and time work, a free ration, and a free kit; while our soldiers received only as many pennies extra working pay as the navvies did shillings. By the contract, too, the firm undertaking the work were to receive bonuses in all of £40,000, in proportion as the various sections of the line were completed.

The additional labour thrown on the troops of guarding the head of the line, and the workmen during their labours, was also extremely heavy. Nothing could possibly have been worse for the men than this. They were exposed to the sun, and had nothing to do but stand about and think. A few tent roofs were sent out to protect them from the sun, but it was not always possible to use these.

I do not think more than from a thousand to twelve hundred yards were laid in a day over this, the easiest part of the country, from Suakin to Handub. The rate of progression in the hills would necessarily be reduced, and at this rate the line would probably reach Berber by the end of August next year, or in other words, the army would have been dragging its weary way along a track, exposed to a thousand hardships and privations, for a period of something like seventeen months, the distance from Suakin to Berber being not unfrequently traversed by camels in ten days.

Another thing. It would be absolutely impossible to build this railway on the telescopic principle—that is, making the railway carry all its own plant forward as it goes—if, indeed, this principle ever worked at all, and also to depending upon it for all the supplies of the army as well.

Under these circumstances the impracticability of running a railway over the thirty-six miles from Suakin to Sinkat, if, indeed, we were ever intended to move in that direction, may be imagined.

There is no doubt that the combination of the civil and military element in the attempt to lay this railway was a mistake. Either the railway should have been laid by the Engineers, as was first intended, or else it should have been carried out by a firm of contractors, representing a financial company in England, backed, if you wish it, by the government, and protected in their work as far as possible by English troops.

A party of about eight hundred *coolies* had been collected by the Royal Engineers in India, for the purpose of laying this line. Most of these men were experienced hands, and used to railway work. They were brought from India to Suakin, and proved of the greatest use, as they worked exceedingly well; but it was ridiculous to put this body of men, with their officers, under the orders of the contractors. Friction was bound to take place, and the experiment failed, and was therefore entirely given up.

The railway, to our thinking, was much too clumsy and heavy to be rapidly laid; and instead of a 4 feet 8½ inches gauge being adopted, the lightest possible form of railway compatible with stability and strength should be selected as the one for general use with an army, so that it would not only be very portable, but more applicable to rough countries, where sharp curves are often a necessity, and where gradients are of frequent occurrence.

During the Afghan war we were able to lay a light railway at the rate of a mile a day, but greater rapidity than this would have to be attained, and a mean of at least three miles a day would be none too much to expect.

The officer in charge of the line of communication found his hands tied in dealing with the contractors, as he was forbidden to interfere in any way with them; and though they on their side were only too ready to accept the help of the soldiers, without which they would have been at a standstill, it was impossible that a large civilian element could pull with the military, unless they were to a certain extent under military discipline, and for that reason under the same rules and regulations as the soldiers. Thus, again, it was found impossible to get along, and the work was accordingly retarded.

I am the last to discount the British navvy. I admire his many good qualities, and above all, his gigantic proportions and muscular development. I have always looked upon the navvy as one of the grandest types of our race, and I think if I were asked to bring forward a number of representative English working men, I should recruit among the navvies. But with all this, I am bound to confess that the navvy as seen at Suakin was not a success. Highly paid, well looked after, easily worked in comparison to the soldiers, and well fed, there was still a deal of grumbling, and none, or very little, of that cheery self-sacrifice and readiness to work of which we saw so many instances among our own men.

I sincerely hope that the many failures in connection with laying the Suakin-Berber Railway may be the cause of the authorities at home taking seriously into consideration the advisability of organising a regular Railway Corps.

A certain number of men attached to the Royal Engineers should be perpetually undergoing training in the various branches of railway making and railway-engineering. Opportunities at home are always close to hand, and could be easily taken up, and there should, therefore, never be any want of a field for operations of the sort. One thing is absolutely necessary, and that is, that the civilian element should in military railway laying be entirely eliminated.

Our wars are almost always carried on in countries not only without railways, but without roads. We have frequently been accustomed to make our own roads in war time, why should we not make our own railways?

With a force of trained officers and men as a nucleus, to be supplemented by paid native labour brought from India, or elsewhere, there should be no difficulty in carrying out work of this sort for an army in the field.

In these days of rapid movements, of quick concentrations, and short wars, every means offered by science, whether it be electricity, ballooning, or railway-making, should be at once adopted. We suffer ourselves to live in a fool's Paradise indeed, if we put off all matters of this sort to the day when we are actually called upon to act.

For the sake of "party," for the sake of courting popularity, for fear of interfering with monopolies and so-called "rights," and on account of a certain dread of what the next election will bring forth, and how we shall appear before our constituents with taxation on the rise, we often forego spending money where money is most needed; and so, after having gone in for a penny wise and pound foolish policy, we find ourselves squandering our soldiers, shedding our blood, and spending millions more than if we had taken the stitch in time at first. "A standing army is a necessary evil" we are told; if it is so, do not be satisfied with spending a mere sixteen millions and possessing a phantom, but spend more and see that the money is well spent.

With our great colonies and dependencies scattered all over the habitable globe, and with all the many heavy responsibilities and duties incumbent upon us by reason of our vast possessions, the absolute perfection of our army and our navy should always have our first consideration, and a Ministry which, for fear of risking popularity with the masses, allows these two services to fall into a state of inefficiency, should be driven at once from office as unworthy of the confidence of the nation. A great writer has said regarding our country, that:—

> While we have everything to fear from the success of the enemy, we have every means of preventing that success, so that it is next to impossible for victory not to crown our exertions. The extent of our resources, under God, is equal to the justice of our cause.

A great war is looming in the far East, and the vibrations of a first shock have already sounded on our ears. Let us be prepared, therefore, while there is yet time.

I'll live tomorrow, 'tis not wise to say;
'Twill be too late tomorrow: live today.

But I am digressing. We were all now looking forward to the general advance, which could not be much longer postponed. There was a sort of fever among the whole army to get on. Anything was better than lying in tents or trenches at night to be speared or shot at, and we one and all longed to be "up and at 'em." Our preparations were nearly completed, the water tanks and barrels had arrived, our stores were well up to the front, and yet there was delay, and we were condemned still to further days of waiting. Not that we sat with our hands in front of us, not a bit of it. There was always plenty of hard work to be done, and there always seemed to be too few hours in the day to get it all in.

I went up to the top of the Right Water Fort one afternoon to have a good look round the country with a fine telescope that was there, and very interesting it was. Half a mile to the front, and stretching right across to the West Redoubt, were our cavalry videttes and pickets. They must have had hot work of it, as they were out all day long standing nearly motionless in the sun. They had a few cases of sunstroke, which the doctors were pleased to diagnose as "exhaustion," and of course they suffered a good deal from sunburn.

There were one or two instances where men who had been out in this way all day, came in with a line across their faces as though cut with a knife, where the sun had caught them below the shade cast by the front of the helmet and opened the flesh.

Beyond the videttes were scattered groups of the enemy sitting or standing about, and perhaps waiting till darkness came on and they were able to make their customary descent on the camp. I could see them very plainly with the glass as one of the party would advance a little, evidently to take stock of what the cavalry outposts were doing. Then after a while he would return again, and there would be a deal of talking and pointing, when the whole lot would retire. They appeared to have a regular system of outposts, and these parties, consisting of from ten to twelve men, were to be seen dotted about all along the front.

We had one of our first doses, about this time, of the "*Hgramseen*," or "the wind of fifty days." It is very unpleasant, very enervating and very hot. This wind blows during this season of the year, and lasts off and on for fifty days, at any time of which it may be expected. One very curious thing about the *Hgramseen* is, that if it begins to blow one day it is absolutely certain to blow for three days, but if it blows over the third day it will continue till the fifth day, when it as certainly drops again. I don't know that it is an unhealthy wind, but it seemed to take all the energy out of one, and it was an effort to go about one's work.

As a general rule I was agreeably surprised with the climate, and though the heat was intense I could do a long day's work without feeling any fatigue. We were feeding better now, and used to send a camel down almost daily to bring up tinned provisions from one or other of the stores in Suakin. We got a variety of these provisions, and I think tried pretty well everything ever prepared either by Messrs. Moir or Messrs. Crosse and Blackwell. Our favourite things were the Oxford sausages and the herrings *à la sardine*, both of which were excellent. Stewed beef steak, haricot mutton, mutton *ragout*, and grouse *aux truffes*, were also among the most appreciated. The tinned vegetables were not at all bad, but we fought rather shy of these for fear of colouring matter.

Never shall I forget one of our party returning one evening with two tins of *foie gras*. Our delight was quite beyond description. We sat down there and then, and with a good allowance of ration bread very quickly put the contents of the two tins out of sight. But there is a sequel to this tale.

"Do you know," said our comrade, "I only gave half a crown a tin for it!"

"Dear me," rejoined we, "what a fool you were not to buy more!

So, it was settled that the very first thing the next morning he was to ride back again to Suakin and buy every tin he could lay his hands on.

By eight o'clock he had returned from his errand, but with no *foie gras* for breakfast, much to our dismay, for I think we had all been repeating to ourselves, *"Foie gras* for breakfast, more *foie gras* for dinner, and still more for supper;" in fact, to our hungry insides it was to be *"toujours foie gras."*

"Well," said one of us, who had been anxiously awaiting his return, "where's the *foie gras?*"

"Well," answered our comrade, with a very long face, "I have been a bigger idiot than I ever thought I could be. Do you know that when I entered the store where I bought the stuff last night, the man rushed up to me saying, "You are the officer who took the *foie gras;* you are the officer who took the *foie gras.*'— 'Yes,' said I, 'I certainly bought two tins of *foie gras* here last night and paid you half a crown for them.'—'Yes,' said the man in reply, by this time almost crying, 'I know you did—I know you did; but they are half a sovereign each and not half a crown!'"

We retired to our tent then with heavy sighs, and contented ourselves with the dry bread which was to have had the *foie gras* on it Perhaps it was just as well it hadn't.

One of our greatest failures with tinned provisions was with brawn.

"Who's for brawn this morning?" said our mess president.

"Why, of course, we are all for brawn," we replied.

The top of the tin was ripped off, and again we were doomed to disappointment.

"By Jove, it's soup!"

And so it was, and yet it had been packed in straw inside a large box. It was soup right enough, though—nasty, thick, greasy-looking soup, with pieces of white fat floating about in it.

Only one of the party tackled it, and he ate his brawn with a spoon.

We heard one morning that a shipload of oranges had arrived in harbour for the use of the troops, and "when practicable," said the orders on the subject, "an orange a day will be issued to each officer and man." "This indulgence, however," added the order, "is not to be looked upon as a right." So, for some days an orange apiece was given to us, and very good ones they were. I never knew what an orange really was before, and no peach on a hot summer's day at home ever tasted more delicious to us dried-up mortals than did those oranges. We simply devoured them, and felt inclined to eat peel and all.

I have never mentioned anything about our postal arrangements. We used to get our letters very regularly, considering all things, and though some necessarily never reached us, there was nothing to complain about. They only took ten days coming all the way from London, overland, *via* Brindisi, Alexandria, Cairo, and Suez, where a steamer of one sort or another met the mails and ran them down to Suakin. Every corps had its own letter-carrier, and a deal of sorting used to go on at the so-called post-office in Suakin, when the mail-bags arrived and were emptied out in piles on the floor.

It was rather like looking for a needle in a truss of hay, and the letter-carriers did not, therefore, always wait till the whole lot was sorted out. In this way one sometimes got a letter two days afterwards, when least expected, and much to the delight of the recipient. When the detachment of the Post-Office Volunteers arrived, everything was very well managed, and much of the previous inconvenience as well as risk of losing letters, both going and coming, was avoided.

We always thought it very hard that we should be called upon to stamp our letters to avoid a double rate of postage being levied on the friends receiving the letters at home. I believe this was claimed at first, though we used to write in the corner, "On active service. No stamps." Afterwards I heard that the ordinary rate of postage was claimed on delivery of the letters in England. It struck us as a little severe that any charge should be made at all. Surely letters from soldiers fighting hard for their country might always be allowed to go free. It is not much we get, and it would be a graceful concession if this boon were granted in future.

Few people can understand the enormous pleasure letters afford to soldiers on active service. When there is so much work and so many hardships to be undergone, a letter, giving a glimpse of the old home, is an untold joy. To hear about what they are all doing, what people think about the war, or even the smallest details of home life, all alike possess an interest quite beyond comparison. The most trivial incidents of everyday life are magnified in one's mind into pieces of momentous intelligence, and none of us, I am sure, ever found letters either too numerous or too long.

The lucky ones who received letters sat down and simply devoured them, and, with a happy smile upon their faces, they would read and read till their eyes seemed as if they would burn through the paper, while they drank in the news of home, of wife, of children. Reading the letters was easy enough, but getting time to write them was quite another thing. The only way was to have a letter always going, and add to it as time allowed.

Newspapers were a great blessing, and we were quite as eager to see the news of the war "on the paper" as the people at home were. And here I feel bound to put in a word about the "war correspondents." A more hard-working set of fellows I never saw. Up early and late, they were always in the front where fighting was going on, and always to be found where bullets fell thickest and where danger was to be met with. Then, after the fighting was over, or, perhaps, after a long march, they would ride miles in the hot sun and sit up half the night to write home the doings of the day.

There always seemed to be a great spirit of rivalry among the different representatives of the press, and there was always a race among them to get their messages off first. The people at home ought to be very grateful to the war correspondent, for he risks all, and sacrifices himself entirely to supply news to be consumed daily at the breakfast-table, or in the quiet and comfort of some club armchair. There is much that he would telegraph home, if he could, but since the appointment of a press censor, he is only able to send exactly what that officer allows him, and no more. In this way many details which should be known at home never reach there until the reason for publishing them has passed away.

What is forbidden in the telegrams is naturally enough written in the weekly letters, but by the time these get into print they are for the most part stale news. It is, of course, absolutely necessary that certain restrictions should be put upon correspondents for many reasons. In these days of universal cables, news of the movements of an army is quickly enough sent home, and there is nothing to prevent its being as quickly sent out again for the information of the enemy; but many unnecessary restrictions are put upon correspondents which might be removed, and many an item of news which should be sent home is now stopped, because it would, it is supposed, create needless alarm. Oh, for the days of the immortal Russell!

Of all the thankless positions in an army in the field, the press censor has the worst. Abused by correspondents at the seat of war, maligned by editors at home, and continually found fault with by his superiors with the army for allowing too much to pass, he must have the temper of an angel, the tact of a consummate diplomatist, and the nerves and constitution of a Hercules, ever to carry on the work and live through it. For every single word that passes along the cables to the newspapers he is responsible, and every telegraphic message has to bear his signature before it can be sent off. Added to which he frequently has other duties of an arduous nature to perform, as those of press censor are combined more often with those of an officer acting on the staff in some capacity or another.

There were three figures which became very familiar to us in the camp. They were often to be met with together, and they would turn up at all times of the day; in fact, they always seemed to be riding about somewhere, looking after some detail here or inspecting some fresh arrivals there.

The first of these was a very tall, broad-shouldered man, with a certain shrewd look in his face, with a kindly manner and a soldierly bearing. The double line of ribbons across his jacket showed him to be a man who had seen a deal of active service, and amongst his ribbons was the most prized of all orders, though now becoming a little too common.

He always seemed very grave, as if he bore on his shoulders the weight of some overpowering responsibility, and he certainly acted on the principle that silence was golden, for he told his staff nothing, and, they say, consulted nobody. One of his personal staff once told me that they never knew an hour beforehand when a move was going to take place, and that this reserve was carried so far that they never even knew what time they were going to have their dinners. Report put him down as a man who had studied deeply, and who was well versed in the science of war. His pluck in action and his excessive coolness under fire were undeniable, but his repute as a general was somewhat slender.

We all liked him because of his many attractive qualities, and above all he was a true friend and a perfect gentleman. He might have been popular, but his somewhat cold manner and habitual reserve rather repelled any advances, and there was none of that spontaneous *bonhomie* and happy manner with his troops, which, while it sacrifices nothing to discipline, wins for a commander the love of his soldiers.

The second figure was different altogether from the first. He was of middle stature, somewhat stout, and with a round, red, good-humoured face. He, too, wore many ribbons, and possessed also the red one of the Victoria Cross. He had a quick, sharp way of asking questions, and a somewhat "stand-off" manner with strangers, though when you knew him there was pleasanter companion or kinder-hearted friend. He possessed also an attractive manner, and a cool, quiet way of taking things, which made him to a certain extent popular. He looked though he had the constitution of a giant, and as if he could stand or go through with anything. He was always perfectly self-satisfied, and even when things went against him, he acted as though it was all *couleur de rose* and rather a good thing for him.

As to any qualifications to command—these were shown in after days. I ought to mention his right-hand man—a true soldier, an energetic staff officer, unhampered by rule and the trammels of red tape, and with the inestimable quality of perfect readiness to accept responsibility and total fearlessness of the consequences. Everybody liked him, and, though he had a quick temper, he never lost it, and if you wanted anything done, he did his best to help you, sinking personal considerations before all others.

As to the third, he was a short, sharp-featured individual, with a pompous and rather disagreeable manner, a loud voice, a quick temper, and a sense of his own importance which defied everything. He was not popular, and he seemed generally to be absorbed in that wonderful thought, "I am." A short answer was all you ever received from him, and one which often fell far short of ordinary courtesy.

There was a fourth I should mention, who held the most enviable place of all. I never met him myself, but I never heard anything but the highest praise of him from his brigade, in which I had many old Eton friends.

I mentioned just now the extraordinary way in which all projected movements of the force were kept a most religious secret, and how even the Heads of Departments never knew until sometimes half an hour beforehand of the intentions of our commanders. I cannot think that this was justifiable in the extent to which it was carried. Secrecy is an absolute necessity very often in times of war, and especially so in a country where the inhabitants are more than ever quick to take advantage of any news, they may get hold of, and where a general is surrounded by so-called "friendlies," always on the watch to carry over to our enemies news of our intended movements.

I am perfectly ready to allow all this, but I think that officers placed in a confidential position are entitled to consideration by reason of that position, and, at the same time, I think it is a slight upon the character of those holding commands when they are not taken into the confidence of their leaders.

I do not wish it to be inferred from this that I think commanding officers and Heads of Departments should be at all times consulted, far from it; I think that there would be a considerable element of weakness in adopting for one moment such a course. But I do think their convenience should be at all times considered, for two reasons—first, because hurrying may thus be avoided; and second, because their men may be saved the strain of work attendant upon sudden movements. Let a general's movements be as sudden and unexpected as possible-indeed, in a warfare such as we were engaged in it is absolutely necessary that they should be so to ensure success—but do not let this suddenness and rapidity of movement be attained at the price of a certain loss of efficiency, as well as much grumbling, when both can be so easily avoided.

No department of the army felt the extreme inconvenience of this excessive reserve more than did the Commissariat and Transport. I often heard many of the senior officers of this branch of the service say that they knew nothing of what was going to happen, and that orders would come in to them one hour which had to be carried out the next. There is no doubt that in all branches of the service in the Sûdan much of the confusion, hurry, and annoyance caused by this mode of procedure would have been avoided if a certain amount of trust had been placed in commanding officers and Heads of Departments. If officers in responsible and important positions are not considered worthy of trust, it is high time that those holding such positions should be replaced by officers that are.

We all knew now that any hour we might hear the welcome news to advance, but we none of us had the least idea in which direction the advance would be, though we inferred it was not to be towards Sinkat, on account of the direction in which the railway was being laid.

That there would be fighting, and hard fighting too, we were well aware, and, from the cool way in which the enemy made his night attacks on us, it was evident that Osman Digna had not profited by the lesson we had given him last year—a lesson, too, from which we gained nothing, when we might as easily have marched on Khartoum and rescued Gordon as withdrawn to our ships. The opportunity then offered has never occurred again, and so through a mixture of vacillation, weakness, and total incompetence, we soldiers were for a second time sent forward to dye the desert sand red with our own and the Arabs' blood, and sow the burning plains thick alike with the graves of the Christian and the Mohammedan.

Years hence the wail of misery which had its birth in all the bloodshed, the slaughter, the sickness, and the suffering endured by our soldiers in that bloodstained frying-pan, the Sûdan, will still find an echo in the land at home, where gaps in happy circles remain for ever unfilled, and where homes are blighted with the crushing weight of a sorrow that will never heal.

CHAPTER 6

The Advance

We were going to advance; the day for which we had all been waiting, working, longing, for the past few weeks, was coming at last. A renewed activity seemed to start up in the camp, and men went about congratulating each other, with a happy smile on their faces, that they were not "going to stick here no more," as they put it.

We knew nothing about what day it was going to be, and of course all sorts of rumours were going the round of the camp. At one time it was going to be "tonight," the next that it had been put off till "tomorrow at daybreak," and so on.

I was awoke on the morning of the 19th of March, after a long night's work, by a friend saying, "Come out and see the cavalry; they are all out just in front of our camp." So up I jumped, and, by way of getting a good view of what was going on, ran up to the top of the Water Fort, and there below me was as fine a parade of troops as anyone could wish to see.

On the left was the whole cavalry force, including the two squadrons of the 5th Lancers and the 20th Hussars, the 9th Bengal Cavalry, and the Mounted Infantry. Next to these were the Indian Infantry Brigade, and on the right were the three battalions of Guards, a battery of Royal Horse Artillery being stationed with the cavalry. After a short inspection by the general, the English cavalry were thrown forward, and gradually spread themselves out over the plain like a great fan, the advance parties keeping up a continuous flow of messages to the main body by means of the ordinary signalling flags.

The 9th Bengal Cavalry acted as a support and accompanied the guns. The Indian infantry were kept out some time, in the event of their being required, but the brigade of Guards was sent back to camp. I do not think I ever witnessed a more imposing spectacle than was presented by the beautiful working of this cavalry force, as they gradu-

Hussars charging with native spears

ally felt their way across the plain towards the mountains and in the direction of Hasheen. The Mounted Infantry were pushed to the front as the force neared the hills, and a few shots were fired at small parties of Arabs who showed themselves from time to time.

It was considered probable that the enemy would be found in force behind the isolated hills which stand out on the plain in front of the mountains, and behind one of which the village of Hasheen is situated.

Our Mounted Infantry ascended cautiously to the crest of this hill, on reaching which considerable bodies of the enemy were seen both in the valley below and along the ridges in front. Only a few shots were fired by the enemy, to which our men replied. An Arab was seen to fall here and there, as they retired up the gorge leading towards the mountains, but they never attempted to stand, and were evidently only a part of Osman's forces, numbering in all not more than a thousand men.

Hasheen was found entirely deserted. It consisted only of about forty wretched-looking huts, a few of which had been evidently quitted in rather a hurry, as there were remains in some of a half-eaten meal.

A thorough examination of the ground was made, and a well discovered. It was also ascertained that water could be obtained a few feet beneath the surface. The enemy never attempted to interfere with our movements, and by our sudden advance we had evidently taken him by surprise.

Before retiring, a letter from General Graham to Osman Digna was placed on a white stick in the centre of the village. In this letter General Graham referred to the respect that England entertained for all religions, and stated that it was her chief desire to maintain friendly relations with the Arab tribes, and to establish peace in the country. After referring to the defeats sustained by the Arabs at Teb and Tamanieb last year, the letter went on to advise the *sheikhs* to submit without delay, and thus escape the punishment and death almost certain to overtake them. This letter was in reply to one received by General Graham from Osman Digna a week or two ago, in which, after recapitulating his many victories and the defeats sustained by the Egyptians under Hicks and Baker, he advises us to withdraw before a like fate overtakes us and we are driven bodily into the sea.

Having thus completed our reconnaissance, orders were given to retire. The village was left as we found it, and, immediately our retirement commenced, was re-occupied by the enemy, who were seen all along the tops of the hills as we marched back towards home. Our losses were only one man killed, and one officer and one man wounded.

Two or three prisoners were taken, and one of them, an old man with white hair, was barbarously cut down by one of the "friendlies" who accompanied the force, before anyone had time to interfere.

The whole force was back again in camp by one o'clock in the day.

One word about the 9th Bengal Cavalry. A more magnificent regiment no one could wish to see. Their loose-fitting dress, made of khaki, with blue *puttees* instead of long boots, and with blue-and-grey turbans as a head-dress, the appearance of these fine, swarthy-looking warriors was enough to strike terror into any foe. They were very grand-looking men and splendid horsemen; but why were they ever sent to Suakin to act as a lancer regiment, when there were so many splendid lancer regiments to choose from in India? Their arms are a sword and a carbine, which they wear on a cross-belt over either shoulder, but beyond a certain amount of practice a few of them may have had in tent-pegging at regimental sports, not one of them had ever had a lance in his hand before.

And yet they were sent off to Suakin to act as lancers in the field, and use a weapon in action which is allowed to be one of the most difficult to handle, and which a man cannot be taught to use properly under two years of constant training and practice. What was the result? Having been provided with their staves through the philanthropy of a native prince when actually on their march down country for embarkation, they arrived at Suakin knowing, naturally enough, nothing whatever about handling a lance; and, to mend matters, two or three of the 5th Lancers were sent every day to give them instruction in the way to use their new weapon.

Of all arms the lance is the best in warfare against a savage nation armed for the most part with spears, as it is a matter of necessity to keep the enemy at a distance. A sword is next to being absolutely useless against a spear and a shield, especially when these are in the hands of warriors who have been accustomed to handle them since their earliest boyhood. The result of suddenly arming a regiment in this way was that, knowing nothing about the use of the weapon, the men, when in action, threw away their lances and drew their swords.

As regards the dress of the 9th Bengal Cavalry, they all wear steel-chain shoulder-bands, which serve as an excellent protection against a sword-cut. Some of our English cavalry officers had steel chains sewn into their shoulder-cords; but why should not these be part of the regular dress of our cavalry, as it is that of the Indian cavalry?

Just as the reconnoitring party were coming into camp, I was telegraphed for to go down, with another officer, to No. 5 Pier, where all the condensed water was pumped from the ships into large iron tanks on the wharf. I had no time to put any food into my haversack, as we had to be off at once. Moreover, the rations had not come up, so I could only take with me a box of meat lozenges. We were down at the pier, which was about two miles from our camp, in under a quarter of an hour, and there we found we had to collect on the wharf adjoining the pier several hundred tins, barrels, and *mussocks* or water-skins, which were being landed at the Ordnance camp about a quarter of a mile off.

We had to help us, a fatigue party of a hundred men from an Egyptian regiment, with four Egyptian officers and about fifty *coolies*. A well-known figure out there also accompanied us, and many were the nights of hard work we did together afterwards. A cheery voice, a happy, pleasant manner, a splendid constitution, and a man who never spared himself, he was more than popular with all of us. A civilian—he had never been a soldier—wearing a grey jacket decorated with the Cape medal ribbon, a round white cap with a peak in front and a curtain behind, and generally to be seen riding a small camel, his figure was familiar to all of us; and some thought he looked a regular guy as he went about here and there, helping things along.

Our orders were to have thirteen thousand gallons of water loaded and ready to march by daybreak the next morning. With such material to work with it looked almost a hopeless undertaking, but it had to be done, and therefore must be done. A more miserable, indolent, useless lot of fellows than those Egyptian soldiers I never came across. Big men, most of them, but so lazy and so slack that it was utterly impossible to get them to move out of the slowest of walks, and their officers seemed unable to do anything with them.

However, by dint of a deal of driving and pushing, we managed to get the tins and barrels on to the wharf just as it was getting dark, and we also rigged up six hand-pumps to pump the water out of the storage tanks into the portable tanks. These portable tanks were made of galvanized iron, and were about three feet long, eighteen inches deep, and eight inches wide. Each one held twelve gallons and a half, and we put their weight down, when filled, at 125 pounds. They were fastened with a screw stopper, which could be secured with a key.

The barrels were of two sizes—the largest held twelve gallons and a half, and the smallest eight gallons. The *mussocks* were water-skins bought in Egypt. They were supposed to hold eight gallons each; but they leaked very much, and after the first time of using them, we always avoided filling them if we possibly could. Who was responsible for their purchase, I don't know, but they never should have been bought. They were supposed to have been passed by a board of officers, who sanctioned their purchase at one pound apiece. Their value could not have been more than a few shillings, and to us they were almost, if not entirely, useless. The water, after it had been in them a few hours, was absolutely undrinkable, and stank. The skins themselves were covered with a brown grease, which stained one's hands, and withal they crawled with vermin.

Just before sundown the camels to carry the water arrived; these were about seven hundred in number, and we parked them in lines of fifty, one behind the other, alongside the field railway, a branch of which ran down to the pier.

A rather amusing thing occurred as the sun sank behind the mountains. The *coolies* one and all dropped on their knees, said their prayers, and then made off at their best pace, as it was contrary to their religion or inclination—I don't know which to work after sunset. We had no time to run after them, however, so we let them go. A fresh fatigue party arrived about seven o'clock, and replaced the one we had been working with all the afternoon. As bad luck would have it, this party was also of Egyptian soldiery, scarcely less feeble than the first. No wonder we administered such a wholesome thrashing to them in 1882, and that they cut and ran directly they saw the tops of our hats.

We began filling the tins at about eight o'clock, and we managed it in this way. A pump with india-rubber hose fitted to it was rigged up in each of the large storage tanks into which a constant flow of condensed water was pumped from the condensing ships. Each of these pumps was manned by two men, and two more looked after the portable tins as they filled them through an ordinary leather funnel, a third screwing up the stopper and making it fast with a key. Then a fresh supply of tins was brought by another lot of men, who took away the full ones and arranged them in rows ready for packing into the trucks on the field railway.

It was not until late at night that we were able to get an engine to draw the trucks up to the place where the camels were parked.

However, we did get one at last, and then we began to run the tins and barrels up the line, and with a part of our fatigue party to unload the train again and place the tins in rows between the camels, two in front of each animal, ready to be put in the *celitas,* or nettings, later on.

It was very heavy work for us, as, though the Egyptian officers did their best to make their men work, we had to do the hardest part of it ourselves, or it would never have been done at all. If we turned our backs for a moment these fellows would sit down on the ground, light their cigarettes, and talk. It really was almost maddening sometimes trying to get anything out of them, added to which, only one of our party could speak Arabic. We had begun the night's work with one of the interpreters attached to the army, but he became tired of the job as soon as it got dark, and we saw nothing of him again till morning.

It was now getting on for ten o'clock, and we had been many hours at work without food, so I suggested going across to the Ordnance camp and begging a crust of bread.

I found my way over in the darkness, but my friends there had nothing of any sort or kind to give me, as they had eaten all their ration of bread for their evening meal; so, there was no help for it but to return to the pier with empty hands as well as empty inside.

I forgot to say that we were lighted in our work by a lamp composed of five incandescent lights hung from the top of a pole. These were worked by "leads" laid on from the *Dolphin*. They gave an excellent light, and I don't know what we should have done without them. It was a curious sight to see this one spot illuminated as bright as day, while all around was inky darkness; the Egyptian soldiers, in their white uniform and red *fezes*, puddling about ankle-deep in water as they toiled along with the heavy tins or pumped away standing up on the tops of the great storage tanks.

There was little to break the silence but the sucking of the pumps, or perhaps a loud remark from one or other of us, more often the reverse of parliamentary, addressed to some of the fatigue party. Every now and then the engine would give a whistle as it started with its heavy load slowly along the line in the darkness. The engine-driver fell asleep at last from sheer exhaustion, so I, by way of a little relaxation, manned the engine and drove the train up and down the line. In this way the night wore on till at length we had filled the last *mussock*.

Then we joined the camels and woke up the drivers, who were sleeping on the ground rolled in their blankets. There were one or two officers with the various detachments of camels making up the whole number, and these soon had their men together and ready to load up; so we dismissed the Egyptians and went to work at once to get the tins on the camels, for it was now nearly three o'clock in the morning, and we should have to march in an hour and a half.

As each section of fifty camels was loaded, we marched them off with orders to halt opposite the Headquarter camp.

During this time, we were working by the electric light thrown on us from the *Dolphin,* which gave a curious weird appearance to the mass of men in their many-coloured garments as they toiled away with a will to get the seven hundred camels loaded before the day should begin to break. Affghans, Soumalis, Punjabis, and Bengalis, all mixed up together, toiled on through the remainder of the night, and the camels grunted and groaned and made the hours hideous with their horrible sounds.

Each camel had two tins or two barrels put on him, so they had an easy load. The Indian camels moved along in strings of three, but the Berbera animals were not tied, a driver looking after three or four of them. Some of the barrels leaked very much, as the wood had become very dry, and the *mussocks,* as I have already said, very soon parted with half their contents. The last section was loaded as the sky began to blush in the east with the presage of the early dawn, and we had still half an hour left us before the day would break. What a night of toil it had been! and what an age it seemed since one o'clock the previous afternoon! Hot, tired, sleepless, and foodless, we had still only half completed our task as yet, and we had still before us many hours of work, of marching, and probably of fighting, in all the heat of the noonday sun.

It will be long indeed before I forget the kindness of a friend who brought me a cup of cocoa as I was mounting my horse to catch up the front line of camels. It is always thus with soldiers—those who have give to those that have not, though the one may be an entire stranger to the other, and though they meet then for the first time, and never perhaps afterwards. It is this *camaraderie* among members of the same cloth which marks the English soldier above all others, and makes the English Army what it is.

I have seen men almost starving, yet share with a comrade what would hardly fill their own mouths three times over; and I have noticed others parched with thirst themselves offer, it may be to a stranger, the cup of precious water before they put it to their own lips. It is in trying circumstances, in times of tribulation, and, above all, in times of war, that the noblest qualities of a man are brought out, and that a spirit unknown before shines at length brilliant in its true colours.

But we had to push forward; the different units of the force were gathering together and forming up into three sides of one vast square, in the middle of which were hundreds of camels, our water detachment being but a quarter of the gathering—mules drawing carts with entrenching tools, teams of horses, ambulances, *dhoolies* with their bearers ready to receive their ghastly burdens, and the various detachments of the field hospitals with their doctors and appliances.

The cavalry were already out in front; the sun was just rising above the horizon, and in a few minutes his heat would reach us, when at length the vast concourse of men and baggage-animals began to move, and the advance had begun. The huge square, measuring some eight hundred yards across, went forward in a cloud of dust without hurry and without noise, save the clank of arms, and with all that marvellous precision of movement attained by perfect organisation and thorough training, for around us was some of the flower of the British Army—a chosen force, perfect in every detail, animated by one spirit, ready for any emergency. So, forward we went in all the—

Pride, pomp, and circumstance of glorious war

. . . . and the advance had begun at last.

CHAPTER 7

Hasheen

The troops composing the great square, in which formation we advanced towards Hasheen, were as follows:—The front face was composed of three battalions of the 2nd Brigade, *viz.* the 49th, 70th, and Royal Marines; the other regiment of this brigade, the 53rd, having been left behind to look after the camp. On the right face were the Brigade of Guards, and the left face was formed by the Indian Brigade, *viz.* the 15th Sikhs and the 17th and 28th Bombay Native Infantry. The troops inside the square, besides the Commissariat and Transport Corps, were the 17th and 24th companies of the Royal Engineers, some Madras Sappers and Miners, two rocket-troughs of the Royal Artillery and a battery of Gardner guns. The cavalry force in front was composed of two squadrons of the 5th Lancers, two squadrons of the 20th Hussars, and four squadrons of the 9th Bengal Cavalry. There was also in front a battery of Royal Horse Artillery and the greater part of the Mounted Infantry.

With the cavalry and mounted infantry covering the front we marched along through the bush, which in this part is somewhat scanty, and did not impede us much. The square moved a little too fast for the baggage-animals, and there being no rear face to it, there was a good deal of straggling in spite of all endeavours to push the camels along. It was a perpetual drive, drive, drive; but very few loads were displaced, and none of the water was lost except through the leaking of the barrels and the skins.

So, with the sun scorching on our backs, we marched along till we lost sight of Suakin, and at length, without opposition, reached the isolated hills to which I referred in the last chapter.

It was now about half-past eight, and we had come a distance of six miles or more. The square was halted for a few minutes, while our generals scanned the hills and mountains in front and settled their plan

The 15th Sikhs

of attack, as it was seen that the enemy did not mean us to have it all our own way as we had had the day before, and that since yesterday he had concentrated his forces and was fully intending to oppose our further advance. The country in front of us was covered with a dense, thorny bush; there were a few rough tracks here and there, but for the most part it was entirely overgrown. Nearer the hills the bush was much higher, quite high enough indeed to hide a man on a horse, but the hills themselves were bare and rugged, and very precipitous.

One large isolated hill, a thousand feet high and a mile and a half long, stood like a great island out of the surrounding bush, and on the other side of this hill was the village of Hasheen. On the right, and three-quarters of a mile from Hasheen Hill, were the mountains, some two or three thousand feet high, which here abut on to the plain, and then turn again in a north-easterly direction towards Handoub, distant about seven miles. Behind Hasheen the range of mountains trends away in a north-westerly direction till they circle round to where the village of Tamai is situated, twelve miles to the south-west.

In front of where we halted stood two conical-shaped hills, one behind the other, and two hundred feet in height, while to the left of this there was a much lower hill, which was afterwards used as the point where the General Commanding took his stand. These hills were to the south of Hasheen Hill, and a mile from it, and were not occupied by the enemy.

The 70th Regiment and the convoys were ordered off to take up their position between the two conical hills above mentioned, and to construct a *zariba* connecting them together. Sand-bag redoubts were to be at once thrown up on the summit of each, to hold two guns of the Horse Artillery battery, and the Royal Engineers and Madras Sappers were soon at work dragging the heavy pieces of timber they had brought with them up the steep sides.

In the meanwhile, the 49th, supported by half a battalion of Marines, was ordered to take the great hill in front which I have called Hasheen Hill. They went forward, and very soon were advancing steadily up the precipitous slopes under a heavy fire from the enemy, who were posted at the very summit. Never hesitating an instant, they continued to ascend the hill, neither pausing to get breath nor waiting to return the enemy's fire till they reached a kind of ledge half-way up. Then they opened on the Arabs, and the rattle of the musketry echoed round the adjoining mountains as volley after volley was poured in.

A few moments only, and then again, the gallant 49th pressed forward, carrying out their advance as if at some parade at home. Steadily they ascended the steep rocky ground in front of them, while the enemy, almost invisible behind the boulders and rocks, redoubled their fire, and sought, if possible, to stem the tide sweeping towards them. But it was no good; the firing at the summit began to grow weaker and weaker, as the 49th and the Marines got nearer to it; and then a few minutes more and the hill was crowned, and a heavy fire at once opened upon the retreating Arabs. Wreaths of smoke wrapped the top of Hasheen Hill, and told that in this part of the field our troops had gallantly carried out the work given them to do.

A more splendidly executed movement could never have been witnessed; it was simply magnificent, and called forth the praise of all who saw it. After a long march, in a burning sun and under a heavy fire, the men moved as if on parade, taking advantage of every bit of cover the ground afforded, and going steadily to their work in a manner that defied all opposition.

While this was going on on the left, the other half-battalion of the Royal Marines was advancing up the ravine formed by the mountains on the right and Hasheen Hill on the left. The bush in this part was densely thick, and it was not without considerable difficulty that they were able to march through it. The half-battalion moved in column of companies ready at any moment to form into square. In front of them the Mounted Infantry were at work driving back bodies of the enemy who kept rushing towards them, till stopped by a volley or two, and then retiring again to renew the same tactics.

The 20th Hussars were operating on the left, while the 9th Bengal Cavalry, with the 5th Lancers, were on the right. The bush was so thick that it was absolutely impossible for cavalry to act with any effect, and I much doubt whether they ought ever to have been used, as they were, in such a country. A squadron of the 9th were advancing by troops on the right flank, when they suddenly found themselves in the midst of a strong body of the enemy. Unable to charge, they simply were ordered to the right-about, and retired at a gallop to get out of the ambush into which they had fallen. In a certain amount of disorder, they fell back, and as they galloped to the rear to reform as rapidly as possible, they were simply run down by the Arabs.

With surprising agility these fellows sped over the ground after the retreating horsemen, seeming almost to fly through the bush as they sprang from place to place. Rushing up behind the horses, they would hamstring the poor animals, and thus bring the riders to the ground.

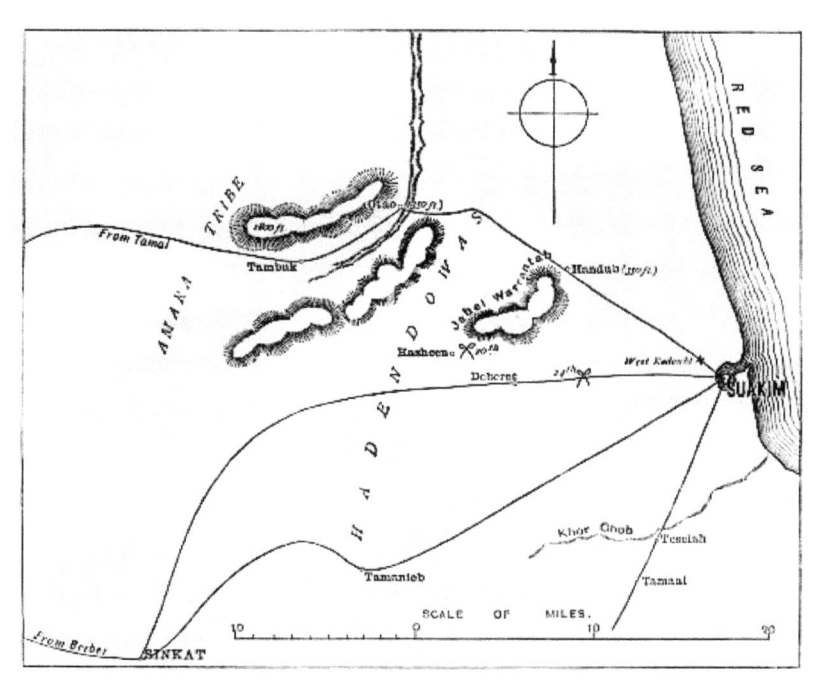

MAP OF THE ENVIRONS OF SUAKIM

There was no time to stop and help those who were in this way dismounted, as the men, owing to the thickness of the bush, were much scattered. They had to fight as best they could, and fall and die when they were outnumbered by the rush of Arabs. Three Arabs attacked one of the dismounted men, who fought hard indeed for his life. Spearing one, and cutting down another with his sword, he was preparing to despatch his third antagonist, when he was himself run through from behind, and thus fell without a friendly arm to help him.

The 5th Lancers had been halted in a somewhat open piece of ground to the left of where this was going on, and waiting his opportunity, their commander, with considerable forethought, delivered his charge on the flank of the pursuing Arabs, going right through them, and then wheeling round and taking them again as he returned to his starting-point to reform. The Arabs practised their usual tactics, and lay themselves flat on the ground when they saw the cavalry approaching, doing their best to hamstring the horses as they passed, but the lance put an end to many of these thus sacrificed to their temerity.

The leader of this little charge, who was a true soldier and thorough type of a dashing cavalry officer, was himself wounded by one of the spears of the 9th, with which an Arab had armed himself. Kneeling on the ground, the fellow kept himself in front of the officer, who was thus rather perplexed to know what he was going to do, so he went straight for him with his drawn sword. The Arab suddenly jumped on one side, and as the horseman passed him, endeavoured to run him through with the lance. So quick was the Arab that the sword was too late to parry the thrust, and the spear was lodged deeply in the rider's thigh, so deeply indeed as to wrench it from the Arab's grasp. With the bridle in one hand and a sword in the other, there was no possibility of withdrawing the lance, which caught in a bush and nearly unhorsed this gallant soldier.

The enemy lost a good few men in this part of the field, and another officer belonging to the 5th Lancers laid four of the enemy low before he emptied his revolver. It was proved again that a sword against a spear and a shield is absolutely useless, and that a lance is the only weapon of offence in this sort of warfare. In a fairly open piece of ground a regiment of lancers would simply annihilate any force of Arabs opposed to them; and if it ever comes again to our having to do battle with this magnificent and warlike race, a complete regiment of lancers should be sent out, and not two squadrons of a regiment in one case, and a regiment unused to the lance in another.

But there was busy work going on in other parts of the field.

A large party of the enemy, some fifteen hundred strong, had made a circuitous march round our right flank, and quite unperceived, suddenly appeared in our rear between us and Suakin, evidently with the intention of cutting off our retreat in the event of their force in front being successful. But the gunners, who by this time had dragged one of their guns into position on the top of each of the two conical hills, viewed them before they were able to get within a thousand yards of us, and in a very few seconds were plunging shell into the middle of them, when they immediately scattered through the bush and made their way back again to where they started from. Artillery has a great moral effect upon the Arabs, and they have a wholesome horror of the "big guns."

About this time news was brought in that large bodies of the enemy were pouring over from the direction of Tamai and threatening our left flank, so the Indian infantry, who before this were stationed in the valley, formed in three sides of a square, were now moved off in this direction and deployed into line. Probably the movement was seen by the enemy, who swung round to the rear of Hasheen Hill and were lost to sight.

The Guards had been ordered to advance up the valley as a support to the 2nd Brigade, and in a huge square they were forcing their way through the dense bush, The Coldstreams formed the front face of this square, four companies of the Scots were on each of the two side faces, and the Grenadiers made the rear face, while a battery of Gardner guns, manned by the Marine Artillery, also accompanied the square. In this formation they were thrown forward, and when they had advanced about a mile were halted with the dense bush all round them. Of course, it was impossible for them to retain their formation intact, and the different faces were broken here and there by patches of the thorny jungle.

From their position they could see nothing of the enemy for some time, though bullets were whistling over their heads in considerable numbers, evidently fired from the mountains, where the enemy were in great force. A party of six hundred Arabs all of a sudden appeared on the right face of the square, and with the utmost ferocity charged down upon it; but the Guards, standing as steady as a wall, received them with a withering volley, which stretched half their number lifeless on the sand. Supported by a large force some three thousand strong, this party renewed their fruitless efforts, and, led in their charges by a youth mounted on a white camel, did their utmost to gain the mastery; but it was utterly useless, for they had opposed to them some of the finest troops in the world.

The roar of the musketry was now general over the whole field, the enemy were firing away in the valley and along the lower ridges of the mountains where the mounted infantry were driving them back, the 49th and the Marines were showering bullets down from their point of vantage, while the rattle of the musketry in the bush in front told of the Guards being hotly engaged. Volley succeeded volley, and amidst the crack, crack, of the rifles, the booming of the guns re-echoed through the mountains, as the Horse Artillery pitched their shells with unerring precision into the enemy wherever he showed thickest and in the greatest numbers.

Another determined attack was made on our right flank, where the 70th were hard at work under a covering party building the *zariba*; but these fellows being charged by the 5th Lancers and 9th Bengal Cavalry, were driven off and great numbers of them killed.

A little before one o'clock, the enemy's fire having slackened, the 49th and Marines were withdrawn from Hasheen Hill and ordered to fall back towards the conical hills in rear, The Guards were also ordered to retire.

No sooner had the 49th and Marines begun to descend their hill, than the top was almost instantaneously re-occupied by the enemy, who opened a brisk fire on our retiring troops, A large force also having ascended the lower part of this hill where it rose out of the valley, opened an exceedingly heavy fire on the Brigade of Guards now also falling back. Their square was much hampered by being absolutely filled with baggage-animals, *dhoolie*-bearers, cavalry, and even artillery, who had all taken refuge inside it, to escape from the effects of the Guards' heavy fire. There was no hurry, and the men moved with the utmost steadiness under the galling fire poured in upon them. Every now and then the square would halt and reply with a volley or two; but they were unable to see the crafty enemy, who took good care to hide himself behind the thickest of the bush, and the rocky ground of the hills. Many a man fell, shot dead, and many were hit; while more than one officer fell, mortally wounded, inside the square.

The dead and wounded alike were all placed inside the *dhoolies*, and this caused a certain amount of delay, as parts of the force were halted to look after the casualties. Falling back in this way was a slow, tedious business, and it has never been revealed why the Guards were

ORDER OF ADVANCE TO HASHEEN.

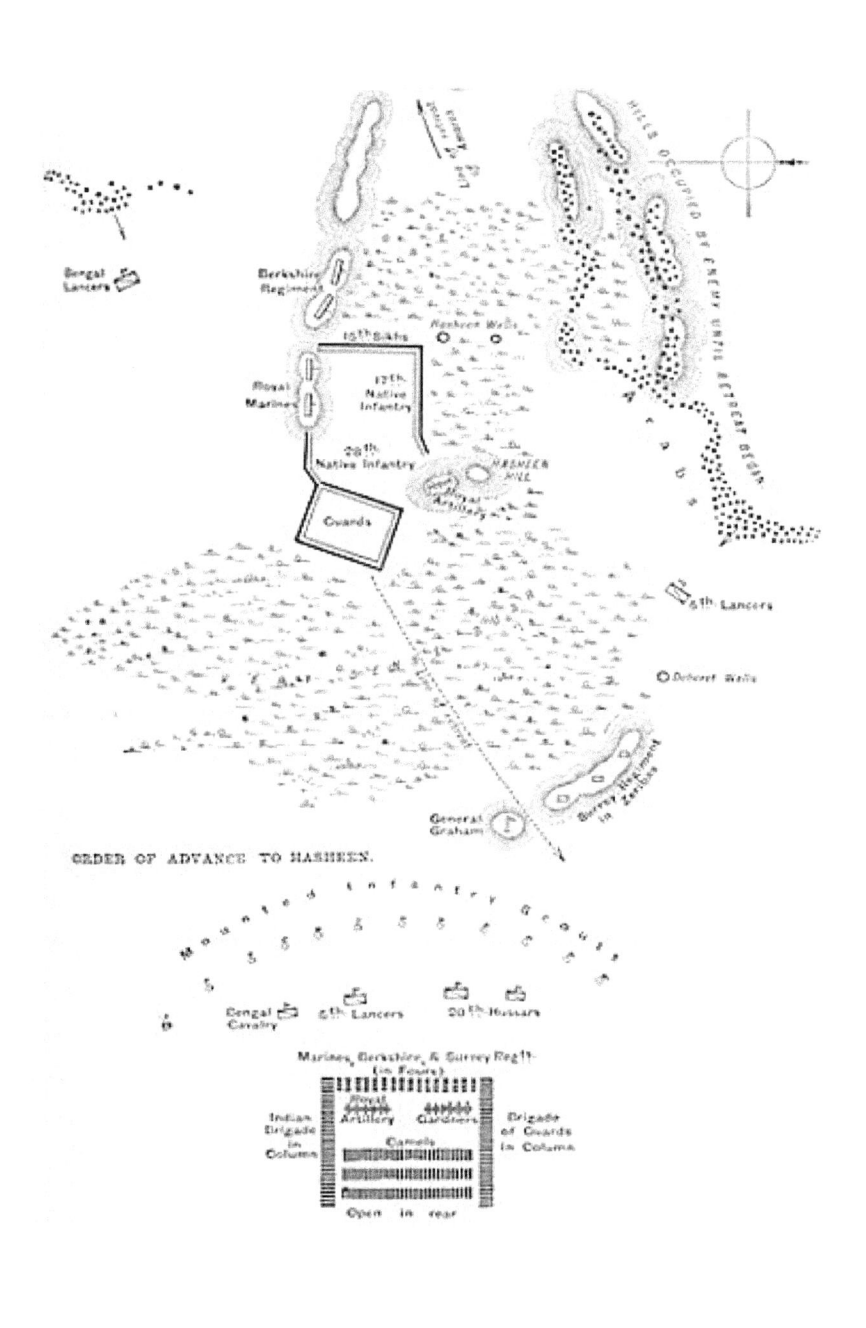

ever put forward into an impenetrable jungle to stand and be shot at. Under the most disadvantageous circumstances they behaved with the utmost coolness, and the majestic way in which they carried out their retreat, over about a mile and a half of the roughest country, beset by an invisible enemy, is deserving of the highest praise. It is not too much to say that had the enemy been better marksmen, and understood thoroughly the use of their rifles, the Brigade of Guards would have been simply decimated.

It was folly first of all to put them in such a position, but this folly was surpassed by the way the retreat was ordered. By the falling back of the 49th and Marines from Hasheen Hill, we gave back to the enemy a position for which our men had fought most gallantly, and from which they were able to annoy us considerably without our being in any way able to reply. With no means of covering their retreat, and with a considerable part of the cavalry actually inside their square, the Guards were exposed for an hour or more to a fire, which, if it had been better directed, would have nearly annihilated them. To run such risks is hardly forethought, and to handle troops thus is not generalship.

With the falling back of the Brigade of Guards and the two battalions of the 2nd Brigade, the firing ceased along the whole line, and the action was virtually over.

There was a report that the enemy was threatening our left flank, and that large bodies were advancing from that direction; but this was found to be groundless, and moreover, there was force enough in that part of the field to repel any attack, as we could just see the Indian Brigade still standing there in line, while their forms seemed to dance in the mirage of the intense heat.

The formation of the force, after the various battalions had fallen back, was as follows. The right was protected by the two hills, and the *zariba*, now almost completed, and held by the 70th. Next to this, the remaining four guns of the Horse Artillery battery took up a position on the low hill to the left, which I have already referred to as being the point where the Staff were stationed. In rear of this was a part of the cavalry. Further to the left were the three battalions of the Guards, and the 49th and Royal Marines; while on the left flank were the Indian battalions drawn up in line at right angles to the remainder of the troops, and in rear of them. The general formation was thus three sides of a square.

Bodies of the enemy were to be seen hovering about the base of the mountains, and on these the artillery opened fire for upwards of twenty minutes. Many of the shells took effect, but the range was a very long one, and it was extremely difficult to see in what measure our fire was successful. No further attempt was made by the Arabs to attack us, and so the men were allowed to sit down and eat their dinners, while the wounded were brought in to the field hospitals and the dead collected and laid carefully in the dhoolies. The doctors had their hands pretty full, and they had to attend to ghastly wounds, for the spears cut long and deep. I am sure nobody will deny the doctors a word of praise for their devotion and self-sacrifice, and for their kindness and gentleness to the suffering.

Present in the very forefront of the action all through the day, they were always at the point where they were most wanted, and many were the cases where lives were saved through their prompt attention which otherwise must have been most assuredly lost. One at least met his death when engaged in this work of mercy, and grand as the death is of a man who falls fighting for Queen and Country, that of one who yields up his life while tending the poor suffering mortals around him on the battlefield seems to me not one whit less glorious.

The water transport had now plenty to do serving out water to the different regiments. Half a gallon was allowed per man, and camels were sent off in all directions carrying the refreshment the men so much needed. We had brought out with the force nearly twelve thousand gallons of water, so that there was not only plenty for everyone, but sufficient to give the horses and mules a drink, though I am afraid from this not being generally known a good many animals went without. The camels had been watered the night before, so they required none.

The *zariba* was being rapidly strengthened, and a portion of the battery of Gardner guns was also being posted inside it, so with the 70th to hold the *zariba*, and the two hills armed with a gun each, the place seemed sufficiently strong to hold out against any odds. Provisions for four days for this force had been brought out, and nearly six thousand gallons of water was stored partly in three large iron tanks and a canvas tank which the Engineers had carried out with them. There was also a considerable store of ammunition, so altogether the *zariba* was well found. The *zariba* was a small one, the two conical-shaped hills being connected by two high hedges made out of the thorny bush running parallel to each other, and about thirty yards apart.

A shallow trench was dug in rear of this hedge, and the sand thrown up against the hedge to give it additional strength. Sentries

A Gardner gun

were placed all along the trench at night time, and the men always slept in such a position that they were ready at any moment to defend different portions of the work. The distance across from the top of one hill to the top of the other was not more than one hundred and fifty yards. A signalling-party was also posted on one of the hills, so that communication might in this way be kept up with Suakin by means of the heliograph.

At half past three o'clock the artillery ceased firing, and there were no further signs of the enemy to be seen. The men were by this time rested, and orders were accordingly given to prepare to march back again to Suakin. It was some time before all was ready, as the various battalions had to be marched into position, and the camels and mules collected before a start could be made for home.

The formation in which our return march was made was the same as that in which we had advanced in the morning. The Guards were on the proper right, marching in column of companies, the Indian Brigade was on the left, while the two battalions of the 2nd Brigade formed the rear or proper front face. In the inside of the square were the transport animals, and the *dhoolies*, and *dhoolie*-bearers carrying our killed and our wounded.

I believe all our killed were brought in and buried the following day at the Christian Cemetery down by the harbour. The wounded were taken to the base hospital, and afterwards transferred to the *Ganges* hospital-ship.

Our losses were officially returned as follows: three officers and twenty non-commissioned officers and men killed, and two officers and forty-one non-commissioned officers and men wounded.

There were several cases of sunstroke and extreme exhaustion, but this is not to be wondered at as the men had been under arms since before four o'clock in the morning, and everyone had had a hard day's work. The march out to Hasheen was a hot and tedious one of over seven miles, then followed the fight and heavy work of the day in a sun which absolutely seemed to singe, and when all this was over there was the march home again through the prickly bush and heavy sand. The whole force worked magnificently and the general ought to have been proud of his troops. They deserved all the praise they got. The honour of the day no doubt belonged to the 49th and the Marines, whose feat of the morning will long remain in our memories; but all alike deserved praise, though some had a better chance of distinguishing themselves than others.

A good many of us were much struck with the tactics of the enemy, who worked on a regular system and evidently a prearranged plan.

First of all, they relinquished the two conical hills to us, and fell back to the superior range in rear, from which they had complete command of the whole ground in front.

Their tactics in the valley were, no doubt, intended to draw us on, as they purposely concealed their main body in the hollow behind Hasheen Hill. In this way a smaller force continued to retire slowly before the half battalion of Marines and the Native Infantry, always just retaining touch and keeping up all the while a tolerably brisk fire. But the officer commanding the Royal Marines, who was an experienced soldier of many a hard-fought field, told me himself that he saw through their little game and halted his half-battalion to await orders.

While they engaged us in the front in this way, they managed to lay in wait for our cavalry, a part of whom they entrapped, while with a considerable force they threatened our right and left flanks simultaneously, and despatched as well a body, fifteen hundred strong, to attack us in rear. Had it not been for the guns of the Horse Artillery on the hills, there is no doubt that this attempt on our rear would have been successful, and the whole of our transport destroyed.

The transport was huddled together on the left of the *zariba*, and without any guard except two companies of the 70th, all the other men being hard at work building the *zariba*. I was told by an officer, who was stationed here all the day, that when he was ordered to get his men together to protect the transport from an attack, which at that moment seemed imminent, he only had sufficient men to put along one side of the mass of animals, and those were a yard apart—an efficient defence this against the impetuous onslaught of a large force of Arabs!

Altogether the generalship on the part of the enemy was good, and it was lucky for us we went out as strong as we did. Most of the men we engaged were of the Hadendowa tribes, but we heard afterwards, that a large force of some three thousand Amarars were drawn up in rear, waiting to see which way the fight went—so much for the "friendlies."

The strength of the enemy was variously estimated at from eight to twelve thousand men, but reports differed materially in different parts of the field. The intense thickness of the bush prevented our seeing what their strength really was, and, added to this, there were large bodies of men in the mountains watching their opportunity. I do not think myself there were as many as ten thousand men present, but I had no opportunity of seeing what the strength of the party was that came over from the Tamai direction.

Their losses must have been very heavy, for added to the execution done by the Mounted Infantry and the cavalry, the 49th and Marines must have slain a considerable number; and further than this the steady and very heavy fire of the Guards' square must have told considerably on the dense formation, in which the enemy made their repeated charges, The artillery fire was also not without effect. The opinion among many was that there must have been twelve hundred of the Arabs killed; but I should fancy a thousand would be nearer the mark. To this must be added the number of wounded, which must of necessity have been considerable also.

With our own wounded brought back to camp, was the youth who led the charges on the Guards' square, riding on a white camel. He was slightly wounded and made a prisoner of, being afterwards taken to the "H" Redoubt Hospital, where he received every care and attention, just as one of our own men. I don't know whether he appreciated a cot provided with sheets, which must have been a somewhat foreign luxury to him, but he was kept in a tent by himself, and had a man continually watching him, both for his own sake as well as for other reasons. His great grief was that his white camel had been killed, and he seemed to find it a hard matter to get over this. I do not think he ever showed any particular signs of gratitude for the kindnesses he received; but this was hardly to be expected from a representative of the race, who hated and detested us most bitterly.

I alluded just now to the way in which the transport animals were left without any efficient guard to look after them. The English portion of the transport was of course not numerous enough to be of any use, added to which they had their work cut out for them to look after the native drivers. A part of the Transport Corps was, moreover, told off to occupy the small hill on the left, which duty should surely have been carried out by someone else, and thus the chance of guarding or defending the camels was reduced to a minimum.

There was another thing at which we were somewhat astonished, and that was that the transport, comprising in all, that day, somewhere about twelve hundred camels, was suffered to march the whole way out from Suakin to where the force made their first halt, a mile from the conical hills, without any guard whatsoever. We have often wondered since how it was the enemy did not take advantage of this, as he might so easily have done by one of his rapidly executed movements.

Many hours were not, however, destined to pass before a fearful fate was to overtake this same transport through the laxity and carelessness on the part of those responsible for its protection, and through an overweening confidence in their own strength.

Our march back was a long business and a very tedious one, for we were all thoroughly tired. A hot sun scorched our backs and the dust half suffocated us, but the camp came into sight at last, with Suakin behind it in the distance, and in another hour, we were passing the line of redoubts and the different battalions were breaking off to their own parts of the camp, while those we had left behind came out to meet us to hear the news or to assure themselves of the safety of some friend.

We rode on down to the Headquarter camp to make our report, and then, just as the sun set, we reached our own tents, having had a spell of work of over thirty hours with little or no food and without a rest of any kind. We were almost too tired to eat, and sleep was all we asked for; but our night was not without alarms, and many shots were fired. I think, though, it would have taken heavy firing indeed to have disturbed some of us.

Our first real fight with the Hadendowas was thus over, though what was gained by it nobody ever knew. The enemy on their side celebrated it as a victory, while Her Gracious Majesty on ours sent a telegram congratulating the troops on their success and thanking them for their gallantry.

All that was gained by the action of Hasheen was the possession of two small hills which we secured without firing a shot, and before the fighting began. It was generally supposed that we marched out with the intention of occupying Hasheen, and of thus depriving the enemy of their water supply in this part of the country; but we never went within a mile of the wells, which had been noticed by the reconnoitring party the day before, and we contented ourselves with leaving a force behind in a barren situation, too small in itself to take any active measures against the enemy, and depending the whole while they stopped there on their friends at Suakin being able to run them out convoys of supplies and water.

To the Arab mind a defeat is not a defeat unless the one force can follow up his advantage and drive home his blow. No wonder, then, that when they saw us retire from the positions we had carried in the morning, and then quietly march off back again to camp in the afternoon, they concluded we had had the worst of it, and agreed to celebrate the affair as a victory. The mere killing of a certain number of their force means nothing at all to them, and unless they are dispersed, shattered, and absolutely driven off the field, it is as much their victory as that of their enemies, and most certainly they do not reckon it a defeat.

As to the moral effect the Battle of Hasheen had upon them, this was illustrated two days after, and showed in an unmistakable way that it amounted to *nil*.

How far our generals were justified in their course it is neither my wish nor my intention to inquire. We in the force only knew that many good men and true fell that day, and we knew also that as soldiers we had done what we were ordered, and done it to the best of our ability; but how far the blood then shed helped us on our way at all, or furthered the object of the campaign, we were at a loss to imagine, and were never afterwards enlightened.

CHAPTER 8

The "Zariba"

As I said in the last chapter, many of us enjoyed a fair night's sleep, and by four o'clock the next morning we were ready for more work, and more fighting if necessary. When I talk of a night's rest, though, I do not mean that we went to bed comfortably, for we none of us took our clothes off, but merely lay down as we were, with our loaded revolvers and our swords beside us, too dead tired for anything else.

I must mention an amusing little episode to do with the way we carried out our ablutions. A few days before we had "come by" a barrel of water, which we annexed for the purpose of having a good bath. We then secured the half of an old water-butt, and filling it nearly full of water, proceeded solemnly to take a tub in it one after the other, and five of us thus enjoyed the first real wash we had had for a very long time. We did not upset the water, though, after our first wash, but kept it religiously, and for the next five days continued to tub in it whenever we had a chance.

By the morning after we returned from the Battle of Hasheen we had been separated from our tub for two days, and when it came to the first one's turn to wash, I saw him at work with an iron cup, skimming a thick glutinous scum from the top of the water, after completing which operation, with the utmost gravity, he as solemnly proceeded to take his tub like a true Englishman. I must confess that the black and putrescent water of our bath that morning defeated me, and I never tubbed again.

It was evident that another advance was contemplated almost immediately, and though no orders were issued about where we were going to march to next, we, in the afternoon of the 21st of March, were told that we were to have as much water as possible loaded up and ready to start an hour before daybreak on the next morning.

Owing to the number of tins we had left at the Hasheen Zariba, we were rather short of means of carrying a large supply of water, but all through that night we worked on again pretty much in the same way as we had done two nights before, and filled every vessel we could get hold of. By four o'clock we were marching off to join the remainder of the Transport up at the Right Water Fort, where also the whole of the troops were paraded before starting.

The force which marched out this Sunday morning, the 22nd of March, was composed as follows: The 49th, the Royal Marines, the Indian Brigade, a battery of four Gardner guns, manned by the sailors, a detachment of the Royal Engineers, and a squadron of the 5th Lancers. There was, of course, as well a proper complement of *dhoolie*-bearers, doctors, and ambulances, an ammunition column, a telegraph-cart, with wires, etc., and a huge number of transport animals carrying supplies for four thousand men for three days.

All were on the move by half-past four o'clock. In front, the 49th and Marines, with the battery of Gardner guns, moved in one square, while in rear was a second square composed of the Indian Infantry, with the whole of the transport.

The orders were that this force was to advance about five or six miles in the direction of Tamai, that is south-south-west of Suakin, and there halt and build a *zariba*, in which the stores and water were to be left, guarded by a portion of the force, while the remainder were to return to the camp with the transport animals as soon as the work had been accomplished. In this way a kind of *depôt* was to be formed well on the way to Tamai, and stores of all sorts were to be massed there by convoys marching out daily from Suakin.

The whole of the force was under command of General MacNeill, and the advance was undisturbed by the enemy, who indeed showed no signs of being in force in the neighbourhood. The first part of the march was through country covered with small isolated patches of bush, but nothing to impede the advance of the troops. Further on, the bush became much thicker and closer, and the cavalry had some difficulty in forcing their way through it, being thus prevented from obtaining a thorough view of the surrounding ground.

Having arrived at length at a point about six miles out, the whole force was halted and three *zaribas* marked out, joining one another, and placed like the squares on a chess-board taken diagonally. The two outside squares were to be occupied by the 49th and Marines, having two Gardner guns in each, while the third or centre square, which was double the size of the other two, was to be occupied by the Indian

Brigade, and was the one in which all the stores were placed.

After a short interval for rest, a part of the force was ordered to pile their arms and set to work at once to cut down the bush and drag it in to build the *zariba*, while others were digging trenches or helping to unload the transport animals and carry the cases of tinned meat and biscuits into the centre square. Later on the men were allowed to sit down and have their dinners, for they wanted a little rest, as the march had been a heavy one, and the work of cutting down and dragging the bush about was exceedingly hard in the intense heat of the sun.

A considerable portion of the force were standing to their arms, while the remainder worked at the *zaribas*. Small pickets consisting of from four to five men each, drawn from the Indian Brigade, were thrown forward into the bush, which was especially thick on the side where the 28th Bombay Infantry were stationed. Beyond these infantry pickets were the cavalry pickets and videttes. The greater part of the transport animals had been unladen, and the stores placed in the centre of the large square. The camels were drawn up in a body on one side of, and about seventy yards from, the *zaribas* of the Marines and the Indian Brigade, and those that had been unladen were waiting for orders to start on their return march to Suakin, according to the pre-arranged plan.

All around seemed quiet; the men continued at their work, and the two small sandbag redoubts at the corners of the *zaribas* of the 49th and Marines were gradually being completed, when a cavalry vidette came galloping in to tell the general that parties of the enemy had been seen not far off in the bush. The general was asking the man in what force he thought the enemy were, when a second vidette came in telling the same story, that the Arabs were collecting in force round the *zaribas*. Then suddenly the air was rent with the most frightful yell; the cavalry outposts came clattering in, dashing through the working parties, and a heavy fire was poured upon us from the enemy, who seemed all at once to have sprung out of the earth where but a second before all had seemed so quiet and so still.

There was a cry all round, "Stand to your arms, men!" "Stand to your arms!" but, alas! some of the men were without arms, for they had put them down on the ground while they were toiling away at their work. There was a rush to the partially formed *zaribas*, and, mixed up together, Englishmen and Indians stood back to back fighting for life against an overwhelming force.

A large body of the Arabs had at the same time attacked the mass of camels and transport animals, who turned round and, like a vast surging sea, came onward towards the *zaribas*, crashing through the bush, swaying with their mighty weight, and trampling down everything in their course as they swept forward enveloped in a dense cloud of dust, maddened and terrified. The Arabs were among them, hacking, hewing right and left, ham-stringing and ripping up the wretched camels, and cutting down mercilessly the poor miserable native drivers who, unarmed and helpless, were hemmed in and carried onward by the flood. Many of our own men and officers, too, were in this way driven forward, unable to extricate themselves or even to draw their swords. Mules, horses, and camels were huddled into one hopeless mass of inextricable confusion, while the air was filled with the screams of men and animals and the roar of the musketry.

The 17th Native Infantry had possession of this part of the ground, the Marines being on their left. It was on this point that the confused mass of men and animals fell. The 17th were for the moment somewhat scattered, but groups of men stood fast here and there, and poured in their fire, in the general confusion, right into the men and animals in front of them. It was a minute before they were able to form up in any way, and then they fired upon friend and foe at once, and men and animals went down before the leaden hail, killed by our own bullets. But the Marines on the left stood firm as a rock, and it was well they did. The enemy dashed onwards, with almost irresistible impulse, falling in terrible numbers before their well-directed volleys, and not being stopped until they were actually touching our bayonets. Led by *sheikhs* carrying white banners inscribed with the *Mahdi*'s name, they charged again and again, rushing up to the face of the square and engaging our men hand-to-hand.

Many of these Arabs would fall before the rain of bullets, but, picking themselves up instantly, they would dash forward with the rest, till, pierced through and through, they reached the square at last, positively riddled by the fire. It was a supremely awful moment, but the English foot-soldier again proved himself invincible, and stood facing the foe—which outnumbered him ten to one—without a waver and without a move, save to load and reload or drive home the thrust of the weapon in the use of which he ranks before all others. So Arab and Englishman hacked and hewed, and shot and thrust, till blood flowed out on the ground like water, and black and white man alike bit the dust or writhed in death-agony on the hot sands of that parched-up desert.

The 49th *zariba* was entered by about a hundred and fifty Arabs, as many of the men were, as I have already said, outside, cutting down the bush. Getting their arms as quickly as possible, two companies of this gallant regiment formed rallying squares, and in this formation none of the Arabs could touch them. They did their best with shot and spear alike, led on, as in other parts of the field, by *sheikhs* carrying banners, on one of which was inscribed the words in Arabic, "Whosoever fights under this banner shall have victory." So crafty were the enemy in the way they attacked these detached portions of our force, that they got round between them and the *zaribas*, as they saw that our men would not be able to fire in this direction for fear of injuring their friends. But cold steel did what the bullet was unable to do.

Nothing could have exceeded the coolness and signal bravery of the 49th, as they fought their *zariba* against overwhelming numbers, who never faltered for a moment in delivering charge upon charge. It was the triumph of perfect discipline, combined with the utmost bravery, over a glorious pluck untutored in the ways of war. Nothing but this saved our force that day. Had there been the least unsteadiness, had there been the slightest hesitation on our side, our force must have been doomed.

Nothing could have saved us but this perfect self-possession and steadiness when taken at a disadvantage. Had it not been for the sterling quality of the English troops, another catastrophe more awful than that of Isandlanha, another massacre more fearful than that of Maiwand, must have occurred that Sunday afternoon. Never did the sterling quality of the British soldier shine out more brightly than it did on this occasion. Never did men face death more resolutely and with greater *sang-froid*. The glory of the British Army has not yet departed, when deeds of this sort can be performed. Happy is the country who possesses such soldiers; the people of England ought to be proud of them, and a general ought to be thankful indeed who has such men at his back to pull him through.

But I must go back. The remainder of the 49th were in an incredible short space of time in position, and a hand-to-hand fight with the Arabs who had entered their square ensued. Some were shot down, while others were run through with the bayonet, till, fighting splendidly, the last of these fanatical and undaunted warriors fell, a victim to his indomitable pluck. One hundred and twenty-two bodies of Arabs were counted actually inside the square after the fight was over, and among them, strewed pretty thickly, were many of our own men, soldier and sailor alike. The Gardner guns had opened on the enemy and swept the ground in front, carrying death and destruction wherever they were pointed, but heedless of danger and with surprising agility the enemy were among the sailors in a second; a few only escaped being wounded, while many, alas! were killed. They fought their guns gloriously, and fell, as British sailors have done before, side by side with their soldier-brothers.

The redoubt in the *zariba* furthest from Suakin was the scene of some of the most severe hand-to-hand fighting; and it was here the sailors suffered most, no less than one officer and ten blue-jackets, who had been working the guns, lying dead in a heap.

I ought to mention an incident of the fight, showing how the enemy are animated by a bitter hatred for us, and how this hatred is not confined to the Arab men alone, but fills the hearts of their women and their children also. For one single instant the smoke cleared off and showed the swarming hordes of Arabs leaping and dancing in the bush, while they rushed onward in endless numbers to demolish us if possible; and as we thus gained a momentary view, there stood out between the two opposing forces a boy, aged not more than twelve years, without signs of fear, actually throwing stones at us. But the Arab fire was growing hot, ours opened again, and the fate of that boy was sealed, not because there was the slightest wish on the part of our men to slay the little fellow, but because one and all were hopelessly doomed before that terrific and deadly hail.

There were women, too, fighting like the men, and dressed in the *Mahdi's* uniform. It was horrible to think of their being there, and worse still to think that they had to fall. But there was no help for it; in the short half-hour that the fight lasted there was no time to pick and choose, and though we never knew till afterwards that there were women in the enemy's ranks, the dead bodies of several lying on the field told more surely than anything else of the bitter enmity there was between us.

The enemy did not, however, confine their attacks to one side of the *zaribas* alone; they were on all sides, and the Sikhs and 28th had a hot time of it. The Sikhs especially behaved most gallantly, magnificent fellows that they are.

They were perfectly in hand the whole while, and stood as firm as rocks, carrying out the orders of their officers and plying their bayonets with the utmost effect. Many Arabs had entered this *zariba*; and indeed, some were seen quietly to trot across it before we were hardly aware that we were attacked. These fellows actually succeeded in running up behind some of our men and in stabbing them while they were still at their work. So, daring was the approach of these forerunners of the force, that the very audacity of their movements caused them to be mistaken for some of our own Soumali drivers, and it was a minute at least before they were detected and shot down.

This more than anything shows how completely we were taken by surprise, and how utterly ignorant we had been of any real danger.

But I must refer back again to what became of the Transport. By far the greater part were killed and wounded at the first onslaught, but when the stampede took place they very soon scattered in all directions, and as far as the eye could reach, all over the plain were camels, riderless horses, mules kicking themselves free of broken harness, drivers running for their lives, and our own men cut off from the *zaribas*, sharing a common fate with the rest, and falling either speared by the enemy or shot down by the reckless fire of some of the Native Infantry.

All those who were at first shut out from the *zaribas* and swept away by the stampede of animals were never able to reach the squares again, as it was utterly impossible for them to approach their friends when they had once opened fire. Many attempted to do so, but they had to turn before the storm and fly with the rest in the direction of Suakin. Many of the cavalry and a great part of the transport men fled for their lives in this way; some managed to leap on to the backs of affrighted animals, and even these had to gallop hard to escape from the numbers of Arabs who attempted to run them down, while others ran on foot, and few indeed of these ever reached the camp alive.

Some escaped a fearful end by hiding in the bush and feigning death, and a lad of ours saved his life in this way by lying down between two comrades who had fallen down killed by the Arab bullets. They continued their pursuit to within a mile of the camp, and thus the whole line of retreat was covered with dead and general *débris*. The first and somewhat exaggerated account of the affair was conveyed to the camp by these refugees, some of whom reached home in time to tell the news in broken, breathless sentences, and then to fall and die.

The enemy's tactics were as well planned as they had been two days before, and they carried out an attack upon all sides simultaneously without any shouting or word of command, and without showing in force for a moment.

Not only this, but seeing our most vulnerable point was the transport, they got round in rear of the camels and other animals, and drove them before them on to the *zaribas*, thus not only being able to slaughter the transport at will, but also to drive them on to us and thus throw our own men into confusion. A further force took up a position on the path along which we had advanced in the morning, ready to cut off our retreat to Suakin, and also to intercept all animals which did not fall before the knives and spears of the attacking party.

A strong reserve, numbering some thousands, was also in readiness to carry out the massacre at the *zaribas*, which they fully expected to effect; and when they had completely exterminated our force here, it was their intention to fall upon the camp before Suakin with their whole force, after which the starving out of the *zariba* at Hasheen would have been merely a question of days. All this we found out afterwards from prisoners, but the disposition of their forces showed us quite plainly enough what their intentions were.

They might, had it not been for the gallantry of our troops, have carried out the first part of their programme, and it was a wonder they did not; but beyond doing a certain amount of mischief among the deserted part of the camp, they would have been simply swept off the face of the earth by the force left behind there, as there was in the camp at the time the brigade of Guards, the 53rd, a greater part of the cavalry, and a battery of Horse Artillery, to say nothing of a mountain battery of seven-pounder screw-guns, as well as sundry other details and detachments which were quite prepared to receive them. There was, indeed, an alarm in the camp that the enemy were coming down, and every preparation was made to receive them; but they never showed up, though large bodies of them were seen from the Hasheen *zariba* moving across in our direction.

The natives and people in the town of Suakin were in a tremendous state of excitement, and the most conflicting accounts were current there about the fate of the troops. Some of the refugees had galloped right into Suakin, where they told the most awful tales of the total extermination of the force, and of the death of the general and all his soldiers.

For an hour or more after the fighting was over, detached bodies of the enemy were to be seen pursuing single animals over the plain towards the sea. They killed most of these, though they took possession of some. Several of the camels and mules, many of which were wounded, made as if by instinct for Suakin, and a few actually succeeded in reaching the camp in an utterly exhausted condition, and covered with blood.

The actual fighting was over in less than half an hour, but the enemy did not turn tail and run—not a bit of it. Many of them merely turned round and walked quietly away, while others withdrew sullenly, keeping up a fire upon us as they went.

The scene around, both inside and outside the *zaribas*, was one utterly indescribable. Little would be gained by trying to describe it, if indeed it were possible, by mere word-painting, to convey the dimmest notion of the appearance of the ground around. The task would be a sickening one to the writer, for it would be to go over old sorrows and old hours of the most bitter anguish of heart. It were better to try and blot out what must always remain, I fear, too vividly in the minds of those who witnessed it; and I, for one, care not to pander to the morbid love for horrors possessed by a few. God knows, there is sorrow, trouble, and affliction enough in this wide, erring, sinful world, without attempting to add to it unnecessarily, or rend the hearts of those of the opposite sex at home, who in their gentleness and refinement know little or nothing of war with all its attendant misery.

Let us draw a veil over this part of the picture, and deal solely with that which tells of bravery, of loving acts of kindness—of cases where the man laid down the arm and nursed the sick and the wounded with the care and the tenderness of a woman. A battlefield may bring out all those qualities of brutality, of almost fiendish brutality, in a man, but it most assuredly brings out as well his noblest instincts. The acts, I say, of mercy, of self-sacrifice, of love, and complete devotion seen on a battle-field shine out as beacons in a night of roaring storm, and serve to guide men in after years who have before thought little, cared little, and considered others little, and whose lives were hardly what they might have been.

I have seen men stand on such occasions with hot tears coursing each other down their cheeks while they gazed on the sufferings of some comrade. I have seen others give their all to the wounded when they were almost starving themselves; and I have known men ready to lay down their lives for a friend at once, cheerfully and without hesitation. Are these noble qualities? Then let all soldiers who have these opportunities when fighting for their country, and take advantage of them, be honoured in Old England as soldiers should be honoured, instead of being often treated with indifference, and more often still kicked out into the streets as "unfit for further service," when they have risked their lives for the country which spurns them when cripples, and finds no home for them when they have lost health and strength in some deadly climate. Our streets tell this tale too often, and our country-side as well. An old soldier is cared for where he has friends, but how about when he has none?

For some hours the troops stood in position lining the sides of the *zaribas*, momentarily expecting a renewal of the attack, as the Hasheen force heliographed to the effect that a large body of the enemy were marching in this direction, many of whom were mounted on camels. Nobody was allowed to leave the ranks, except those employed bringing in the wounded to the doctors, who, as usual after a battle, had their hands full. Our dead were all placed together in rows inside the *zariba*, and those of the enemy were carried outside ready for burial the next morning.

Boxes of biscuits and tinned meat, water-tins, trusses of compressed hay, and a multitude of other things, were strewed about outside in all directions, and as much of this as possible was collected together, while the few remaining camels and mules were also brought inside the *zaribas*. Many of these luckless animals were to be seen hobbling about wounded, or standing up slowly bleeding to death. The inside of the *zariba* seemed to be stained everywhere with blood, and almost everyone was spattered with it. Many men, for the first few moments after the fight was over, simply fell down from exhaustion and dropped off to sleep, so with their bloodstained jackets it was difficult to tell who was wounded and who was not.

It was impossible to drag the dead bodies of the animals outside the *zaribas* that night, as everyone was too tired to do anything but look after the wounded. Of course, the inside of the *zariba* was littered with every imaginable thing—broken rifles, spears, shields, swords, parts of kits, helmets, empty cartridge-cases in thousands, blood-stained caps and jackets, bayonets twisted in all sorts of shapes, and thrown away as useless, and sundry other things too numerous to mention.

Thus, occurred in one short half-hour, and suddenly in all the quiet of a Sunday afternoon, one of the bloodiest fights ever chronicled.

Just when our people at home were sitting in the stillness, perhaps, of some village church, listening to the voice of a pastor offering up the prayer to God, "from battle and murder, and from sudden death, good Lord, deliver us;" or, perchance, singing the words of some favourite hymn, or even, it may be, repeating the prayer for us soldiers; we were fighting and falling fast, while many a spirit was in one second wafted upward to appear before his Maker. It was as well they knew it not. On what to them must have been a peaceful sabbath morn—

> *That trysting-place of God and man; that link*
> *Betwixt a near eternity and time—*

....was to us a scene of bloodshed and of death, of man fighting with man for very life, ay, and dashing out all semblance of the creature that God has set up here in His own image. To look on a scene such as we saw that day at those blood-stained *zaribas* is to be seized with a horror of war, and to say with the poet in all sincerity

> *Avaunt thee, horrid War, whose miasms, bred*
> *Of nether darkness and Tartarean swamps,*
> *Float o'er this fallen world and blight the flowers,*
> *Sole relics of a ruin'd Eden! Hence*
> *With all thy cruel ravages!—fair homes*
> *Rifled for thee of husband, brother, son;*
> *Wild passions slipp'd like hell-hounds in the heart,*
> *And baying in full cry for blood; the shock*
> *Of battle; the quick throes of dying men;*
> *The ghastly stillness of the mangled dead.*

I remember the words of a great man who said:—

> While you are engaged in the field, many will repair to the closet, many to the sanctuary; the faithful of every name will employ that prayer which has power with God; the feeble hands which are unequal to any other weapon, will grasp the sword of the Spirit; and from myriads of humble, contrite hearts the voice of intercession, supplication, and weeping will mingle in its ascent to heaven with the shouts of battle and the shock of arms.

And thus, the force was delivered that day from a slaughter almost unparalleled in the annals of war, from a catastrophe which would have carried weeping and mourning into a thousand households, and made our country shake to her foundations, while people mute with horror looked each other in the face and realised, as one realises the meaning of some faint far-off sound, what war really is.

The darkness at length closed around the *zaribas* and shut out from the eye for a time the ghastly sights around. There was perfect silence inside the three squares as a quarter of the force stood lining the hedges and peering into the night. No lights were to be seen except where the doctors worked incessantly at the mass of suffering around them. The dawn was breaking long before they had completed their sickening task. Many of the enemy had their wounds tied up with the same tenderness as if they had been our friends, and I think some of the most fearful wounds were those inflicted by the Snider bullets of the Indian troops. One had not, unfortunately, to look among the enemy only for these wounds, for many of our men will carry to their graves the results of the momentary panic.

While one quarter of the force guarded the front of the *zaribas*, the remainder slept on the bloodstained ground, ready at any moment to jump to their posts. There was one alarm that night due to a mule breaking away from the picketing lines, and being chased by one of the native drivers across the centre *zariba*. In a moment the whole of the men were in their places, firing away into the bush as fast as they could, so much had their nerves been shaken by the terrible events of the day.

The "Cease fire!" was sounded, and immediately the former death-like stillness reigned around, broken now and then only by the neighing of a horse, or the grumble of a camel, or, what was worse, by the shrill and piteous cry of some wretched wounded Arab, calling "*Moya! Moya!*" "Water! Water!" as he lay in tortures in the bush. Then the sound of a voice would come from afar off, answering the wounded, as parties of the enemy scoured the bush and carried off their friends. Since dark the signalling party had been flashing an endless succession of messages to the camp, and all night long this continued without intermission. Lists of the killed and wounded were in this way flashed in to headquarters, as well as many a message to friends there, assuring of safety, and asking that the welcome news might be forwarded home to England.

It was not until after ten o'clock that the moon rose and threw her white light over the field. The scene looked, if possible, doubly ghastly now, and the dead could be seen lying all round in hundreds, while numbers of the enemy lay actually in heaps close up to the *zaribas*.

The weary hours of the night dragged on slowly, as we lay on the ground listening for any sound and starting at the faintest noise. At last, the sky in the east began to show signs of growing red, and never was dawn more welcome to men than it was to us that morning. The night with all its anxiety was past, the constant dread of an attack in the darkness was over, and it mattered little what the day brought, for we were ready now.

When the noise of the first heavy firing was heard in the camp, and volumes of dust were seen flying high in the air, there was a rush to any point of vantage where a view could be obtained of what was happening to the force that had marched in the morning. It looked as if a fearful catastrophe had happened; the fire was very rapid and "independent," and there was at first none of that regularity in it betokening steadiness and obedience to commands. The volumes of dust that filled the air showed that either the cavalry were charging, or that large bodies of the enemy were traversing the ground with great rapidity.

Then from out of the volumes of dust and smoke appeared a mass of fugitives, men and animals, and everywhere all over the plain were to be seen riderless horses, mules, and camels, flying for very life. At first it appeared as though the whole force had been scattered, but the rapid firing still continued, and then after a while gradually settled down into steady volleys. It was all right then; the men were steady and in hand, and those volleys told us of security and of fearful slaughter.

There was immediate activity in the camp, and before the first fugitives arrived the whole of the force there were under arms. One battalion of Guards had started in the morning as escort to a convoy carrying out stores to the Hasheen *zariba*, but the other two battalions were at once paraded, and, together with a battery of Horse Artillery and a strong force of cavalry, marched in the direction of the *zaribas*. This force did not, however, go out more than about two miles, as the firing had entirely ceased. About six in the evening it was accordingly marched back again to camp, bringing with them in their *dhoolies* many wounded, who had sunk down in their flight from loss of blood and exhaustion.

Every preparation was made in the camp to repel an attack, and a greater part of the force was under arms and on the watch all night, while guns were got into position and tents were struck to clear the ground. It was a night of great anxiety for those in camp, owing to the uncertainty about what had actually happened. Many of those who had escaped gave conflicting accounts of the fight, while many friends were reported killed by them who turned up the following day all right. It was not, however, till towards evening of the next day that a true account of the affair reached the camp, and anxiety was set at rest.

There are one or two things which need a reference to do with this fight at the *zaribas*. The first in importance is the clogging of the Martini-Henry rifles. Years ago, when first these rifles were issued to the army, every instructor of musketry was asked to send in a report upon the way they worked in his regiment. The common fault found with them then was that the extractor failed in the performance of its proper functions, and that a rifle was often rendered momentarily useless on account of the inability to extract the cartridge-case after firing without either repeatedly working the lever or drawing the cleaning-rod and forcing the case out by pressure from the muzzle.

With regard to the cartridge itself, fault was found with its construction; but we were informed that the cartridge was only experimental, and would be replaced by a better one later on. However, that may be, the clumsy built up and bottle-shaped cartridge has been in use in the army ever since, and no other cartridge has ever been supplied; and more than this, a price is given per thousand for the empty cases returned into store. Thus, the cartridges are refilled and the error continued *ad infinitum*. As a musketry instructor, I used to dress all my markers with the money I obtained for the old cartridge-cases, and thus I was a party to the sin; but I see no reason why all these built-up cartridges should not be got rid of at target practice, and reloaded as often as you like, provided they are not issued to men going on active service.

It not unfrequently happened that the base of the cartridge was torn right off by the jaws of the extractor, when the rifle was at once rendered utterly useless. The sand and the temperature may have had a certain amount to do with the jamming, but the fault lay principally in the extractor of the rifle and the form of the cartridge. The extractor ought certainly to be improved upon if this rifle is to continue the arm of the services; and a drawn copper cartridge-case, unlubricated, should take the place of the present one. Many men have lost their lives through these two things in our late wars; and though years ago reports, as I say, were made by those best able to judge on the defects of the weapon and the cartridge, no notice was ever taken, and thus through a love of cheeseparing economy, and a penny wise and pound foolish policy, valuable lives have been sacrificed.

Another thing to which I think attention should be drawn is the bayonet. We hear a lot about the wonderful quality of British steel; but why are our soldiers armed with a weapon which, when put to the test, simply doubles up like so much soft metal? Surely, above all others the weapons we give our soldiers to fight with should be of the best possible quality.

A man going covert shooting is not contented to go out armed with a thirty-shilling gun from Birmingham, neither is a man going pig-sticking content to have a soft piece of metal at the end of his staff; but it seems perfectly natural to those at home to send our soldiers out into the field to fight their country's enemies with a rifle which is liable to be rendered utterly useless at any moment, and a bayonet as much use to them as if it were made of hoop-iron. Every soldier's life is valuable, and our soldiers are not so numerous that we can afford to sacrifice them to the love of economy of some, and the short-sighted policy and indifference of some few more.

A jammed rifle may be of use to the man who can go in with the bayonet, but how about a rifle with a bent bayonet in front of the muzzle? The first is bad enough, but in the latter case the weapon is rendered utterly useless. In every fight in the Sudan campaign there were many instances of both of these faults, and surely it is time, therefore, some notice was taken of a crying evil which may land us in a terrible plight when we become engaged in a European war. Our swords want looking to as well; the present pattern cavalry sword is made of bad metal, the job of some contractor. All bayonets and swords should be called in and a fresh issue made of weapons, each of which have been put through a severe test similar to that through which Mr. Wilkinson puts his celebrated blades, to the satisfaction of the purchaser.

The Gardner guns often appeared to jam, but of course, in a complicated weapon of this kind, the conditions under which it was tried in the Sûdan were a severe test. The expansion of the metal from the heat, and the dust which was always flying about, were sufficient in a great measure to account for its failure; but I think the cartridge was also at fault here. Later on, in the campaign another form of Gardner gun came out, consisting of two barrels, enclosed in a cylinder filled with a fluid, instead of the five exposed barrels as in the ordinary pattern gun. I am not aware that this gun ever came into action, but it was tried at Suakin with good results.

The ammunition was of two kinds in the Suakin force—a fatal error. Why cannot the Indian troops be armed with the Martini instead of the Snider? One word about the revolver. The calibre of the regulation pattern revolver a short time ago was .450, but it has lately been changed to .455, so that there were again two different sizes of ammunition here. Moreover, the ammunition was of an inferior quality, and I heard on one occasion of three miss fires out of six-a nice thing to happen when everything may depend upon a shot! The calibre of the revolvers should be increased; the present bullet is not sufficient to stop a man unless he is struck in the head or the heart, and an Arab shield made of crocodile skin or rhinoceros hide would, we found, turn a revolver bullet at forty yards.

A revolver is ten times more use than a sword, provided it is fitted with the Webley patent, enabling the user to reload without difficulty. All cavalrymen, gunners, and sergeants of infantry should be armed with them, and prizes offered for good shooting, as practice with the weapon should be encouraged. A revolver is a most difficult weapon to use with effect, and it is useless in the hands of a novice.

Before closing this chapter, the losses in the *zariba* fight have to be chronicled. As to the loss sustained by the enemy, they must have had, at the lowest possible computation, twelve hundred killed. We collected and buried a thousand and more of these poor fellows, nearly all of whom were the *Mahdi*'s men and not the common Hadendowa tribesmen, as they wore the white blouse and straw cap which makes up the uniform of the Prophet's soldiers. For every man killed there must have been at least one wounded, so two thousand four hundred killed and wounded would be within the mark.

As to our own losses, they were very heavy and especially so in transport animals. The official account which I obtained from a friend, better than all others able to judge, was as follows:

Seven officers killed and five wounded. Sixty-six rank and file killed and one hundred and twenty wounded, and one officer and one hundred and twenty-four men missing. Besides this, we had in the water column alone one hundred and seventy-nine native drivers killed and missing out of a total of considerably under three hundred who started in the morning; and it would not be too much to say that there were fifty more drivers killed in the Commissariat convoy. As to the loss sustained in animals, I am unable to give any figures regarding either mules or horses, but our loss in camels was six hundred and eighty-two; our gross loss on this and the succeeding day being eight hundred and twenty camels.

The value of these animals may be estimated as follows: The Egyptian camels for the most part were bought at prices averaging £20 apiece, and they then had to be brought to Suez and shipped to Suakin, so that when delivered at the Camel Depot, Suakin, their cost to the country must have been £25 per head. The Indian and Berbera camels were bought at a lower figure, but taking into consideration the distance they had to be brought, they must have averaged at least £20 per head. It will never be known how many of each class there were out that day, but our water transport was mainly composed of

THE AUSTRALIANS AND THE ATTACK ON THE COMMISSARIAT

Indian camels, and we lost over four hundred of them; so, taking two-thirds of the animals killed at £20 apiece and the remaining one-third at £25 apiece, the nett loss to the country in camels would stand at £17,765. This, it must be remembered, is exclusive of horses and mules, and there were a great number of these killed besides.

It remains a fact that cannot be contradicted that this terrible loss of life was due to the fact that the force was surprised. There is no doubt too, that one squadron of cavalry was wholly inadequate either to form an efficient protection, or, in a country such as that surrounding the *zaribas*, to give timely notice of the approach of the enemy.

The place selected for the halt might have been better chosen by Headquarters. Had the line of country more towards the sea been adopted, the enemy, if they had attacked at all, would have done so at a disadvantage, for in this part there is much less bush, and we should therefore have been apprised of their approach. We should have been also in an equally good position as a halting-place on the road to Tamai, and more protected from attack while the *depôt* was forming. Instead of this, the force was marched into a dense jungle, thus giving all the advantage to the enemy and putting a surprise at a premium.

It is easy to appear wise after the event, but I am merely writing here what occurred to the minds of all of us actually at the time.

I was told afterwards that our Intelligence Department out there had received news through their spies that it was the intention of the enemy to attack us that day, and that they would watch their opportunity. From the source I heard this, I believe it to be the truth.

Chapter 9

Convoys

Almost before day had broken everyone was astir in the *zaribas*, and parties were sent out at once to search the bush for any of our dead and wounded. Two or three of the enemy's banners were picked up, and any rifles collected and brought in. Most of the banners taken had inscriptions on them; some were white with red edges, others blue, and one was black. The enemy were seen hovering about the *zaribas*, and two or three times in the morning they opened fire, when the men were immediately ordered to stand to their arms. Under these circumstances it was difficult to get on with any work. Large holes were being dug in the sand to bury the dead in, as this, for sanitary reasons, had to be attended to at once, and the air was already filled with a sickly smell.

Our killed were buried with the greatest decency circumstances would permit, and the officers were interred in two separate graves. We had, of course, to bury the Arabs as best we could; huge holes were made and as many placed in them as possible, the sand being afterwards heaped high over the grave. It was impossible to do anything with the enormous number of dead animals; those nearest to the *zaribas* were dragged away, and some covered in; but our only hope was the birds, who very soon congregated in great numbers. Many wounded Arabs still lay about near the *zariba*; it was dangerous work, though, walking near them, as they invariably endeavoured to reach passers-by with any weapon they still possessed.

A young officer was killed by one of these wounded Arabs shortly after the fight; he went outside the *zariba*, and as he passed by the hedge forming the side of the defence, a wounded Arab raised himself from the ground and ran him through the back with his spear. The officer turned round and re-entered the *zariba*, but he was unable to speak, and fell down dead almost directly afterwards. One of our men, too, taking pity on a wounded Arab, gave him his water-bottle. The Arab took the bottle and drained it, and when he handed it back, he accompanied it with a thrust from a knife, which dangerously wounded the man, in return for his kindness. There were other instances of this kind, but I mention the two cases above in order to show how deep-seated was the hatred of the Arabs for us, and how perfectly ready they were to die, happy if they could first only get an opportunity of dyeing their spears in the blood of an *infidel*.

It is not to be wondered at that our men, after experiences of this sort, killed the wounded as they lay on the ground, and it is unfortunately only too true that this occurred on several occasions. I have no wish to plead in their defence, however much provocation they may have had; on the contrary, I think this course was unnecessary; and though war must always have, to a certain extent, a brutalizing effect upon men, I do not see why members of a civilized race should pay off barbarians in their own coin.

To do so is to descend to their level, and to be as much barbarians as they are. The Arabs endeavoured to take advantage of us when they were wounded because they were impelled by a wild fanaticism, and there is no doubt also that they mutilated our dead; but this is no reason why we should do the same, unless it were in individual cases of self-defence.

We should shrink with horror from mutilating a dead body, but to kill a wounded man is worse. The Arabs knew no better, but we did. Kindness they did not understand, and gratitude was foreign to them; the first they looked upon as weakness, the second as an impossibility from a Mohammedan to a Christian. The only extenuating circumstance I can find to do with this killing the wounded is, that our men were for the time demoralised by the fierceness of the fighting, and lost control of themselves; and I believe many were embittered by seeing friends fall after the fighting was over.

However, this may be, the practice was not continued, and was of course immediately discouraged and forbidden by the officers. I do not wish the reader to imagine that our men went out into the bush and killed the wounded off indiscriminately; this was not the case. Many wounded Arabs, on the contrary, had their wounds dressed by our doctors, and were given food and water, being afterwards carried out into the bush again to be fetched away by their own people. Many of the Arab wounded entreated our people to kill them, in order that they might be despatched to a happy land by the hand of the *infidel*.

At about twelve o'clock in the day (23rd of March) a strong force arrived at the *zariba* from the camp, consisting of the brigade of Guards, some cavalry, and mounted infantry, enclosing a large convoy of water and stores. This force was not attacked during their march out along the line of flight the night before. All along the road there were lying dead men, horses, and camels; but no halt was made to bury any of these, as the general wished to reach the *zaribas* as soon as possible.

After an hour or two for rest it was arranged that the grenadiers, together with the whole of the Indian Infantry, should accompany the convoy back to camp; the Scots and Coldstreams being left behind in the centre *zariba*. Preparations were shortly after made for the return, and a huge square formed, the grenadiers bringing up the rear. All the wounded that it was possible to send in were sent with this square, a large number of *dhoolies* and *dhoolie*-bearers having been brought out.

Shortly after three o'clock, everything being ready, orders were given to commence the march back to the camp.

And now began a hurried and most ill-managed affair. There were a vast number of camels to be taken back to camp; as, besides all those we had brought with us in the morning, there were also the whole of the animals collected in the *zaribas* after the fighting was over; and together with these there were many mule-carts, ambulances, and our long train of wounded.

About two miles after leaving the *zaribas* our leaders began to think that, hampered as we were with this vast collection of animals, we should not reach the camp before darkness set in unless means were taken to increase the pace. Orders were accordingly given to press forward as quickly as possible, and a general thrashing of the wretched transport animals began; not, however, carried out by the Transport themselves, but by those inexperienced in the management of camels, and ignorant of the pace a camel can travel.

In this way loads were dropped and not picked up, saddles were torn off and lost, as no halt was made to reorganise the convoy, and speed was attained at the sacrifice of everything else. What was the result? Our march, instead of resembling the return of a victorious army, resembled only a disorganised rabble retiring as rapidly as they could before a pursuing foe. Confusion was everywhere, order there was none; and the camp was reached at last just before sunset in a state of disorganisation. In our wake were empty boxes, parts of saddlery, exhausted camels, and in fact the ground might have conveyed to the Arabs the appearance of a general rout. "Get on, get on," said our superiors; and we did "get on," but at what sacrifice? Had it not been for the Grenadiers who, as I said just now, brought up the rear in line, the confusion would have been ten times worse.

The Sikhs did good service as well; but the whole thing was a disgrace to any civilized army, and reflected only renewed mismanagement on the part of those responsible. I have endeavoured to give a mild impression of this return of ours to camp, but there are many who might paint it in far more glaring colours. I confine my remarks to the simple impressions of an eye-witness.

That night we were hard at work loading up water again for the convoy, starting the following morning at daybreak, as we very often at this time worked all night long, and then marched and fought all day. It was hard work, very hard work in that climate, where it was always intensely hot, where there was never a cloud in the sky, and where food and water were scarce. The heat had become very much greater since our arrival, and every day the sun seemed to be growing in strength. Sickness was much on the increase, and men were dropping fast from sunstroke, exhaustion, and fever; for the never-ending fatigues, escorts, and "sentry go" was telling on the men very much.

It was the intention of the general to collect a great quantity of stores of all kinds at the *zaribas* preparatory for the further advance to Tamai, consequently every day all through this week convoys of provisions and enormous quantities of water were sent out there. This convoy work was very heavy on all concerned, as the march was a long one, being over five miles out and five miles home, over burning sand and through thick and thorny bush. Moreover, the convoys were almost always attacked going out or coming home, and not unfrequently both ways, so little were the enemy overcome by their two very recent defeats.

The escort this particular morning was composed of the 15th Sikhs and 28th Bombay Native Infantry, with a party of Madras Sappers, and a body of cavalry consisting of a squadron of the 9th Bengal, and another of the 20th Hussars. The orders were that they were to march out three miles, and commence to cut a "drift" and form a *zariba*. A force was to be sent out from the *zariba* to meet them and take over the convoy. The home force was not interfered with on their march out, reaching the point where they were to construct their *zariba* without seeing anything of the enemy.

About eleven o'clock a battalion of the Guards (Coldstreams) and the Marines, left the *zaribas* to meet the convoy half-way, and were almost immediately fired upon by large parties of the enemy who were seen to be swarming in the surrounding bush. Most of the bullets flew high over the square, but one officer and one man of the Marines were wounded.

The two parties met at about two o'clock, and the two wounded were given over to the Indian infantry, who then recommenced their march home.

The Guards and Marines, accompanied by the cavalry, were twice attacked on their way back to the *zaribas*. Not long after leaving the Indian regiments, large bodies of the enemy suddenly dashed from the bush and charged down on our force with the utmost impetuosity. The cavalry clearing the front, enabled the Guards and Marines to open fire, which they did with the utmost effect, the enemy after a while retiring into the bush again and out of sight. For some while it was supposed that another heavy attack similar to that of Sunday was intended, as great numbers of the enemy were seen both from the squares as well as from the *zaribas*; but after the first rush, when many of the Arabs got close up to our bayonets and engaged our men hand-to-hand, they did not for a time attempt to renew the attack, contenting themselves with firing long shots at us from the bush.

The enemy having retired, the force again moved forward, but was a second time attacked shortly before reaching the *zaribas*, though not by large numbers. The losses sustained by the enemy must have been, from all accounts and from the bodies we saw lying about on the following day, upwards of two hundred killed; while we on our side had three killed and thirteen wounded.

From the *zaribas* considerable bodies of the enemy were seen drawn up on the right while this attack on the convoy was being carried on, and their strength was variously estimated as from four to six thousand men. Endeavours were made to reach them with the Gardner guns, but they were just out of range. Had there only been a part of the mountain battery in the *zaribas*, they could have plied them with their shells with the most deadly effect, and *destroyed* numbers before they could have withdrawn into a position of safety.

The bravery displayed by the enemy on this occasion was as marked as on all others. They simply appeared perfectly callous of the punishment they received, and their heavy losses of only two days before did not seem to have affected them in the least. As to our having established a funk among them, that was pure nonsense. Their valour was as marked as it was before, and they were only embittered by the chastisement they had undergone. Women and boys were again seen in their ranks supplying the fighting men with arms and ammunition, and altogether the number of men who appeared ready to fight for the cause of the *Mahdi* seemed to be absolutely unlimited. It certainly looked as though there were plenty always prepared to charge our squares, or to throw themselves on to our bayonets, in spite of the example made of those who had come before.

The following morning another convoy was despatched to the *zaribas*, carrying a large supply of water.

It was on this occasion that our balloon was first used, and it was also memorable as being the first occasion on which we had ever made use of a balloon on active service. The balloon, which was of goldbeater's skin, covered with a netting, was taken up to the Right Water Fort the night before and unpacked in the ditch, when filling it was at once commenced, so that it should be ready to ascend by daybreak next morning

When I reached the Water Fort just before daylight, after a hard night's work loading up water, I found the balloon inflated and quite ready for the ascent. I was rather disappointed at its size, and fully expected to see a larger one. The basket or carriage beneath the balloon did not seem capable of holding more than one person.

The actual measurement of the balloon was twenty-three feet in diameter, and its weight altogether ninety pounds. When filled it contained seven thousand cubic feet of gas, brought all the way from Chatham, a distance of nearly four thousand miles.

Very soon after our convoy was formed up ready to start, the balloon began to rise slowly to a height of about two hundred feet, being fastened to the ground by two lines attached to the car.

An admiring crowd of natives witnessed the ascent in silence, and did not seem in the least surprised, much to my disappointment, as I had expected to see them struck with amazement at the sight of a man floating about in the air. However, these natives seem astonished at nothing, and I do not believe they would have been surprised if they had seen a regiment provided with wings and suddenly begin to fly. Whether the extreme unexcitability of temperament of these people is the result of dullness of intellect, or that they are altogether emotionless, I do not know, but they were not taken by surprise at the sight of the balloon, looking on the whole while with far less interest than is shown by an average London crowd witnessing the departure of a party of gentlemen in a balloon from the lawns of the Crystal Palace.

I fear that the excellent stories concocted for the delectation of the people at home about the Arabs being struck dumb with horror at the sight of the balloon, or flying in masses and hiding themselves from the sight of this terrible apparition, are nothing more or less than humbug. The behaviour of the "friendlies" may be taken as being that of the Arabs, who were neither dismayed nor deterred from any action they may have determined on by the sight of the balloon flying in the air above them. When the convoy was ready to move, the balloon, still two hundred feet up, was made fast to a cart in the centre of the square.

It was rather difficult to avoid jerking the cords which held it, and thus running the chance of breaking them; but extreme care was taken when crossing any rough pieces of ground, as it would not have been pleasant for the occupant of the car if he had suddenly found himself floating quietly towards the mountains, miles beyond the reach of any friends.

Communication was kept up with the balloon by means of written messages, and it was not long before a letter came down telling us that the enemy were still pursuing the stampeded camels down towards the sea and killing them as soon as they got up with them. The enemy could also be seen in force retiring in the Tamai direction; and later on, a large body of them were standing gaping up at the balloon only three or four hundred yards distant from the convoy, though quite unseen by us on the ground.

The force reached the *zaribas* at last unmolested, when the balloon was hauled down and packed up, the gas being as far as possible saved for future use. Thus, the first ascent may be chronicled as a success.

The convoy returned to Suakin in the evening without firing a shot.

The stench all around the *zaribas* was simply terrible. It was absolutely impossible to bury the dead camels lying in hundreds in the bush, and there are few things that stink more fearfully than a dead camel. I have known them to scent the air strongly when their bodies have been at least a mile off. Added to the camels, many of the enemy's dead remained unburied about the country; our friends, the birds, too, were surfeited with their loathsome meal, and hopped about lazily or stood unable to move or get out of one's way, being simply gorged to repletion.

Life in the *zariba* was almost unendurable. As much shelter as possible was obtained by sticking blankets or waterproof sheets on to spears, thus making a sort of awning. Any shade that could be got behind the cases of stores or the forage-bags was seized upon at once, as the heat all day was terrific.

Water was sparingly issued, and at one time the ration was reduced as low as one pint per man in the morning and another pint in the evening. This, to wash in, cook in, and live on, was little enough when all the food that could be got was *bouilli* beef and hard biscuit, which last it was impossible to eat without first soaking. Why the ration of water was reduced so low I know not, as there were upwards of forty thousand gallons stored in the *zaribas* in large tanks buried in the sand. I remember hearing at this time of a bottle of soda-water fetching half a sovereign; the purchaser did not, however, proceed to drink it at once, but, slowly and solemnly pulling out the cork, he washed his face in it.

And here I want to correct a wrong impression which we saw afterwards was much commented on in the papers sent out to us from home. It was reported in one that the supply of water was accumulating very slowly at the *zaribas*, and the troops there were on short allowance, as through some bungling empty tins and barrels had been sent out in one convoy. To this it is only necessary to give a most emphatic denial; it was absolutely impossible that it could have happened. Every tin was locked, after being filled, by a responsible person, who was more often than not an officer; special parties being told off by us to look after this important point.

The filled tins were afterwards placed in rows along the railway, another officer seeing them put in the trucks previous to their being taken on to the camel lines; and an empty tin could not have escaped him. Every tin and barrel was shortly after placed in the *celitas* and packed on the camels. I am therefore absolutely certain no tin or barrel ever started in our convoys empty. Some of the barrels leaked very much, and there may have been robbery; but the other assertion is absurd, and it probably was a story started by some person who got mixed up in his hot haste for information between the outgoing convoy with full tins and the returning convoy with the empty ones. Thus, in his excessive zeal to discover a mare's nest, he may have tumbled against an empty load, and started a false report detrimental to a department who worked harder than any other all through the war, and never failed.

The condensed water was good enough when it was fresh, but after being kept a day or so in the tins it began to smell and became filled with a white slime. I never heard how this slime was accounted for. Certainly, condensed water will always extract its salts from other bodies if possible, and the material of which the tanks were made, galvanised iron, or the solder, may have had something to do with it; but however, this was, the water was not wholesome, and I cannot help thinking that some means might have been adopted by which it might have been in a measure aerated.

Sickness was increasing very rapidly at this time in the *zaribas*, there being several cases of enteric fever. The disease most prevalent was dysentery. I put this down almost entirely to the want of fresh meat, which might so easily have been sent out from Suakin. The *bouilli* beef which, as I mentioned before, was rather salt, was principally the cause of it, and why the army was ever supplied with such uneatable and unsuitable stuff is wonderful indeed. I knew many cases where men actually threw their rations away rather than run the chance of increasing their thirst by putting such stuff in their mouths. A few potatoes were issued, but why was there not a plentiful supply of lime-juice served out daily? It would have been as simple a thing as possible to have allowed the troops at the *zaribas* a ration of fresh meat at least twice a week.

A few oxen or sheep might have been driven out with the convoys and slaughtered on arrival at the *zaribas*, if it had been considered unadvisable to send dead meat out in carts. This last method might, too, have been easily managed, as a plentiful supply of ice was always procurable from the ships. Instead of this, the men were fed on an eternal supply of tinned meats, till everyone was simply nauseated with the stuff and turned from it with loathing and disgust. An eminent medical man out there told me that dysentery might have been almost entirely avoided had fresh meat been sent out twice a week, and that, from certain symptoms he observed, he discovered that the force in the *zaribas* was bordering on scurvy. A nice thing to happen when there was a plentiful supply of fresh meat only six miles off!

The sick were always sent in by the returning convoys, and every care taken of them while at the *zaribas*, the doctors being simply indefatigable.

A telegraph wire had been laid along the ground when we advanced on Sunday, but this was always being cut by the natives, who had a wholesome horror of wires after their experiences of the mines laid round Suakin. This difficulty was overcome by building a crow's nest at the *zaribas*, which served the double purpose of a signalling station and a lookout post. All messages were sent in to the Right Water Fort, from which point they were forwarded on to the different parts of the camp. The signalling party at the *zaribas* were very hardly worked, and were often up till late at night, when the lamps took the place of the heliograph.

Of course, it soon became apparent to the Arab mind that the force in the *zaribas* was dependent for supplies on the camp, and no doubt their having grasped this was the cause of the perpetual attacks on the convoys. We heard through our spies that Osman Digna had given orders to the effect that the *zaribas* were not to be attacked, but that everything was to be done to harass the convoys, and all energy was to be directed towards intercepting them if possible. Hence, they scarcely ever left us alone.

The convoy escort duty fell doubly heavily on the troops at this time, as, besides the labour entailed on throwing provisions and water daily into the *zaribas*, and thus collecting sufficient supplies for the advance on Tamai, the Hasheen *zariba* had also to be kept going in food and water. So, convoys were running in both directions. On Wednesday, the 25th of March, it was therefore determined to withdraw the force from the Hasheen *zariba* altogether, and that evening the 70th and other details returned to camp, escorted by a party of Mounted Infantry. During their retreat the enemy were sighted and a few shells fired into them, but beyond this the march was uninterrupted.

The *zariba* was destroyed before leaving it, and nothing then remained of our fight at Hasheen beyond the graves down at the harbour of the poor fellows who had fallen in that most objectless action.

I say "objectless" because few of us ever understood why lives were sacrificed for so small an end.

We did not take the wells at Hasheen, and thus interfere with the enemy's water supply. The position at Hasheen did not protect the right flank of the force advancing on Tamai, or the line of communications either in the Handoub direction or the Tamai direction, for it was many miles away from both. As to the protection it afforded to the flank of the force at the *zaribas*, it was pretty evident on Sunday, the 22nd of March, that the Hasheen force was impotent to act in this direction. How far an isolated force of one battalion was intended to protect the line of communications may be judged of by the fact that it was withdrawn before the advance on Tamai began, and as soon as it had been determined that the army was to strike for Es Sibil.

The force left at the Hasheen *zariba* was an isolated force, a weak force, and a useless force in the position it was placed. It absorbed a number of men who were much wanted elsewhere, and increased the amount of convoy duty when everyone in the whole army was overworked as it was.

So, the Hasheen *zariba* was destroyed, and the Battle of Hasheen rendered as barren in results as it had been objectless in aim. The many acts of bravery performed on that day, and the gallant conduct of our troops, will always remain a monument to the British soldier, while the battle will only be recalled to mind by the graves of those who sleep beneath the sand.

The usual convoy was despatched at daybreak the next morning, and we rather expected to have a fight because we had been allowed to go in peace the day before. Our convoy was a large one and our escort strong, and as by this time we had cut a fairly open road all the way out to the *zaribas*, we were quite ready to give the Arabs a warm reception if they came on.

Sure enough, after getting about four miles out a heavy fire was opened on us from the bush, and several of our men were struck, but the greater part of the bullets flew over our heads.

About four thousand of the enemy then attacked us furiously on all sides with their usual astounding bravery.

Many of them jogged in their peculiar manner right up to the square before they fell, while others walked quietly back again into the bush after endeavouring to penetrate our ranks. Their coolness under fire was simply astonishing, they seemed to care nothing about it; and it was marvellous indeed that day after day men could be found to charge three or four battalions of infantry in the face of the awful slaughter that invariably took place.

Scores and scores of them fell on this occasion as on others, and remained there unburied to taint the air with sickening odours.

Once or twice on our return march from the *zaribas* we found the enemy had scraped together a thin covering of sand over the bodies of those slain in the morning, and these were very often unavoidably uncovered again as we traversed the path home.

Out at the *zaribas* the stench was something frightful. The wind had blown away the sand, and thus partially uncovered the heaps of slain, leaving swollen and distorted limbs to fester in the sun.

Added to other diseases contracted at the *zaribas*, many suffered terribly with their eyes, from the poisonous dust and the perpetual white glare of the sand. I knew men who were completely blinded in this way, and who did not recover their sight until many weeks afterwards. Ophthalmia and similar diseases were prevalent, and there were, of course, many cases of sunstroke. I think the greatest number on one day occurred in one of our convoys, when we had thirty men knocked over by the sun alone. I saw cases where men dropped down suddenly, as if they had been struck a heavy blow on the head.

The day of the general advance was, of course, kept a profound secret, and we only inferred it must be before long from different little incidents around us.

The masses of stores that had now been collected at the *zaribas*, the bringing in the Hasheen force, the striking of the greater part of the camp, as well as the numberless reports that were flying about, all pointed to the fact that a big fight would come off very soon. One thing only was considered likely to defer the advance for a while, and that was that our Australian brothers had not arrived as yet, though they were expected almost daily. We all thought that if the enemy would only meet us at Tamai in force, we should then have an opportunity of fighting a decisive action, and crippling Osman to such an extent that he would be unable to carry on the war any longer.

If this was likely to be the case, it seemed hard that we should start before the Australians arrived, and there was an earnest desire on the part of the whole army that they might come in time to share any fighting with us, and thus have an opportunity of showing the material of which they were made. We all looked forward to their arrival tremendously, and were prepared to give them a fitting welcome on landing.

We were very busy all Thursday night preparing for Friday's convoy, but very early in the morning orders came down saying that there would be nothing sent out to the *zaribas*, and that the troops would be employed striking their camps and sending spare baggage in to the caravanserai at Suakin. Friday came, therefore, as a welcome day of rest after a week of marching, of fighting, and incessant toil. The truth was that everyone was overdone; the perpetual marching backwards and forwards to the *zaribas* during the day, in a sun heat of over 160°, the large number of men required every night for picket duty, and the numbers also on night fatigues of various kinds, was rapidly undermining the strength and nerves of the men, and rendering the whole force unfit for work.

It was, therefore, wisely determined to give us all a day off; but I do not mean by this that we had a complete holiday, for there was quite enough to be done to make up an average day's hard work without marching a convoy.

We were very busy packing up a few things we wanted with us, such as a second flannel shirt and another pair of socks, and so on; but the largest part of our baggage was made up of a—

> ......*simple box of deal,*
> *Directed to no matter where;*
> *And on it was this mute appeal,*
> *With Care!*

There was something else we painted on this box of deal, though, just by way of satisfying any over-inquisitive minds, and at the same time putting to rest the suspicions of the hungry, and that was "Military Documents."

It was a great feat that, and the cause of much merriment, as we quietly emptied everything out of the box, and put in with the greatest care a bottle or two of whisky, several tins of Brand's essence of meat, cocoa and milk, potted meats, and sardines. With this store we thought four of us would be able to hold out as far as Tamai and back, and have some to give to hungry friends besides.

There were the wildest possible rumours going the round of the camp to explain why the advance was put off. The first was that the *Mahdi* had been made a prisoner by King John of Abyssinia, and that Osman had therefore decided to give himself up, and was expected in camp either tonight or tomorrow morning. To back this up, a flag of truce was said to have been seen flying in front of the camp; but this afterwards proved to be an old deal biscuit box distorted in the mirage. The government, we were told, had decided to give up the war, and had telegraphed out to stop the railway at once.

Of course, there were all sorts of stories about war with Russia and our future destination; how some regiments were to be sent on to India, and how the rest of the force was to be conveyed at once to Cyprus ready to operate in Asia Minor. One hour war had been actually declared, another that it had not, and so on. But these reports caused a deal of amusement, and gave us something to talk about; and though few of us believed a word we heard, we used to discuss the news with the utmost gravity.

Saturday's convoy reached the *zaribas* without any particular incident, beyond being fired upon by the enemy at a distance, and the return was equally peaceable. Each convoy always brought back a number of sick, who were generally taken down to the base hospital at "H" Redoubt, and transferred to the *Ganges,* or *Bulimba,* on the following day.

If we who had been living for the most part in camp longed for the advance on Tamai, it may be judged how much more eager the force in the *zaribas* were to get out of their pestilential surroundings. The Scots Guards had been replaced by the grenadiers, but the rest of the force remained the same as at first. There was nothing to be done to break the monotony of the life there. There was, of course, occupation, and the *zaribas* could always be improved and strengthened, but excitement there was none; the enemy never ventured to attack them, and on two or three occasions only did they fire a few shots.

Beyond this the day was only relieved by the meal of eternal "soup," and the issue of water, or the watching for the approaching convoy. There were a few newspapers of a certain antiquity to be read, and the rest of the day was made up in trying to make work to employ time. It was, of course, impossible to go any distance away from the *zaribas,* as the enemy were always on the watch to cut off any who showed themselves.

In camp we had for the most part struck all our tents and were bivouacking at night on the ground. I was very much struck with the heavy dews at night-time, and once or twice in the morning the coat in which I had wrapped myself before going to sleep was quite wet through. The dew did not show on the sand at all, probably because it absorbed it at once, but it soaked through a blanket or coat. The only way to account for it was, I suppose, that the intense heat exhaled by the sand met the colder air coming in from the sea in the early morning, and thus condensation took place.

We never felt any ill effects from it as it dried very quickly. There were a good many cases of severe rheumatism, but this was most probably due to the extreme variation in temperature between the sun heat of the day and the cooler air of the early dawn, when the thermometer sometimes fell as low as 60°.

We never had any renewal of the night attacks on the camp, though a party were on one occasion detected crawling towards the Ordnance store. Precautions were not lessened, and strong pickets and double sentries were mounted as usual; so, at length we lay down on the ground at night with the most comfortable pillow, a saddle, under our heads, and slept till morning with an easy conscience, but very often somewhat empty insides.

Chapter 10

Tamai

"Bravo Australia!" I think this was what we all felt as we saw the colonial contingent arrive in camp on Sunday, the 29th of March. We gave them a regular hearty reception, and they were cheered all along their road out, while the bands of the various regiments in camp headed the column playing many a tune familiar to all Englishmen and Australians alike. The contingent were a fine-looking lot of fellows, and appeared as if they were as fit as possible for work. They all wore the familiar red serge coat, albeit rather strange out here, but they very soon changed into khaki like the rest of us. Everyone from the highest to the lowest was anxious to get a glimpse of them, and their arrival quite brightened us all up, as we were at that time rather depressed by our general surroundings.

In after years, no doubt, this event will be a landmark to look back to. Let us hope the readiness with which our Australian and Canadian colonies came forward voluntarily, and extended to the mother country the hand of help, when surrounded with a sea of troubles unparalleled in her history, may serve as a warning to our foes of the latent strength of the British Empire, and at the same time be the beginning of that great Imperial Federation which is to bind the whole together in one indissoluble union for the protection of our commerce, the defence of our possessions, and the supremacy of our country's flag.

The contingent were inspected by the general on arrival in camp, and I am sure he echoed the thoughts of all of us when he said:—

> In the name of the force I command I give you a hearty welcome. You are our comrades-in-arms, who will share the perils, toils, and, I hope, glories of this expedition. We honour the feeling which led you to leave your pleasant homes to war against the desert and its savage inhabitants. You are soldiers as well as

Englishmen. The eyes of our common country are on you, and I am sure you will do credit to the splendid colony which sent you out, and the race to which you belong.

Cheer after cheer rent the air after this, and we hoped the contingent were as pleased with their reception as we were to have them in our midst.

They were very proud of themselves, and evidently delighted at forming part of such a splendid force as we were in the Sûdan. I shall never forget a man, fully six feet six inches high, with a back as broad and as flat as a billiard-table, and with a long black beard on his face, coming up to me and saying, with the utmost pride in his manner, "I am a representative of the New South Wales contingent; can you direct me to the camp?" The way he drew himself up when he said, "I am a representative," showed at once that he thought the New South Wales contingent ranked first, and the rest nowhere.

A spirit like this is worth a regiment of soldiers; and, though I wish to be no croaker, I fear there is too much cause to say that the day when every English soldier thought there was only one regiment in the service and only one company in that regiment—his own—is fast passing away. And why? Because of the never-ending meddlesome interference which can and will leave nothing alone, which strikes at *esprit de corps* and destroys it root and branch, which sacrifices everything to the recommendations of ignorant theorists, who bow down and worship the image of a false economy, and fawn to the powers that be.

The next two days were days of great weariness, as nothing is so trying to soldiers as inaction. Plenty of occupation and hard work is the surest way to maintain the health and spirits, and therefore the efficiency, of an army in the field.

I do not know why the advance was delayed. We were quite ready, and there were plenty of supplies of all sorts at the *zariba*, and water enough for the whole force for two days and more. Still we delayed, and still the wearisome succession of convoys continued to march along that dreary track to the *zaribas*. It was no use collecting a larger supply of water out there, as it went rotten if kept in the tins more than two days. We had plenty of transport in spite of our having lost so many camels, so this could not be the cause of the delay. The Transport is always made the scapegoat in war-time, and the shield behind which to hide the faults and shortcomings of others; but in this expedition it never failed, though success was gained only by superhuman exertions and willing sacrifice on the part of those who bore the brunt of the work and received scant notice.

The enemy seemed now to have drawn off towards the mountains, as they never even attempted to molest the convoys. We supposed that Osman was concentrating at Tamai, and in fact we heard he had strongly entrenched his position there, and fortified it with many rifle pits, so we looked forward to a real set-to this time. Our hopes were therefore somewhat damped by a story that one of our spies had come in and reported that Osman Digna had only about two hundred followers at Tamai, all the remainder of his forces having dispersed to their homes. This obtained a certain amount of credence, from white flags having been seen flying both towards Tamai and in the Hasheen direction. One of these flags proved to be a party of the enemy burying their dead of Sunday last.

A further countermanding of the advance led to further rumours, and I fear also a certain amount of grumbling, in camp. It was reported that the Amarars were leaving Osman in bodies, giving as their reason that, while they failed to see what they had to gain by fighting against us, being beaten every time, they could, on the other hand, earn good wages if they went into Suakin, by working on the railway or at the wharfs. The result of this was that Osman Digna threatened them with total extermination if they severed their allegiance with the cause. A sanguinary fight thereupon ensued between the Amarars and the Hadendowas. How far this was the case we were unable to judge, but our spies assured us that Osman had been almost deserted, and had retired from Tamai in the direction of Tamanieb.

On the 31st of March (Tuesday), the Mounted Infantry and the Bengal Cavalry were sent out to the *zaribas* in the afternoon, ready to reconnoitre towards Tamai on the following day. Another small body of cavalry was despatched in the Hasheen direction, and returned in the evening, having seen nothing of the enemy.

Early in the morning of Wednesday, a party of cavalry and mounted infantry marched from the *zaribas* in the direction of Tamai. Having advanced a distance of five miles or more, they discovered that the report of the spies, that the enemy had quitted Tamai and fallen back, was not the case at all, and that they were still occupying that place in great force. This news, on their return, was received with the utmost satisfaction, and it was immediately heliographed to the camp.

Orders were issued that night that the whole of the troops, with the exception of one battalion of native infantry, were to parade the following morning at three o'clock, and that three days' provisions and as much water as possible were to be taken out with the force.

It is needless to say with what joy we received this order after the past few days of inaction, and how hard we worked that night, getting things ready for the general advance and the big fight we hoped would shortly follow. At four a.m. we were all on the move, traversing the now well-worn track to the *zaribas*. We moved very slowly, owing to the numbers of animals accompanying the force. The formation adopted was, as usual, a large square; but we saw nothing of the enemy, and by nine a.m. had reached the *zaribas* in safety.

After a rest of about an hour and a half, a further advance of five miles was made in the direction of Tamai. It was very hard work, as every man carried two days' rations, besides a full allowance of ammunition. The bush was thick and thorny, and the sun broiling. A few men fell out from exhaustion, but these came to after a drink of water, as everyone was too eager about the coming fight to think of the heat, or the weight of the load, or anything else.

The balloon had been inflated at the *zaribas*, and accompanied the force, but the day was all against ballooning, as there was a strong wind blowing, which threatened to swing the occupant of the car out of the thing altogether. A few groups of Arabs were reported as being visible, but at length it was thought better to haul the balloon down. This was accordingly done, though not without getting it badly torn in the thorny bushes around us.

Our halting-place was not reached till well on in the afternoon, when we at once began to build a *zariba*. From the hill near us, known as Teselah Hill, a view of Tamai, now only two miles off, could be obtained. The eminences round us were at once occupied by half-battalions of various regiments, and a gun or two was also got into position. The ground was much rougher than that surrounding the *zaribas*, and further on we could see that it was covered with large rocks and boulders. From where we were a few of the enemy could be seen along the opposite ridges, but they did not attempt to interfere with us at all.

While we were thus hard at work making our position secure for the night, the Mounted Infantry were sent forward to reconnoitre the country between us and Tamai. Proceeding cautiously along, they at length reached the village without opposition, though parties of Arabs were seen watching them at a distance. While they were engaged looking about them and inspecting Tamai, a brisk fire was suddenly opened on them from some rough ground in front, and this for the moment rather disconcerted the men; but a general survey of the hill was made, and some of the huts inspected, after which our force withdrew, having achieved all they had been sent out to do.

It was thought by some that a night attack would be made upon us, and all precautions were therefore taken to avoid a surprise.

Soon after dark a somewhat heavy fire was opened by a body of the enemy, and this continued for a while, till at one a.m. the grenadiers, who were out forming part of the advanced pickets, answered with a volley or two, and the gunners sent a few shells at them. This very soon silenced their fire, and the remainder of the night was passed in peace. Why the enemy hit so few of us is very wonderful, for even allowing for inaccuracy of aim, the mark we presented to them, packed, as we were, like sardines in a tin, ought to have insured their doing a certain amount of execution.

Our casualties during the night were only one man killed and two men wounded.

The next morning, at an early hour, preparations were commenced for a further advance, and the Guards, Marines, 49th, Australians, and Sikhs were formed up ready to march on Tamai.

At eight o'clock we were on the move, formed in three sides of a square, with the Mounted Infantry and cavalry scouting in front. A few scattered parties of the enemy were seen, and these fired at us at long range. They kept themselves wonderfully under cover, and it was almost impossible for us to hit them as they retired dodging from one big stone to another.

Tamai village was eventually reached without our being attacked or seeing anything further of the enemy. The village was only quite a small place, built on a flat piece of ground standing rather above the surrounding country. It consisted entirely of huts, and there were no stone buildings of any sort.

There had evidently been large flocks of sheep and many cattle there recently, and, like Hasheen village, the place had been left in a great hurry, as many of the huts were in the greatest confusion; drinking-vessels, bead ornaments, copies of the *Koran*, and odds and ends of all sorts being left about everywhere.

We did not halt at the village for any length of time, as our general was anxious to secure the wells in the hollow, or *wady*, on the other side.

After leaving the village, I am glad to say that for once the cumbersome square formation was relinquished, and the troops advanced

The Australian contingent at Suakin

as for attack. We could see the enemy were in tolerable force on the opposite hills, and as we approached nearer, they opened fire on us, though always keeping themselves well under cover.

It was almost impossible for our skirmishers to touch them. One of these fellows had established himself behind a big rock, and quietly fired shot after shot with a certain amount of accuracy in his aim. An officer, I think belonging to the Coldstream Guards, happened to have with him a Winchester repeating rifle, and, putting his sight to a thousand yards, he took a steady aim, and in another second, we saw the intrepid Arab who had been annoying us knocked head over heels.

Our disappointment may be imagined when, on reaching the springs or wells, we found, instead of the running stream we had been told to expect, only a well or two which had evidently been recently filled in by the enemy. The engineers were set to work to dig out the wells, while a portion of the force was sent forward to drive the enemy from their position on the hills. This was easily effected by the Marines and the 49th.

All the water found was of a dark brown colour, utterly unfit for human consumption and insufficient to water even a few animals. This was a grievous disappointment to all of us, as I, for one, had been told by a friend who was at Suakin all through the winter months that he had often seen through a good glass a stream of water running down this same *wady* and sparkling in the rays of the sun. That there is a running stream here at one time of the year is beyond a doubt true; but what we found in the month of April was a different thing altogether, being merely a few small wells holding little water, and a small stagnant pool of putrid liquid which could hardly be called water at all.

While the Marines and the 49th were driving the enemy back in one part of the field, the remainder of the force were engaged dislodging them in another; but there was no real fighting, and the enemy never showed up in force all day.

It now became evident that Osman had determined not to face us, and that he had retired towards Tamanieb, seven or eight miles further south. It was very disappointing, after all the work we had had; but whether or not the enemy tried to draw us on, or that they had come to the wise determination of harassing us by carrying on a guerilla style of warfare, I do not know; we had certainly come all that way for no purpose, and there was nothing for it but to return home again.

On our way back to Teselah Hill we set fire to Tamai, which was thus very soon burnt to the ground. A few rather interesting things were taken from Osman Digna's hut there, and amongst others a hand-illuminated copy of the *Koran*, done on separate sheets of a thick paper, and held together in a rough sort of portfolio.

It would have been quite impossible for us to hold Tamai in the face of the utter inadequacy of the water supply, and it was therefore decided to return forthwith to the *zaribas*.

Our losses during the day, not including the casualties of the preceding night, were, altogether, one man killed, and one officer and nine men wounded.

It was a very tedious and hot march back again that afternoon to the *zaribas*, where we found the 28th Native Infantry had not been molested in our absence. We left Teselah Hill about two o'clock, and did not reach the *zaribas* till after six p.m.

There were a few cases of exhaustion from the heat, and some of the men, as soldiers always will, had drunk all their water at starting. I saw this happen over and over again during the campaign, and no amount of experience ever seemed to teach them better. We always found it best to put off drinking water as long as possible, never touching it until it was absolutely necessary, as when once we had moistened our lips the craving for more was almost irresistible. The cavalry continued their march into camp, but the remainder of the force bivouacked that night at the *zaribas*.

I have never devoted any remarks to the Mounted Infantry. A hardier and more willing lot of fellows it would be difficult to find anywhere; they were always to the front, and you would see them galloping about in the bush or clattering up the hills on their little Arab horses, who suited them down to the ground, and were just the animals for the job. There is one thing though, which I think calls for a remark, and that is the manner in which the Mounted Infantry were utilized during the campaign. Every Mounted Infantry man is armed only with a rifle, and he carries his ammunition on a cross-belt, *bandoleer* fashion.

It is a recognised thing with them that they are not to engage the enemy under four hundred yards, unless driven to do so by circumstances, their duties being to harass the enemy at a distance by the accuracy of their fire, and to move rapidly from point to point. They were, however, in the Sûdan continually used as cavalry, which, there is no doubt about it, was a grave mistake. They are utterly unsuited for the work for several reasons, but principally because, in the event of their being attacked by cavalry when mounted, they are practically unarmed, as they carry no swords. It is no doubt a great difficulty to know how to separate the two organisations of Mounted Infantry and cavalry, and to keep each intact in its own individuality.

If you give a Mounted Infantry man a sword you practically make a cavalry man of him, as both then are armed almost identically. To keep Mounted Infantry as a distinct force, and to separate them entirely from the cavalry, the only way is never to use them for duties for which they are unsuited. When the cavalry is hardly worked, there is a great likelihood of the Mounted Infantry being taken for outpost duty, and the ordinary routine of vidette work; but for these duties they are unsuited, and, moreover, were never intended.

In our next big war I conceive that Mounted Infantry will play, to a certain extent, an important part. The force is only still in its infancy, and now is the time that arrangements should be made to give it a distinct place of its own in the army, and not make it up, on the spur of the moment, of units from various regiments, and then in the field require it to perform duties for which it is utterly unfitted, and for the performance of which we have already an organised force in our cavalry. To fire and scuttle away, and never to engage the enemy at close quarters, should be the two rules for the guidance alike of Mounted Infantry men themselves, and those who utilise them.

After the two exceedingly severe days' work entailed upon the troops by the advance on Tamai, everyone slept pretty soundly in the *zaribas* that night, and nothing took place to disturb the general quiet.

The next morning the whole force, with the exception of the 28th Native Infantry, who were left behind to look after the *zaribas* till the stores there could be withdrawn, marched back to their old quarters in front of Suakin.

The enormous concourse of men and animals may be imagined when I say that, besides a fighting force of 8,175 men, there were also 752 camels, over 1,000 mules, 1,773 drivers and followers, eight ambulance waggons, a number of mule-carts, a great many *dhoolies*, and two field-hospitals, together with seventeen wounded and thirty-three sick.

When one considers what it means to feed such a force as this, and provide water every day for nearly 12,000 throats, miles from the base, and in a country where there is nothing but dried-up bush and parching sands, the work, to say the least of it, seems a heavy one.

All our toil and labour in collecting supplies at the *zaribas* had now gone for nothing. I do not know what the general thought, but many of us likened ourselves, on our return to camp that day, to the soldiers of a certain king of France, who amused himself marching much such an army as we were, in point of strength, to the top of a hill and down again.

The day after we got back to camp was Easter Sunday, and we were allowed a day of comparative rest.

On the following morning, at 4.30, an enormous convoy of baggage animals, numbering over two thousand camels and fifteen hundred mules, escorted by four battalions of infantry, marched out for the last time to the *zaribas*, to bring in all the stores and the garrison, and to a certain extent to destroy the place. With the exception of a few trusses of hay everything was brought in, the convoy returning to camp shortly before six o'clock in the evening. The 28th Native Infantry had been fired at for nearly three hours the previous night, but only one man and two mules were wounded. The mere fact of the enemy having dared to follow us on our retreat from Tamai, and to open fire again on the *zaribas*, shows how little real moral effect our operations had had upon them.

Thus ended our connection with those three *zaribas*, dyed so indelibly with the blood of so many brave men on both sides.

The campaign thus far seemed barren of results indeed. How far any plan was carried out by these marches here and marches there, I know not; but many able men thought it would have been much better had we made the line of the railway the line of our advance, and avoided the loss of life and excessive toil entailed by marching after Osman Digna wherever he chose to lead us. Had we acted in this way, Osman would have been bound to attack us, or lost for ever his prestige with his followers. He would have fought then at a disadvantage to himself, and with a corresponding advantage to us; and we should have been able to devote our energies the whole while towards pushing on the railway, which was, after all, one of the principal objects of the expedition.

Many men who had spent years of their life in the country, travelling about and studying the character of the natives, were of opinion, even before we landed at Suakin, that this latter course would have been the one adopted by our leaders. But here we were, after many weeks spent in marching about the country, back again at our starting-point, doing exactly what it was supposed we should do, even before the troops left England.

It appeared evident that, as far as fighting was concerned, the campaign might now be considered over, and that we need not expect any serious opposition from Osman Digna.

Our spies also informed us that Osman had been almost entirely deserted by most of the tribes, and had retired with a few hundred followers to a point between Sinkat and Erkowit.

While the stores were being withdrawn from the *zaribas*, the remainder of the troops were busily engaged concentrating the whole of the camp along the line of railway, which had now reached as far as the West Redoubt, a distance of nearly four miles from Suakin.

A force, consisting of the Coldstream Guards, the Australian battalion, 17th Company Royal Engineers, two guns of the Mule Battery, and a troop of cavalry, marched, early the same morning, five miles out in the direction of Handoub, where a *zariba* was formed. This *zariba* was known as No. 1 *zariba*, and was constructed partially to protect the line of railway, and also as a halting-place and *depôt* midway between the West Redoubt and Handoub, which place was to be our next object.

The enemy had actually begun to renew their night attacks on the camp, and, the first night we returned, a party attempted to rush the Marines, but were discovered and fired upon before they could do any damage. How little they had profited by the severe chastisement they had at all times received may be judged of from this fact.

The force at No. 1 *zariba* moved forward the morning after their arrival there, their place being taken by the Scots Guards, with a large convoy of stores and provisions.

It was not expected that the enemy would offer any serious opposition to our advance on Handoub, but every precaution was taken, as the bush at the foot of the hills is remarkably thick. The Mounted Infantry scouted the ground in front, but only a few Arabs were seen watching our movements from a distance.

It was a terribly hot morning, and the men suffered very much on this tedious march through the heavy sand. Handoub was at length reached, and occupied without any opposition at all. The place, which consisted only of a few huts, was entirely deserted. The wells, altogether five in number, were found to contain a fair supply of somewhat brackish water. One of the five gave a rather better quality than the others, but a plentiful supply of drinkable water was obtained by digging in the bed of the *khor*. It was not, of course, free from the brackish taste, but a little citric acid mixed with it overcame this. Water was sent out to Handoub by the convoys, in the same way as we had been doing before; but we hoped that, as soon as the railway reached there, this part of our labours would be over. All along the side of the line four-inch pipes had been laid to carry water to the front, and patent pumps had been sent out to force it any distance.

Handoub is the first halting-place on the traders' route from Suakin to Berber, and is situated at the foot of a low isolated ridge or spur of the Waratab Mountains, which here run down into the plain. It is twelve and a half miles north-west of Suakin.

After an interval for rest after the hot march, a *zariba* was commenced between two small hills which commanded the village, and a gun was also mounted on the top of each hill, so the position was as secure as it well could be, and, with the Australians and Coldstreams to defend it, could have held out against any numbers.

The following day a large convoy was sent out to Handoub, escorted by a squadron of cavalry; the remainder of the troops being engaged in cutting "drifts" and making a broad track in the bush for the railway.

This drift-making was terribly hard work in the burning sun, as the wood of the mimosa and acacia is very tough indeed, and it is almost impossible to get at the stems of these stunted bushes, owing to the thorns. The way our men managed it was to sling a rope round a bush, and then, while two men hauled on the rope to pull the branches on one side, a third would attack the stem with an axe. When the bush was cut down it had to be dragged out of the way by more men; so, the work was altogether very slow and very hard.

I think the most tedious work of all was guarding the head of the railway. A force of cavalry and infantry was told off for this duty each day, and while some of the men were placed on sentry, the rest were allowed to lie down on the ground, ready at any moment in the event of an attack. A few tent roofs were sent out, to protect the men from the sun; but as these were insufficient in number, many of the men would lie down on the sand, and go fast to sleep in the full blaze of the sun.

With nothing to occupy them and little to think about all day long, the men had nothing left to do but to go to sleep. A guard of this sort was absolutely necessary to cover the working parties, but the Arabs never interfered with us, and so there was not even the excitement of a little skirmish to while away the time. I really believe some of the men would rather have been engaged on the railway fatigue, or in cutting the "drifts," than as covering party to the workers.

There was rather an amusing story told of one of the navvies at this time. The line had very nearly reached No. 1 *zariba*, and of course there was a large quantity of sleepers, fish-plates, rails, etc., collected in front, to be used up as the railway proceeded. One morning a navvy happened to go out rather earlier than usual, and found an Arab asleep among the sleepers.

While he was debating in his mind what he should do with the fellow, the Arab suddenly woke up, and in the twinkling of an eye sent his spear flying at the somewhat astonished navvy. Stepping gracefully on one side, the navvy is said to have caught the spear as it passed him. Walking up then to the Arab, without more ado he planted a blow, with his clenched fist and in true English fashion, right between the fellow's eyes, which knocked him about ten yards into the bush. Having settled him in this way, the navvy walked up to his prostrate and insensible foe, and brought him in a prisoner.

One of our Indian drivers who had been missing ever since our fight at Hasheen, turned up in camp in the middle of this week, having been a prisoner all the while in the hands of Osman Digna. His story was that, when he was about to be killed by some of the Hadendowas, he declared himself a Mohammedan, and thus saved his life. He was taken to Tamai, and after the fight at the *zaribas*, the Arabs returned there with seven more of our native drivers, who had been cut off in their flight to Suakin. He had had an interview with Osman Digna, who, he said, had given orders that Mohammedan prisoners were to be treated with kindness. He also said that, although on the day we visited Tamai there were only a few men there, there was a large force further on in the mountains, but that they were all badly off for food.

The 2nd Brigade was moved further up the line as the rest of the force advanced, and pitched their camp about two miles from the No. 1 *zariba*, in readiness for a further advance when required.

We were daily engaged running convoys out to Handoub, and occasionally we had for our escort only a small body of cavalry. This did not seem altogether a wise measure, considering the lesson we had already learnt from treating the enemy with too much indifference. On one occasion our friends in No. 1 *zariba* watched us, expecting every moment to see us attacked, as a few hundred Arabs were seen on the hills quite close to our line of march. It was curious thing, that, although we never knew exactly where the enemy might be, our returning convoys not unfrequently moved without an escort at all.

Another serious loss in camels would have crippled our transport very considerably, but still these risks were run, and the safety of our camels left to chance.

In our advance to Handoub, we were accompanied by Mahomet Ali, the friendly *sheikh* of the Amarar tribe, who had been endeavouring to persuade the Amarars to come in in a body, though not with much success. After the short campaign last year the "friendlies" had suffered severely at the hands of Osman Digna, as soon as we had sailed away in our ships, and they were naturally not altogether inclined to run the chance of the same thing occurring again. They therefore demanded that we should guarantee their protection before they submitted. This it was impossible to grant, as we had no idea what the future policy of the government might be with relation to the Sudan.

On the 13th of April the Mounted Infantry reconnoitred the country as far as Otao without meeting with any of the enemy.

Two wells were found containing a small amount of water, and it appeared probable that more might be obtained by digging. The ground all the way from Handoub to Otao, a distance of five miles, is more open, the bush being much less thick. On the 16th Otao was occupied by the Scots Guards, with two guns and a squadron of the 5th Lancers. Nothing was seen of the enemy.

There was a good deal of sickness now among the troops, principally from dysentery and sunstroke, but enteric fever was also increasing, and one or two cases had terminated fatally. The work was very hard, as it always must be in wartime, the weather was frightfully hot, and the climate not of the best, so what with the want of good food and water and the incessant labour from dawn till dark, the percentage of sick was slowly rising, and the hospitals were filling apace.

The campaign dragged slowly on, and there was no fighting to relieve the drudgery of the day, the long marches, or the never-ending convoys. A good fight would have brightened us all up, but it was evident now that Osman Digna did not intend to try issues with us again.

We heard he was doing his utmost to collect his followers, but the tribes were all engaged up in the mountains sowing their crops. A few scattered bands still hovered about the country, but these generally made off when any of our cavalry or Mounted Infantry approached, and the whole country appeared deserted.

The most extraordinary rumours reached us from England, about the government being pressed to withdraw from the Sûdan altogether, and give up the destruction of the tribes, against whom we had no real quarrel. We hardly credited this, though, and we could not believe that the enormous outlay and loss of life would have been allowed unless the government had had some decided aim in view.

Berber seemed a very long way off to us, and we still had two hundred and sixty miles left to do. I do not think we ever imagined for moment that the railway would be carried all the way, and with the hot season now beginning we thought we had quite enough before us to get to Ariab, before the autumn. How much of the force would eventually reach Berber in time for the advance on Khartoum was a matter of the vaguest speculation, the general idea being that we should not participate at all in this part of the programme, but merely occupy a point to threaten the enemy's flank and cut off their retreat in this direction when Khartoum had fallen.

So, as I say, the days and hours dragged on, the hospitals filled, the sick were sent away homeward, and those that were left toiled on in their now ragged clothes from sunrise till sunset.

Chapter 11

Hospital

A *dhoolie* is a comfortable conveyance. I was carried some miles in one. I was to have been sent down to hospital in a cart drawn by a pair of mules, till someone suggested this would be a painful experience. So, a *dhoolie* was sent for, and shortly after I was lying inside it, with my water-bottle for a pillow and my small amount of kit following behind on a camel.

Let me explain what a *dhoolie* is to those who have never seen one. Suspended from a thick bamboo pole some ten feet in length is a light iron frame six feet six inches long and three feet broad. Across this frame is stretched some stout canvas, while at the ends and sides a similar piece of material, about six inches broad, is fixed round to prevent the occupant from falling out. The corners of the iron framework are fitted with short legs, so that when then *dhoolie* is put down the person inside does not touch the ground. Curtains, two feet six inches high, go all round the *dhoolie*, fitted at the top to a cane framework, the roof being made of a swinging sort of awning of thick canvas.

The bearers are eight in number, and two work at a time at each end of the pole; so, there are two reliefs, and no stoppage need be made. These *dhoolie*-bearers are Indians regularly trained in the art of carrying the sick. They move at a sort of running shuffle, taking care to break the step so as to stop any swinging of the *dhoolie*. The sort of shuffling noise these fellows make with their feet will, no doubt, recall many sad experiences, and maybe also hours of much suffering, to those who have been carried in a *dhoolie* in war-time.

"Goodbye, old chap," from a friend, and "*challow* Quarantine Island" (go on to Quarantine Island) to the bearers, and I was on my journey to one of the hospital-ships in the harbour.

I do not know how far I had gone when the *dhoolie* was quietly put on the ground, and I heard the bearers sit themselves down and begin talking.

Theirs happened to be one of the many languages I was unable to talk, and, moreover, I was too ill to raise my voice much above a whisper; but, pulling aside one of the curtains, I saw I was near some tents, and as there was a sergeant standing by, I made signs to him to come to me. The only answer I received from this individual was, "You bide where you are;" so no doubt he did not recognise me as an officer—how should he in the rags I had on?

At length I managed, by pointing to my bearers the direction in which I wished to go, to start them again, and nothing particular occurred for the next mile save the periodical changing of the reliefs.

After a while I was again put on the ground, and this time found myself at the Base Hospital at "H" Redoubt.

"What have you got here?" says a sentry to the bearers—the English soldier always thinks everyone must speak his language. "Oh, a officer, is it? Well, what's the use a-bringing on 'im 'ere? I tell ye he's for Quarantine Island."

But by this time a doctor had come up, who very kindly asked me whether I should like to go on by train, as the "Flying Hadendowa" would be passing directly. Thinking that the *dhoolie* would be more comfortable than the somewhat primitive Suakin-Berber railway, I said that on the whole I would rather stick to my *dhoolie*. Thus, I lost my chance of a ride on this famous line, which someone *naïvely* described as a line which begins nowhere and ends nowhere else.

This time I really did get to Quarantine Island; and when my bearers stopped again another doctor pulled my curtains aside, and, shaking me by the hand, said, "You will have to wait a bit, but we will have a boat for you presently; meanwhile we will draw these curtains aside, and you will get the air." So, I lay like this for half an hour, surrounded by all the bustle and the dust of that busy landing-place. Many came and stared at me, and passed remarks the reverse of inspiriting.

"Well, he's a gone coon, anyhow," said one. "Lor', don't he look ill!" said another. "Sunstroke," said a third. "I tell ye he isn't sunstroke," said a fourth; "'e've been wounded," and so on. They settled it between them somehow or other, but how made little difference to me.

The boat came at last, and then, being unable to move, I was rolled out of the *dhoolie* into the dust, and picked up and put in the boat. Ten minutes' pulling brought me to the hospital-ship. I was carried up the side, and in another minute found myself on a comfortable bed in a cabin all to myself, too ill to care much about anything, and too tired to do anything but fall asleep at once. I shall never forget the peace, quiet, and contentment of the first few hours in that small cabin. The air blew in cool through the port, the silence was only broken by the plashing of the water against the ship's great sides, and with this music in my ears I fell asleep.

They were very kind to us in hospital, and everything that could be done was done for the sick and the wounded. It seemed very odd to hear a woman's voice again, and we ought all to be very grateful for the loving care bestowed upon us by the lady nurses.

There were many of these, both in the shore-hospitals as well as in the two hospital-ships, and their scarlet capes and cheery faces did much to brighten up the different tents and cabins. We often talk of the way we soldiers are ordered off here and there at short notice, but I think few soldiers ever started for foreign service with shorter notice than did some of these lady nurses.

I knew of one, aged not more than one and twenty, who received her orders for Suakin at nine o'clock one night and had to be ready to sail the next morning at seven. What can we say of such devotion as this, of a readiness to share with the soldiers their trials and hardships, to tend them when sick, and to soothe them in their hours of greatest suffering? To brave all the horrors of a military hospital, and to fight at the same time against a climate, requires a noble spirit indeed, and women who are able and willing to undertake such duties, forgetful of self, and mindful only of the sufferings of others, should rank among the very highest of their sex. Women teach us many things, but above all they teach us unselfishness.

One of the greatest drawbacks to our hospital was the enormous number of rats. I awoke one night to find upwards of a dozen in my cabin. They were the most confidential rats I ever saw, and they seemed to know perfectly well that, being a cripple, I was unable to get at them. They would take a jump right across from the bunk on one side of the cabin on to the top of me; but I got accustomed to them at last, and quite content that they should enjoy themselves so long as they did not crawl over my face.

Besides the rats, there were thousands and thousands of cockroaches of all sizes, the largest measuring an inch and a half long. Some people would have objected to these more than the rats, but I preferred anything to the cold paws of a rat on my face. That was really objectionable, and, what was worse, it generally woke one up with a start.

There were cases of all sorts in hospital-wounds of the most curious and interesting description, the doctors said; cases of sunstroke, many of dysentery, fevers of various kinds, affections of the eyes, smallpox, and even cholera. The smallpox patients were kept on a lighter at the entrance to the harbour, and I never heard of more than two cases of cholera.

I think the one I pitied more than most was an officer who had served his country in the Crimea and in China, and who had had a lengthened experience in the Sûdan besides. A finer soldier and a kinder-hearted or more genial man I never met. He was suffering from an acute attack of some disease of the eyes which rendered him for the time blind. Being, of course, unable to read, and having nothing to occupy himself with, he used to wander up and down the saloon all day long, and when night came he was unable to sleep for pain. One day a ship started for home with invalids and he was ordered in her, but at the last moment they had no room for him, and he was condemned to another week or more on the hospital-ship. He never murmured, he was always cheerful; but when the ship came at last and took him away, he reached England but to die.

There were many cases as sad as this, and many died ere reaching home—victims to a climate and to the hardships of war.

Denied the glory of a death in the heat of action, they succumbed to the foe that slays in greater numbers than either the spear or the bullet—a death less glorious, perhaps, but a life given for Queen and Country just the same. The sorrows following after a war are, for the most part, localised. The nation feels not as a whole the loss of its soldiers; but they feel who find gaps where formerly stood cheery, manly forms, who miss the ring of the voice they loved so well, and the light heart and ready grip of the hand. The day will come when the troops will return, the towns will be gay with many-coloured flags, bands will play and crowds will cheer, and who among all the concourse that watch that homecoming will miss the forms of those who come not?

Our friends came to see us in hospital when time would allow, but many were too far up the country now to come down easily to Suakin. Let me give one instance of the way one soldier helps another. I was lying on my bed one hot afternoon, the temperature even in the cool of the hospital being 88° all through the day, when in comes a friend, saying, "Here are your letters, old chap. Goodbye; I can't stop."

That friend had ridden many miles in all the fierce heat of a noonday sun, and when overdone with work, to bring me what soldiers value most on service—home news.

May I thank him here?

And now my story is almost over. One night they told me they were going to send me home. I don't know that the news was good news, for I would far rather have come home with the rest; and though the war was said to be over, I did not like leaving friends behind.

The next morning, early, we were put on board a lighter and towed off to the ship that was to take us home.

We were put on board with our baggage, and stood for some time on the lower deck waiting for our cabins to be told off to us.

We were a motley-looking crowd certainly as we stood or sat there in our ragged, worn-out clothes. There were a good many of us.

Men with bandaged heads, with arms in slings, with battered helmets and torn jackets. Men looking ill and worn, and with that peculiar expression of countenance begotten of days of fatigue, of nights of anxious watching, of hours of suffering, and times of great privation.

Why does not one of our great artists paint a picture such as this? The world would rave about it, people would stand by the hour and gaze at it, crowds would wonder at it, and women would weep over it, while some might faintly realise the sufferings of the men who are content to go out with a smile upon their countenances, to brave hourly, daily, nightly, death in its most horrible forms, and then to return, some of them, a shadow of their former selves.

"Soldiers," said one of England's greatest generals, "your labours, your privations, your sufferings, and your valour will not be forgotten by a grateful country."

We pray this may be so.

Suakim, '85

By Norman Robert Stewart

A soldier's life is full of surprises. The end of February, '85, saw me on tour of inspection with my general (A. H. Murray), and on the very day we reached Banda, he received a wire from Army Headquarters, Simla, directing me to report myself at once to Brigadier-General John Hudson, who was appointed to the command of an Indian contingent about to start for Suakim, and with which I was to proceed as D.A.A.G. This was truly joyful news, but it was a great upset to our plans; as Banda was off the line of railway, and the general's health was indifferent, I disliked leaving him. However, he was not to be persuaded to return with me, so after sending my horses off by road, I said goodbye to him the same night, and never saw him again, as he died very shortly afterwards, to my deep regret. On arrival at Jubbulpore, I found a telegram from General Hudson ordering me to proceed to Bombay to superintend the embarkation of the troops.

Two days and one night I devoted to my affairs, and the third morning saw me in Bombay, where, I soon discovered this embarkation job meant seeing everyone else off and leaving by the last transport myself. The embarkation staff at Bombay did all the work, but for the 10 or 12 days I was there I had to spend all my time at the docks, and constitute myself as a sort of "Court of Appeal" in the event of disputes between the regimental authorities and the local embarkation officers.

My time came at last, and I found myself on board the Indian Marine steamer *Tenasserim* with a detachment of the 9th Bengal Lancers, the Madras Sappers and Miners, and any odds and ends, in the shape of departmental staff officers, as companions. After an ideal passage we reached Suakim on the evening of the 14th March, and were ordered by signal to join the other transports at anchor some miles down the coast, where we would receive further instructions regarding disem-

9TH BENGAL CAVALRY

barkation, which took place the following day.

On landing I was put in charge of the water supply of our contingent, the arrangements for which were in the hands of the Naval authorities. It turned out an easy task, as every evening certain tanks were told off to brigades, and one had merely to pass the *number* of the tank on to the unit concerned, and see that the regimental authorities carried out their orders. The *bhisties*, or water carriers, drew water morning and evening, by which time the supply was exhausted, when the condensing ships set to work and refilled all the tanks during the night. The arrangements were carried out with mathematical precision, and not once was there any failure, which speaks well for the Naval system.

The supply provided was a liberal one, and was quite sufficient for that luxury, "the daily bath"; but when it came to marching, the labour was great, as the water had to be carried in zinc cylinders holding 10 gallons each, two of these forming a mule load. In filling these cylinders, the fatigue parties had to be very carefully watched to prevent waste, as we only carried the exact ration for each man for drinking and cooking purposes. The rule was to fill up these cylinders overnight, and so have all in readiness for the march. Each cylinder had two strong bands, to which rings were attached, corresponding with hooks on the pack saddles, so all that had to be done was to lift two at the same moment and hook them on to the pack, and then pass a rope round the ends of both under and over till a compact load was made well up on the animal's back.

All ranks understood how precious the supply was, so took particular care in adjusting these loads. In addition to the supply carried on mules, each unit had a water cart or carts, drawn by mules, at the end of which was a tap which enabled water bottles to be refilled on the line of march if the same turned out particularly distressing or prolonged. These carts were invariably under special guards with instructions that no water was to be drawn except under the orders of the responsible officer in charge of the regimental supply.

Only on one occasion did I see these orders abused, and that was by the Australian Contingent on the march to Tamai, which was a real corker, and the lesson they learnt was one not to be forgotten, for on reaching their destination they found themselves short, whilst others were enjoying the benefits of their untouched supply. However, we managed to spare them a drink all round, with the warning they were not to expect the same consideration again—a warning which to their credit they bore in mind.

Just at first there was a good deal of "shifting" of camps, as every night we received visits from "snipers" and others, who crawled in on all fours and speared many an unwary sentry or follower in a manner which was truly astounding, considering the precautions taken. One night these gentlemen grew bolder and rushed a large guard of the Berkshire Regiment, well in rear of the entire camp, and under the very nose of one of our gunboats. They managed to kill several of our men, and got off themselves with slight loss, but not without leaving behind one of Osman Digna's most important lieutenants, a loss which caused that chief considerable regret, for the next day he sent in a letter offering a sum of money for the man's body, which I need hardly say was not complied with.

Later on, we tried every device we could think of to put a stop to the sniping, but with poor results. On one occasion a mine was laid on a spot surrounded by a low wall, from behind which the Arabs frequently took up their position to pepper a searchlight on the walls of the town. This mine was so laid that anyone entering the enclosure must assuredly be blown up, and we thought we had caught them at last, but to everyone's surprise it was again made use of, and no explosion followed!

The next morning a party of Engineers went out to ascertain the cause of the failure, and on approaching the spot the officer in charge halted his men, whilst he advanced to inspect the wires, the slightest touch of which would explode the mine, but with fatal results, for the next moment there was an explosion, and the poor fellow was blown to atoms. After this accident the ground was carefully examined, and two points were clearly demonstrated.

Without doubt men had been there the previous night, and had not only disconnected the wires, but re-connected them before leaving, and this on a pitch-black night; proving to us that not only had they, through spies, learnt our plans, but possessed men thoroughly conversant with the handling of electric wires. It was well known that amongst Osman Digna's following there were several mechanics and others who had served under the Egyptian Government, and whose education he was now apparently making good use of.

On the 19th a reconnaissance was made as far as Hashim, which was entered by the cavalry and mounted infantry, and at whom only a few shots were fired.

The following day practically the whole force, with the exception of the Shropshire Light Infantry, paraded at daybreak, and advanced on Hashim about 6.30.

With the Cavalry Brigade and Mounted Infantry in front and on the flanks, the 2nd Infantry Brigade in line of columns formed the front of a three-sided square, with the Guards' Brigade and Indian Contingent in columns of companies forming the right and left faces respectively, inside being the Gardners, rockets. Engineers, and animals. On reaching some lows hills due East of Hashim the Engineers and East Surrey Regiment occupied these, and proceeded to form a *zareba*, whilst the remainder of the 2nd Brigade, supported by the Indian Contingent, with the Guards in reserve and the cavalry on each flank, were ordered to attack the Dhilibut Hill, which was occupied by the enemy.

The Berkshires formed for attack, with half a battalion of Marines in support, the remainder of whom advanced to the right of the Berkshires, followed by the Indian Contingent, with the 15th Sikhs extended in line, and the 28th Bombay Infantry and 17th Bengal Infantry in column in rear of right and left flanks of the 15th Sikhs.

The hill was so steep the Berkshires had almost to "crawl" up some of it, so the advance was necessarily slow. The summit was held by the enemy's riflemen, and it was quite impossible to form any correct estimate of their strength. Without a halt the 49th advanced inch by inch, as it were, whilst we all looked on, and a prettier piece of work I never saw, as they were under a hot fire all the time. The enemy clung to the heights to the last, and eventually bolted along the spurs in rear and across the *khor* behind the village of Hashim, under the heavy fire of the Berkshires, who had gained the hill.

As soon as this was accomplished, the Marines and Indian Contingent swung half right and occupied the ground south of Hashim.

Whilst this was going on two squadrons of the 9th Bengal Lancers were engaging the enemy making for Tamai, and others who were apparently coming from that direction with the intention of getting round our left and rear. One of these squadrons being dismounted had to resist a nasty rush of the Fuzzies at considerable disadvantage, hampered as they were with carbine, lance, and sword, till the mounted squadron came to its assistance, but not before it had lost nine men and a water cart with its followers, some of whom were killed, whilst the rest were made prisoners.

On the extreme right the 5th Lancers and remaining squadrons of the 9th Bengal Lancers made several effective charges at bodies of the enemy who were attempting to turn our right.

After remaining in the *khor* for some two hours under a dropping fire, which knocked over a few men, the Indian Contingent was ordered to retire, covered by the 2nd Brigade, followed by the Guards and Horse Artillery, who kept up a heavy fire on the enemy, who seemed to spring from the bowels of the earth in all directions, occupying the ground we vacated within an interval of time that was astonishing even in thick bush.

Our losses were one officer and eight men killed, and three officers and 36 men wounded. What the enemy suffered is impossible to say. They appeared and disappeared as if by magic, and only in a few cases did I see any fall to our withering fire. The cavalry, on the other hand, claimed having killed many, and one *sowar* of the 9th B.L. is reported to have slain seven to his own cheek!

The troops returned to Suakim after a long day of 12 hours, leaving the East Surrey Regiment in *zareba*, which turned out a very happy move, as it practically put a stop to sniping at night.

This was the first occasion our Indian troops had experienced what bush fighting meant, and on the whole they seemed to enjoy it. Considering the conditions, the work of the mounted troops appeared excellent.

On the 21st the force was given a day's rest prior to breaking up Osman Digna's gathering at Tamai to the South-west of Suakim. For this purpose, the following troops paraded on the morning of the 22nd, under the command of Major-General Sir John McNeill:—

1 Squadron 5th Lancers.
1 Battalion Royal Marines.
Berkshire Regiment (49th).
1 Field Company R.E. with Telegraph Section.
Detachment Naval Brigade with 4 Gardner guns.

Ammunition column.
15th Sikhs.
17th Bengal Infantry.
28th Bombay Infantry.
1 Company Madras Sappers and Miners.
Sir John McNeill's Staff:—
A.D.C., Lieut. Hon. A. D. Charteris, C. Guards.
Brigade-Major, Lieut.-Col. W. F. Kelly, Royal Sussex Regiment.
Commanding Indian Contingent, Brigadier-General J. Hudson.

Staff Indian Contingent, Maj. R. McG. Stewart, R.A., A.A. and Q.M.G.; Bt.-Major N. R. Stewart, D.A.A. and Q.M.G.; Major A. J. Pearson, R.A., D.A.A. and Q.M.G.; Major J. Cook, Brigade-Major; Captain C. Muir, A.D.C.

The force was formed up before daybreak, and marched at daylight, the 5th Lancers scouting in front, followed by the British and Indian troops in two squares in the order named.

The object of the advance was to proceed some seven miles and there form a *zareba*, to be held by the British troops, on the completion of which the Indian Contingent were to return to Suakim with the empty transport, this *zareba* being the first of a series to be built on the way to Tamai or Tamanib.

Inside the Indian Contingent square were all the animals carrying water and provisions. It marched in echelon to the British square, which being more compact and mobile, had to halt continually for the more cumbersome square in rear. The "going" was so slow we hardly seemed to make any progress, and Suakim was still in sight when we began to feel the effects of the sun, and by the time we had covered five miles man and beast seemed to have had enough, so it was decided to halt and build the first *zareba* where we stood.

The precautions considered necessary having been taken, fatigue parties from each unit were sent out to cut the bush, the loads were removed from all animals, and the work of building the required *zareba*s was commenced. These were three in number, the leading one for the Berkshires, the centre one for animals, followers, stores, etc., and the rear one for the Marines. At the corners of the Berkshire and Marines' *zareba*, pointing towards Tamai and Suakim respectively, it was intended to have two Gardner guns in position;

Personally, I was engaged erecting canvas tanks and looking after the water supply generally, so did not pay much attention to what was going on elsewhere. The work I was superintending was completed a little after 2.30, when I rode up to General Hudson, who with his staff was eating lunch, and reported to him accordingly. Being mounted, he ordered me to warn the regiments of the Indian Contingent to fall in where they stood preparatory to marching back to Suakim.

At the time the 28th Bombay Infantry and two companies of the 17th Bengal Infantry were facing North, the 15th Sikhs West, and six companies 17th Bengal Infantry South, the intention being to march back in a hollow square with the animals inside, it being known at the time that communication with Suakim was being kept up by squad-

CORNER OF THE SQUARE

rons of the 20th Hussars and 9th Bengal Lancers.

The Marines' *zareba* was complete, the Berkshires nearly so, and the one for animals only partially so, though enough bush had been cut to complete it and join up all three. The Marines were inside their *zareba*, and half a battalion of the Berkshires in theirs, but the Gardner guns were not in position. The other half battalion of the Berkshires were in the bush some distance S.E. of the Marines' *zareba*, and between them and the left of the 17th N.I. were picquets of that regiment. In front of all facing Tamai were the 5th Lancers. The animals were in front of the 17th N.I.

Major von Beverhoudt, commanding the 17th N.I., had just drawn his regiment up in line some 50 yards clear of the Berkshire *zareba* when some of the 5th Lancers came galloping in by the left flank of the 15th Sikhs and right of the 17th N.I. and on in the direction of Suakim. As no enemy was to be seen, and all was quiet, the last thing to enter my mind was an impending fight, more especially as only a few minutes before I had seen General Hudson at lunch and noticed Sir John McNeill chatting with a group of officers. For these reasons it is hardly surprising little or no notice was taken of the galloping lancers. The next instant, however, the Arabs were rushing us from every direction. In front of them were soldiers in shirt sleeves running to the cover of their *zareba*s for all they were worth, and quicker than thought there was a fire which was absolutely deafening, and a scene that beggars description.

All seemed to grasp the situation except the 17th Bengal Infantry, who only had to open fire as they stood, instead of which this regiment for the moment seemed paralyzed, remained at the slope, and actually watched their commanding officer being killed by an Arab, who jumped up behind him on his horse's back and plunged a spear through his body! Still the men fired not, and appeared incapable of action, so great was their consternation. The next instant they began to look about, and then step back, breaking their formation, and lastly, they went. It wasn't a case of a stampede, it was more "a bolt at a walk." Anyhow, nothing could be done with them, and God knows their British officers did all in their power as well as many of their native officers and non-commissioned officers.

After a few yards had been covered the walk broke into a run till the mass of these men got jammed in the gap on the right of the 28th Bombay N.I., where two companies of their regiment were, and the Marines' *zareba*, where some of them did use their rifles. A great number, however, went through the gap and joined the runaway followers, who had been in the first instance carried by the force of the *sepoys* of this regiment, a force I had myself experienced, for they nearly lifted me and my horse bodily off the ground. The whole affair was only a matter of seconds, and in describing it, it would be untruthful to call it by any other name than "panic"; without doubt the regiment was panic-stricken and useless.

The men being drawn up for the purpose of marching quietly back to quarters were completely taken unawares, and seemed incapable of pulling themselves together or realising a "battle" had started. In spite of the excitement, it was painful to watch the look of astonishment, despair, or fright, whichever you like to think it, on the majority of the faces one could take in at a glance. A few men certainly did shake themselves free of their comrades and open fire, but it was too late, and they were too few.

The Arabs, although on the heels of the last men, had now to face the fire of both *zareba*s, and a small body of Madras Sappers and Miners, fortunately brought up by their C.O., Captain Wilkieson, at a most critical moment, were checked just long enough to prevent the mass of men getting through and attacking the 15th Sikhs and 28th Bombay Infantry in rear. Had this rush not been checked at the "biscuit boxes" the fire from the South and West faces of the Marines' square must have caused many casualties to our own side. To give some idea of how rapidly all this occurred, I may add Sir John McNeill had barely time to seek shelter inside the Berkshire *zareba*, whilst his A.D.C. was wounded by a spear thrust.

When the first shots were fired some men in their shirt sleeves who had been cutting scrub, and others belonging to the picquets on the left or Southern flank made a rush for the *zareba*s past the 17th Native Infantry, which may have started the panic, but the excuse is a poor one, as the majority of these men were merely rushing to get their arms.

What would have happened had the enemy pushed their attack home at this point is mere speculation, but the story of McNeill's *zareba* would be incomplete if I omitted all reference to the fortunate check the enemy received by the few rounds fired by the Madras Sappers and Miners, for had they followed in great numbers—and there was some danger of this happening for all we knew—the fire of the Marines would have taken the 15th Sikhs in rear, and the result would have been too awful to contemplate. As soon as all the Arabs who had penetrated the ground between the two *zareba*s had been killed, I found my way to my general behind the right flank of the 15th Sikhs, whence one was able to watch the fight to the end.

The 15th Sikhs and 28th Bombay N.I. had no protection in front of them. The fight was now at its height, and only a few yards separated our men from the Arabs, who were pressing the attack home to such an extent that more than once the Sikhs had to use their bayonets, charging out by companies a few yards, to enable them to make their weight tell, and back again into the line to pump in more lead on the next rush. It was a truly marvellous sight. Our fire was simply terrific, it was impossible for men to load faster, and yet it didn't seem nearly fast enough, for several hand to hand fights were going on all along the line of these two regiments, and at the same time every face of the two *zareba*s was engaged nearly as heavily as our two regiments in the open.

The bush was so thick, in spite of the large quantity of scrub we had cut down, that it was quite impossible to guess how much longer the fight would continue. It was a very anxious moment, practically the whole of our reserve ammunition had been carried away when the mules stampeded at the commencement of the fight, and the men were already asking for more, in fact some had fired every round. Another very serious matter was the condition of the men's hands, as the rifle barrels were now almost red hot. As regards ammunition, the Marines and Berkshires were better off, as they had their regimental reserve to fall back on.

In front of the 28th Bombay Infantry the scrub was thicker than elsewhere, besides being only a few yards off, giving absolute cover to the Arabs. Any unsteadiness on the part of this regiment would have been fatal to us.

We now had time to look round and see what had occurred in other parts of the field. Beginning with the Marines' *zareba*, all had gone well there, the *zareba* had been rushed on every side, but not an Arab managed to get inside. The site of the animal *zareba* was full of our dead, the enemy's, and at least 100 camels, but the saddest sight of all was inside the Berkshire *zareba*. The majority of the Berkshires who were outside cutting scrub rushed for the corner where the Engineers were putting the finishing touches to the sand-bag parapet for the Gardners, and with these men jumped at least 100 Arabs, who first attacked the Naval Brigade men with the Gardners, and practically killed all. Here also Lieut. Newman, R.E., superintending this work, was killed.

To wipe out these 100 Arabs the rear ranks of the Berkshire were obliged to turn about and fire point blank, and the consequence was in slaying the foe many comrades were also sacrificed. The face of the Berkshire square was only 65 yards, so it is easy to realise the effect of the fire of the rear ranks turned about.

The firing ceased as suddenly as it commenced, and hardly a man was to be seen. The stillness after the deafening noise of our fire was almost unbearable. Fortunately, there was lots to do. The work of completing the *zareba*s had to be restarted, the wounded and dead had to be sought and attended to, and lastly the fate of the half-battalion of the Berkshires in the open had to be ascertained, as well as that of the picquet of the 17th N.I. , and we were glad to find both had come well out of the fight, and had accounted for many of the enemy, besides escaping the murderous fire of some of the faces of the Marines' and Berkshires' *zareba*s.

The Arabs attacking from the South, after clearing the scrub, made use of our camels as cover, and in this way advanced right up to the biscuit boxes and South face of the Marines' *zareba* till all the animals were shot down by our fire. The sight of these poor wounded and killed camels and mules was enough to sicken the strongest—poor patient beasts that had not the sense to bolt, or tell friend from foe.

At the outset of the fight most of our mules carrying ammunition and medical stores were collected outside the E. and N. faces of the Marines' *zareba*, and stampeded at once towards Suakim. With these were many followers, private and public, medical subordinates, warrant officers, and war correspondents, who once the firing commenced could not possibly retrace their steps on account of our fire, so bolted after the mules, and soon met their fate, excepting those who were able to outrun the Arabs till they met succour in the shape of the squadrons of the 20th Hussars and 9th B.L. patrolling between our force and Suakim. The line of retreat of those fugitives who fell marked the road for many a day.

The loss of medical panniers was a very serious matter, and many ghastly operations had to be carried out without anaesthetics.

We managed to recover a few boxes of ammunition, which when issued gave each man, I think, some 10 rounds for further attacks!

Considering the fight only lasted some 20 minutes, our losses were heavy, eight British officers killed and three wounded. Including these our total amounted to 150 killed, 174 wounded, and 148 missing.

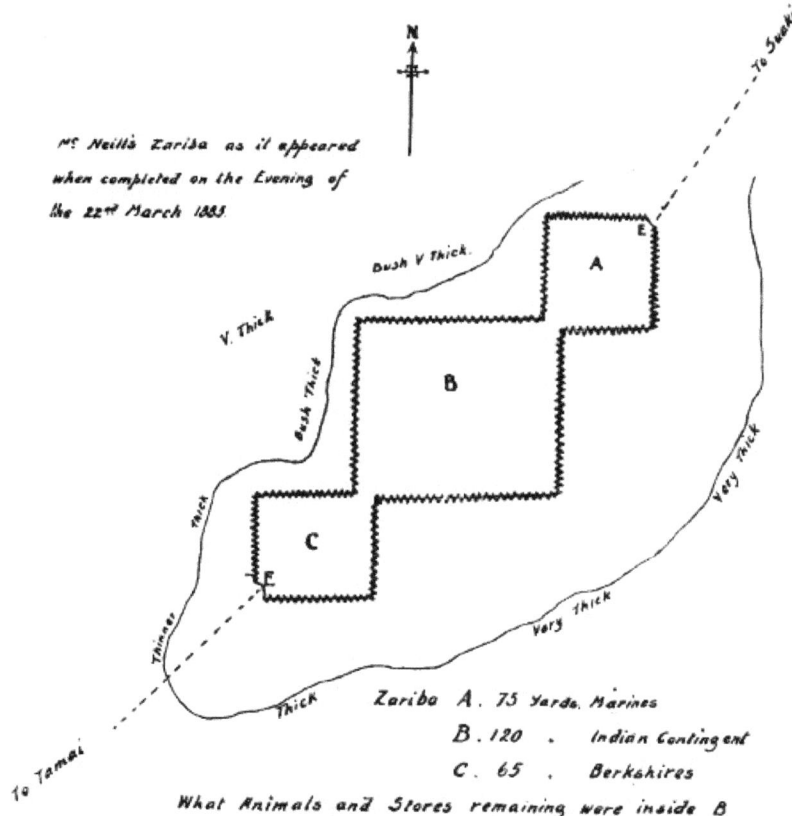

McNeill's Zariba as it appeared when completed on the Evening of the 22nd March 1885.

Zariba A. 75 Yards. Marines
B. 120 " Indian Contingent
C. 65 " Berkshires
What Animals and Stores remaining were inside B
E & E 2 Gardner Guns at Each

The company of the Madras Sappers and Miners suffered the severest losses. Out of three British officers one was wounded and two killed.

Before dark the *zareba*s were completed, and the different squares were told off (as shown in plan opposite), and, excepting one alarm, when a few precious rounds were fired at nothing, the night passed quietly. The Indian Contingent being without food and great coats, were not sorry when relief arrived next day.

Besides our own dead, we buried hundreds of the enemy in long, deep trenches. Lieutenant Swinton, of the Berkshires, was buried in a grave inside their *zareba*, and the rest of the officers in a separate grave from the men outside on the morning of the 23rd. Over Lieutenant Swinton's grave a cairn of stones was erected, which curiously enough was respected by the Arabs after the *zareba* was finally vacated some weeks later. During the evening the telegraph line was cut, so communication with Suakim was suspended till darkness admitted of our using lamps, when fuller particulars of the engagement were signalled.

On the morning of the 23rd General Graham relieved the Indian Contingent with the Coldstreams and Scots Guards.

The whole story of McNeill's *zareba* spells "Surprise," for without doubt it was a complete surprise, and no one was more surprised, I should say, than our gallant commander, a man who would sooner have risked his own life a dozen times over than recklessly thrown away that of the last-joined recruit. Sir John McNeill was the bravest of the brave, and brave men are not careless of the lives of others.

Later it was stated the 70th Regiment, occupying the hill well to the north of our line of march, from their elevated position, watched the movements of the enemy, and reported the same by "helio," but who to? I remember seeing the flashing, on the march out, and I also remember shells being fired, from one of the vessels in harbour, ahead of us and to our right, which certainly pointed to an enemy being in view of someone. But putting these facts together, I personally came to the conclusion the 70th were sending messages back to Suakim, and the guns were firing in response to these messages, which were unconnected with us. For us, marching through thick bush, it would have been no easy matter to flash back to the 70th Hill.

One thing which did surprise me very much was the little use made of our staff officers to procure information from the front. One or more might easily have advanced with the cavalry. The job would not have been a very pleasant one, but two or three dismounted men by stooping down could have gained the requisite information and then have withdrawn in ample time to prepare the force against surprise. It was certainly not the country for cavalry to remain seated on their horses, as the lancers apparently did, for mounted men could see nothing of foot-men moving rapidly through the bush with "cat"-like precision and noiselessness. If the story is true that Osman Digna did send in a written threat of his intention to attack our troops if they attempted to *zareba*, and this intelligence was not repeated to Sir John McNeill, all I can say is, it was a most regrettable omission on the part of someone. But apart from this, in my judgment the methods adopted by our force up to the time of the attack were of the "happy-go-lucky" order, as the precautions were meagre in the extreme.

I don't think the fight of the 22nd March has ever been treated with the importance it deserved. Had more troops wavered, it seems to me highly probable the entire force would have been annihilated, and under the circumstances of the case we have much to be thankful for that the 15th Sikhs and 28th Bo. Infantry stood their ground as they did. Judging from the rewards which were bestowed on the units which composed this force, I am inclined to think this day's fight was officially reported on in terms quite inconsistent with the gravity of the situation.

Looking back to that day, after an interval of 23 years, I am more convinced now, than I was at the time, that McNeill's *zareba* was as fine a fight on both sides as any during the long years our troops struggled for supremacy in the Soudan. The only excuse I can find for treating this fight as a small matter was a reluctance to admit it was "a complete surprise." With no spirit of controversy have I written this account, I am merely expressing my feelings of the day. If others think little of McNeill's *zareba* let them, but in justice to the troops who stood and fell, I am quite unable to write on the subject in more modest terms. If any of my readers have a thought that this is a self-advertisement let me refer to the opening paragraphs where I point out my duties on. that day consisted of erecting canvas tanks and fill in these with water. For the rest of the time, I was merely an onlooker in the same sense as my *bhistie*, who stood by my horse during the fight as calmly as if he were watching a field day!

The contention that the Indian Contingent were to build an intermediate *zareba* on the 22nd March on the return trip to Suakim and occupy it with one regiment I am unable to believe for more reasons than one. In the first place I have no recollection that anything of the kind was hinted at; secondly, I don't think any arrangements were made for provisioning a second *zareba*, or were water tanks taken out for this purpose; thirdly, if my memory is correct, no regiment of the Indian Contingent carried either great coats or cooking utensils; and lastly, is it reasonable to believe we would have taken laden animals out eight miles to carry the same loads back four? The first time I ever heard of this suggestion was on reading a few weeks ago the *History of the Soudan Campaign*.

The loss of Lieut. Richardson and four men of the 5th Lancers, reported missing, was very sad, and as far as this officer was concerned, romantic in the extreme. The story goes that on the evening of the 21st he received a letter from his bride-wife saying she had dreamt he had been killed. He took this so much to heart that before retiring for the night he said goodbye to some of his brother officers. The following morning, he was sent with a handful of men to the front scouting, and I think I am correct in stating he and they were never seen again. Anyhow, they were returned amongst the missing, and not till months after did we come across their bodies, when recognition was only possible through what remained of their uniforms. The telegram announcing the news of this officer's supposed end, when placed in the hands of his wife, caused her to drop down dead.

The Indian Contingent were not sorry to get back into camp on the afternoon of the 23rd, when they received a great ovation from their British comrades. The 17th N.I. were detailed for duty in Suakim, as they were more or less suspected of "nerves."

On the 24th a convoy was sent out towards McNeill's *zareba* escorted by the 9th Bengal Lancers, 15th Sikhs, and 28th Bo. Infantry, which was met half way by the Coldstreams and Marines, who were attacked on the way back to the *zareba*, losing one man killed, three officers wounded, and 25 men and followers wounded, besides over 100 camels, which clearly proved the Arabs had some fight left in them, in spite of having lost some 3,000 killed and wounded on the 22nd!

On the 25th the usual convoy went out, but was not molested; but on the 26th a large convoy, escorted by two guns R.H.A., two squadrons 5th Lancers and 20th Hussars, 9th Bengal Lancers, the grenadiers, East Surrey Regiment (70th), Shropshire L.I., 15th Sikhs, 28th Bo. Infantry, under the personal command of General Graham, was rushed without result, which went far to show the enemy were beginning to think better of the game, for on the two succeeding days the convoys were in no way interfered with.

It turned out, however, they were now collecting elsewhere, for on the 1st April the officer commanding at McNeill's *zareba*, reported that Tamai was occupied by the enemy, having obtained his information from the Mounted Infantry, so orders were at once issued, for a force to start the next morning at 3 a.m. This force consisted of 304 officers, 6,884 rank and file. 1,111 horses, 171 mules, and 1,639 camels, and did not move off till 4.30 a.m., owing to some of the troops having paraded at the wrong spot. The whole was under the command of General Graham. The advance was in one large square, the front face being three companies in line, with sides of 700 yards, with all the animals inside the square. On reaching McNeill's *zareba* a halt was made for breakfast, dropping stores, etc., and picking up the troops stationed there, who were replaced by the 28th Bo. N.I.

At 10 a.m. another start was made, and a captive balloon sent up, which turned out a complete failure. At 5 p.m. we reached the Teselah Hill, where we at once *zarebaed*. The cavalry and mounted infantry were sent back to McNeill's *zareba* to spend the night, with orders to rejoin in the morning. Picquets were posted, and we spent a quiet night, excepting a few rounds which were fired into the square at midnight, which was put a stop to by one round from the Horse Artillery. One private of the East Surrey was killed, two man of the Berkshires, and two Australians wounded.

On arrival at the Teselah Hill these N.S.W. men resented the idea of hiding behind a *zareba*, which they considered a waste of energy. The fact was they were utterly pumped by the march, and had consumed nearly all their supply of drinking water, and only wished to lie down and rest themselves. When the firing commenced at midnight, they were all there, and wanted to rush out and engage the enemy!

On the morning of the 3rd the troops were drawn up as shown in sketch ready to march off as soon as the cavalry and mounted infantry arrived, which they did at about 8.30. The ground was undulating and sandy, with practically no cover, excepting patches of grass in the hollows, so with mounted troops in front there seemed no necessity for this "square" formation, which must have been very trying for the four battalions in column forming the rear face. It had the merit, however, of making "surprise" absolutely impossible.

When we reached the "*khor*," which was nothing but the deep broad bed of a river, and quite dry, the square was ordered to wheel to the right, by which time the Mounted Infantry were exchanging shots with the Fuzzies. This change of front brought us over the wells, the only water supply of Tamai, a place consisting of a number of

CAVALRY

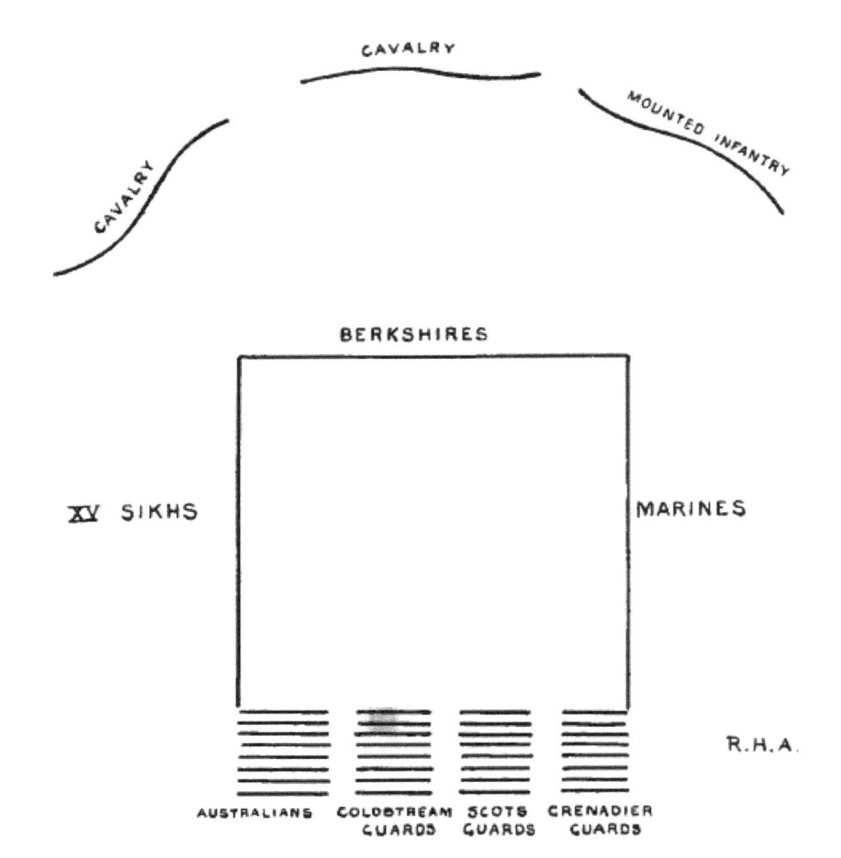

CAVALRY

MOUNTED INFANTRY

BERKSHIRES

XV SIKHS   MARINES

                                                               R.H.A.

AUSTRALIANS COLDSTREAM SCOTS   GRENADIER
             GUARDS   GUARDS   GUARDS

mean-looking huts with grass roofs. The square halted, the Berkshires and the 15th Sikhs were ordered to occupy the heights on the far side of the *khor*, from which they were able to scatter the few hundreds of the enemy in sight, and there was nothing left for the force to do but march back, as the water supply was quite inadequate for our wants. On the return march the huts were set on fire, and soon there was a continuous "popping" of ammunition, which had been secreted in the grass roofs, proving the Fuzzies had made a hasty bolt of it.

It was a most disappointing day, as we were led to suppose the Arabs would certainly put up a good fight at Tamai; but that old fox Osman Digna had no intention of being caught in the open. The only place they could have made a stand was in the *khor*, but our artillery would have soon shelled them out of this. On arrival at the Teselah Hill the men had their dinners, after which we started for McNeill's *zareba*, which was reached about 6 p.m., after a fatiguing march through sand nearly the whole way. Our losses were one man killed and one officer, 14 men, and one follower wounded.

General Graham and his staff rode on to Suakim, whilst the force under General Freemantle spent the night at the *zareba*, and returned to Suakim the next day, the 4th, leaving the 28th Bo. N.I. with two Gardners manned by the R.N., under the command of Colonel Singleton, 28th Bo. Infantry.

On the 6th a large convoy, escorted by four battalions, went out to McNeill's *zareba* to remove all stores prior to the evacuation of that post, whilst the Coldstream Guards, N.S.W. Infantry, 17th Company R.E., 2 guns 5/1 R.A., and 2nd Company M.I., a total of 68 officers, 1,649 rank and file, 54 horses, 190 mules, 327 camels, and 349 followers, proceeded to No. 1 post under General Fremantle and *zarebaed*. This formed the first of a string of posts to be occupied along the projected railway line. During the rest of the month the force was entirely employed building posts and on convoy work. As the posts were occupied the troops at Suakim were continually shifting camp to remain as compact as possible, and by the 26th the force was distributed as follows:—

	Officers.	Men.	Followers.	Horses.	Mules.	Camels.
Base	108	2063	1890	231	1018	2126
Head Quarters	169	3857	2041	1195	1701	1077
Handub	96	2004	2301	642	195	2076
No. 1 Post	1	34	3	5	2	—
Head of Rail	46	1116	30	72	88	70
Octao	63	1511	911	162	405	644
Tambuk	43	905	138	42	80	76
Total	526	11490	7314	2349	3489	6069

To supply so many men and animals with water in a country where there was practically none was no light task, considering it had to be carried to the posts.

The navvies brought out from England to build the line of railway to Berber caused us much amusement. Every shovelful of sand they threw up seemed to bring down two with it, causing many unique expressions of disgust; but the climax was reached when our Indian *coolies* were formed into gangs to work with their British comrades. The Indians could not realise the use of the wheelbarrow, which when filled they immediately hoisted on to the heads of two and carried bodily off to the bank under construction.

This completely beat the British workmen, and produced remarks which I wish I could repeat. The navvies were certainly splendid specimens of manhood, and looked their best in the suitable working kit provided for a tropical sun, but which was completely disregarded on the Sabbath, when one and all turned out in small cloth caps or bowlers, corduroys, and the thickest blue cloth double-breasted pea-jackets I ever saw! How they existed in garments of the kind under a sun so fierce was beyond understanding.

One day we received warning that our camps were likely to be attacked at night. Special guards were placed round the camp of the navvies, who were warned what to do in case of attack, and at the same time advised to arrange amongst themselves for one man per tent to be awake during the night. The scorn with which they received the advice was more than comical; they merely pointed to their picks and shovels and said, "To hell with your n———s!" Not a man among them missed his full night's sleep. They were there to work, and if anyone interfered with this, they would know the reason why!

They were capital fellows, but a great anxiety to the authorities, and no one was sorry when they were safely put on board homeward bound. Their camp songs at night before they turned in were truly delicious.

The 28th Bombay Infantry, looking ahead, and thinking the regiment might be employed in these particular parts for a period of three years, which, I believe was the estimated time for the Suakim-Berber Railway, very wisely determined to make themselves as comfortable as possible, so brought over with them the whole of their mess property, including mess tents, *shamianahs*, etc., as used in India during peace, as well as a complete active service equipment. The consequence was their mess was the centre of attraction, where any morning you might see officers from all the British regiments enjoying a quiet read of the papers in comfort, and soon became known as "the Guards' Club."

Later, when we were turned into an army of occupation, this foresight on the part of the officers of the regiment was well rewarded, as they were able to cater for a large number of honorary members, who otherwise would have had to live in discomfort on the food cooked by the one body servant allowed by Regulations, and spend a miserable, lonely existence. Here again could be seen the handiwork of Westmacott, an organiser whom nothing defeated! It was always a pleasure to dine at this mess, where everything was done well, and where you were sure of a hearty welcome from a particularly go-ahead body of officers, who were equally good in the field. For their services at Suakim the regiment was turned into "Pioneers" in '88, gaining further laurels on the Punjab Frontier and in Tirah.

After, the breakup of the Headquarters and the departure of Sir Gerald Graham, Sir George Greaves assumed command; to him was left the final arrangements connected with the force of occupation, which was to remain in Suakim under Sir John Hudson. Sir George was a man who made things move, a rapid thinker and worker himself, intolerant of delay and shilly-shallying in others, during his short command all were kept fairly busy, and in record time he had all in order, after settling every conceivable point mortal could think of in the interests of those remaining behind. The result was Sir John found everything in working order.

The troops were hutted, arrangements for ice machines (chiefly for the use of the hospital), and water supply had been carefully thought out, and we were left in comparative comfort to face the hot season. The ice machines were not quite a success at first as we only managed to make the water cold, so the British India ice ship *Bulimba* was chartered for a further term till mechanics, who thoroughly understood the machines, could be spared from the Nile, where similar ones were turning out ice regularly.

The command now devolved on Sir John Hudson, which consisted of the original Indian Contingent excepting the 9th Bengal Lancers, only one squadron of which remained, besides the 1st Shropshire Light Infantry, wing of the Sussex Regiment, some guns. Mountain Battery, and the newly-formed Camel Corps. The heat during the day was terrific, and used to go up to 125 deg. in our Headquarters' house.

Owing to the scarcity of vegetables, scurvy broke out amongst the Native troops and followers also a very fatal disease called *berri-berri*.

Special arrangements had to be made for the supply of green food from Suez and Aden, which improved the health of the men considerably.

We still had a very large camel transport, the feeding of which caused much anxiety. To an army of occupation, they were of no use, whilst the difficulties of grazing were enormous and extremely harassing to the troops, necessitating large guards, in spite of which camels were lost and men and followers were killed by the ever-watchful Hadendowas, so it was decided to get rid of them at any price.

Our first effort turned out a lamentable failure, and would have been comical but for the fact it was almost brutal. Some local merchants were approached with a view to purchasing. At first all went well, as we found a ready market at Jeddah, on the opposite coast of the Red Sea, but later the Turkish authorities refused permission to land any more, due no doubt to the fact we were at war with a Mahomedan race. Then a Greek came forward and assured us he could either dispose of his purchases or arrange for their feeding till he could get rid of them, so to this man we sold a batch of 100, as an experiment at, I think, Rs. 25 a head.

A few days after the sale he satisfied us he had got rid of them, and we were just handing over another batch of 100 when a report came in from the Water Forts, the stench out there was so unbearable the men could not stand it any longer, as all were sick. On going out this report was found to be only too true. A detachment of cavalry was ordered to proceed at once and ascertain the cause, which was soon discovered. About half a mile from the Forts the troopers came across the skinned carcases of, 100 camels exposed to the rays of a burning sun. Our Greek friend had done us. Under cover of night, he drove the poor beasts out, skinned them, and made a clear profit of 100 *per cent*, out of the hides, and we had the pleasure of burying this putrid mountain of flesh!

Our next attempt was not very much better. We sent out a deck load of these poor beasts, on one of our transports, and threw them overboard after first shooting them. This turned out failure No. 2, as it only attracted large numbers of sharks inside the coral reefs where the men used to bathe!

Attempt No. 3 turned out more satisfactory for a time, as they were taken out to sea, and in this way, we thought, the difficulty had at last been solved. Not for long, however, for soon reports came in from Mail steamers running up and down the Red Sea complaining of the many carcases they ran into, which stuck to the bows of their vessels, causing endless annoyance and inconvenience. There was nothing left but for the government to carry them back to India. As these animals could not have cost less than Rs. 100 each the loss in sea transport must have been a heavy one.

With the hot weather our staff dwindled down. Pearson was invalided. Cook went on leave not to return, and McGregor Stewart's five years of staff terminated, so I found myself promoted to A.A.G. and Chief Staff Officer, with Major Hare as D.A.A.G. for British troops.

The office work was very heavy, as we had to keep up a double correspondence, *viz.*: with Cairo and Simla, but it was a training and experience any man would have been glad of. I can truly say the general and his staff never knew what it was to be idle for a moment, so time did not hang heavy, and in spite of the intense heat everyone was fit, for after the sun went down the temperature cooled, and all enjoyed the comforts of sleep at night, which made up for the trials by day.

After the excitement of almost daily expeditions of the first months, the duties of occupation were dull, but all ranks found some compensation in the "extra pay," for the authorities were good enough to allow us the choice of drawing our salaries in gold or silver, and as the sovereign fetched locally something like Rs. 15 not many rushed for the familiar *rupee*. This additional "pay" for the native ranks and followers kept all "*koosh*," as we say in India, and although leave was open to the officers, not too many availed themselves of the privilege, they preferred to make "hay" under the burning sun, as opportunities of the kind don't often fall to the lot of the "soldier man." On the whole I never remember a happier garrison than the Suakim one of '85.

There was no lack of amusement, the fishing in and just outside the harbour was excellent, and under the guidance of the cheeriest of the cheery, "Dickie Westmacott," of the 28th Bombay Infantry, hardly a week passed without a gymkhana, whilst polo was played regularly. Cricket on a coir matting pitch was also indulged in, and the mess of the 28th Bo. Infantry was an attraction for all, run on lines other regiments might well copy. Here again one could see the handiwork of Westmacott, who was as good a man in camp as he was soldier in the field; in the latter he was hard to beat, and proved this years later in the Tirah Campaign, when, as a general, he showed *how* rear-guard actions ought to be fought, and *where* generals *ought* to be when these actions are going on, the best loved "soldier" I have ever struck.

Sir John Hudson, in addition to commanding, was acting Governor of the Red Sea Littoral, during the absence of Colonel Chermside, and was fortunate in having as a Lieutenant Brewster Bey, of the Egyptian Customs Service. What he didn't know about Arabs wasn't worth knowing. Nearly all the time we were in occupation, McNeill's *zareba*, or rather the ground on which the fight took place, for we razed it before evacuation, was held by the Arabs as their nearest outpost. Here they squatted for months, and in defiance, erected a long pole with an empty kerosine oil can on the top, which glittered in the sun to make us aware of their presence. They retained some of the wretched followers they caught on the 20th March belonging to the water carts of the 9th Bengal Lancers, and for the rescue of whom we were most anxious.

Brewster amongst his spies had an old Arab lady, to whom was entrusted the delicate duty of securing the escape or release of these unfortunates. We offered a generous reward, and more than once did the old lady nearly succeed. On a small piece of paper, I wrote a short message in Hindi and Urdu, which she managed to show the prisoners, and in return she brought back acknowledgments, and on one occasion a slip to say they were, at the moment, being fairly well treated, as their duties chiefly consisted in carrying water from long distances and gathering fire wood, adding that they had picked up a little Arabic, which, improved their lot. The old lady was at times absent two and even three weeks, and more than once showed signs of severe treatment. However, she was in no way deterred, and at last returned with the news she had fixed the escape for a particular night.

To assist her we were to send a small party out which was to approach close to the camp, with a larger one in rear in case of accidents. She managed so well that a start was actually made, when one of the party lost heart and burst out sobbing, which attracted the attention of that portion of the sleeping guard, which could not be bought over, and the result was failure, much to my sorrow, as it was almost the eve of my departure, and the release of these poor souls before leaving was my one wish. Fortunately for the prisoners, the attempted escape was not suspected. At first, we rather discredited the old lady's story, but later she brought in a written account from one of the prisoners explaining the failure. At this moment I forget if the release was effected later or not, but I rather think some of the men did escape.

In the month of October Sir John Hudson heard the Contingent was to be relieved by another, chiefly from the Madras Presidency, as also the staff, so he asked me, as a favour, to remain on, as he did not look forward to the prospect of having no one with a grasp of affairs to help him run the show. After considering the matter 24 hours, I agreed to remain, and he despatched a wire to the H.E. the Commander-in-Chief in India, begging he might retain my services, and in reply received a cable stating the request would be considered if a written application was forwarded by the outgoing mail, with reasons in support of the request. This was complied with, and I settled down to a further spell of Suakim.

Some three weeks later I was returning, from a fishing expedition down the coast when we noticed with surprise a steamer entering the Suakim Harbour from the Indian side, a rare occurrence. As we entered the harbour some hours later, we could see Sir John waiting at the landing stage, and as I stepped off the launch he greeted me with the words, "Your relief has arrived," the explanation being that our Mail boat carrying the request to Simla for my retention struck a coral reef and remained fast for a tide, thus missing connection with the Mail steamer at Aden, and led the Simla authorities to believe either Sir John or myself had changed our minds!

After a consultation with the newly-arrived A.A.G., the general sent another cable, explaining the circumstances, and adding the new man much preferred the billet in India he vacated. The answer came that it was too late to make any change, but Sir John could keep me as an additional A.A.G., till the last transport, so in this way I remained an extra month, and was able to go into the working of the office with my successor.

On the 19th November I embarked with almost the same detachments I went out with, *viz*., a squadron of the 9th Bengal Lancers and the Madras Sappers and Miners, after taking a regretful farewell of Sir John Hudson, who had now been joined by Lady and Miss Hudson. I think I can safely say the months I served as A.A.G. to Sir John were quite the most delightful I ever experienced as a staff officer. He was a very particular man, but always just and considerate, and in an independent command was extremely strong, and always ready to take any amount of responsibility, and being governor of the place and district, his hands were considerably strengthened.

Our transport on the return journey was a British India steamer, which proved a comfortable sea boat, but a real bad mover against the head winds we experienced going down the Red Sea, when our average for days was not more than seven knots per hour, and as a consequence there was every chance of our running short of water and fodder, so when off Aden we decided on putting into that harbour for these necessities, and proclaiming our wants by signal, which brought the commissariat officer on board in a condition nigh apoplectic. His face was a picture, the idea of coming to a place like Aden for water and grass! I agreed with him it was an uninviting spot, but preferable to dying of thirst at sea, to saying nothing of the loss to government in the event of our having no fodder for the horses.

After a certain amount of haggling he supplied our wants, but took an absolute delight in telling me that "as sure as God made apples" the government would make me pay the piper, for taking the vessel out of its course and claiming excess rations, as the ship's papers clearly showed we had started with the regulation supply! I thanked him for the supplies as well as his gracious words; but I took the precaution to post a report of my action to Sir John Hudson, and kept my commissariat friend thirsty till it was time for him to clear off! As a matter of fact, when we reached Bombay, we had none too much of water or grass.

During the voyage some of the Madras Sappers were attacked by that hateful disease *berri-berri*, and lost, I think, five men, including a Native officer, who had done excellent work, and was present at nearly every engagement. This company suffered from the complaint at Suakim, but no one anticipated an outbreak at sea. The disease being almost confined to fishermen on the sea coast, who seldom enlist, was hardly known to our medical officers, and was only diagnosed by an officer of the R.A.M.C., who at one time served at Cannanore on the West Coast of India, and as well as I remember the recoveries were nil, so one could not help feeling anxious when it attacked the men on board. I am glad to say, however, it did not spread.

The 5th (Royal Irish) Lancers During the Nile Expedition, 1884-1885

By Walter Temple Willcox

In September 1884, the 5th (Royal Irish) Lancers was called upon to furnish 2 officers and 43 N.C.O. and men to join the Heavy division of the Camel Corps being formed for service with the Nile Expedition.

The detachment was selected from volunteers, and left Dublin on the 19th of September, under the command of Major L. M. Carmichael and Lieut. H. Costello, for Aldershot, whence they proceeded to Southampton, and embarked on the 26th of September for Egypt.

This sudden despatch of troops to the Nile was due to the government having at last determined that it was necessary to rescue General Gordon from his perilous position at Khartoum. General Lord Wolseley was to concentrate his troops for the attempt at Korti on the Nile. On looking at the map of the Nile it will be seen that at Korti the river makes an enormous bend to the North between that place and Khartoum.

For this reason, it was determined that from Korti a double expedition should be despatched, the Desert Column commanded by General Sir Herbert Stewart to move straight across the desert, following a line of wells to the Nile at Metammeh, and a Nile Column commanded by General Earle to follow the river to Aber Hamed and Berber, with a view to co-operating with the Desert Column for the relief of Gordon at Khartoum.

For Sir Herbert Stewart's Desert Column, a Camel Corps drawn from the Cavalry and Infantry was to be organised. The Cavalry portion was to be composed of detachments from the Cavalry Regiments in Great Britain, subdivided into "Heavies" and "Lights;" while the Infantry part was drawn from the Brigade of Guards, the Royal Ma-

The Camel Corps

rines and Mounted Infantry of regiments in Egypt.

The following was the eventual composition of the Heavy Camel Regiment of the Corps:

STAFF.

Lt.-Col. the Hon. R. TALBOT, First Life Guards, Commanding.
Capt. Lord ST. VINCENT, 16th Lancers, Adjutant.
Surgeon FALVERY, A.M.D., Surgeon.
Lieut. G. LEIGH, First Life Guards, Acting Quartermaster.

O. C. DETACHMENTS	SUBALTERNS	DRAWN FROM.
Major the Hon. C. Byng	Lt. Lord Rodney	1st Life Guards
Capt. Lord Cochrane	Lt. R. J. Beech	2nd ,, ,,
Major Lord A. Somerset	Lt. Lord Binning	Royal Horse ,,
Capt. A. L. Gould	Lt. R. F. Hibbert	2nd Dragoon ,,
Capt. J. W. Darley	Lt. C. W. Law	4th ,, ,,
Major W. H. Atherton	Lt. St. J. Gore	5th ,, ,,
Major W. Gough	Lt. J. F. Burn-Murdoch.	1st Royal Dragoons
Capt. W. H. Hippisley	Lt. R. Wolfe	2nd (Scots Greys) Dragoons
Major L. Carmichael	Lt. H. Costello	5th Lancers
Major T. Davison	Lt. W. B. Browne	16th ,,

Each detachment consisting of 43 N.C.O. and men.

The detachments making up the Light Camel Regiment were drawn from the 3rd, 4th, 7th, 10th, 11th, 15th, 18th, 20th, and 21st Hussars. Each detachment also of 43 N.C.O. and men.

The Guards' Camel Regiment was formed from the Guards' Brigade and a detachment from the Royal Marines; and the Mounted Infantry Camel Regiment, from infantry battalions in Egypt.

The men selected for this service had all to be marksmen or first-class shots, not under twenty-two years of age, medically fit, and good characters. They were armed with a rifle and sword bayonet, and wore a bandolier over the left shoulder holding fifty cartridges. The dress was a Khaki serge jumper, cord breeches, *puttees*, ankle boots and a pith sun helmet.

The Heavies and the Guards detachments embarked on the 26th. of September in the P.O. steamer *Deccan* and sailed the same day for Alexandria, arriving there on the 7th of October. From there they went to Cairo and then on to camp at the Pyramids. On the 13th, the Heavies moved by train to Assiot and thence by steamer up the Nile to Assouan. Here they were fitted out with camels and marched for Korti, where Lord Wolseley was concentrating the two expeditions for Khartoum. It was a weary, trying march up to Korti, and many a soldier was sadly learning that the camel is not a pleasant beast to ride. There was a man, however—a sailor—in the Nile Expedition, who admired a camel he rode exceedingly, because, being pitched up out of his saddle incessantly, and caught dexterously as he descended, "the camel had only missed him twice throughout an afternoon."

The troops working up the river in their barges were also experiencing a trying time.

The following general order shews the anxiety of the commander to accelerate the passage of the expedition.

> To the sailors, soldiers, and Marines of the Nile Expedition.
>
> The relief of General Gordon and his garrison, so long besieged in Khartoum, is the glorious mission which the queen has intrusted to us. It is an enterprise that will stir the heart of every soldier and sailor fortunate enough to have been selected to share in it, and the very magnitude of its difficulty only stimulates us to increased exertions. We are all proud of General Gordon and his gallant and self-sacrificing defence of Khartoum, which has added, if possible, to his already high reputation. He cannot hold out many months longer, and he now calls upon us to save his garrison.
>
> His heroism and his patriotism are household words wherever our language is spoken; and not only has his safety become a matter of national importance, but the knowledge that our brave comrade needs help, urges us to push forward with redoubled energy. Neither he nor his garrison can be allowed to meet the sad fate which befell his gallant companion in arms, Colonel Stewart, who, when endeavouring to carry out an enterprise of unusual danger and folly, was treacherously murdered by his captors. We can and with God's help will—save General Gordon from such a death.
>
> The labour of working up this river is immense, and to bear it uncomplainingly demands the highest soldier-like qualities, that contempt for danger, and that determination to overcome difficulty which in previous campaigns have so distinguished all ranks of Her Majesty's Army and Navy. The physical obstacles that impede our rapid progress are considerable: but who cares for them when it is remembered that General Gordon and his garrison are in danger? Under God their safety is now in our hands, and come what may we must save them. It is needless to say more to British soldiers and sailors.

The middle of December found Lord Wolseley and his troops collected at Korti, and the final arrangements for the Desert and the River columns being rapidly completed.

The camp at Korti was a pleasant place after the long and toilsome journey by boat and camel. The tents of the Camel Corps were pitched under spreading groves of trees extending to the banks of the river, which there took a winding course in broad still reaches. The days were occupied with field days on camelback in the desert, and by "stables" three times a day, this latter duty chiefly consisting in picking the ticks out of the camel's hide.

Meanwhile affairs at Khartoum were evidently approaching a crisis. The *Mahdi* had occupied Omdurman, only a few miles from Khartoum, and had summoned Gordon to surrender the city. The answer was:—"If you are the real *Mahdi*, dry up the Nile and come over and I'll surrender;" whereupon, rumour has it, that the *Mahdi* accepted Gordon's challenge, and having collected his forces and chanted some spells, sent them all into the river, with the result that enormous numbers were drowned, and the remainder scrambled back half dead.

After this, severe fighting was continually going on round Khartoum, but the gallant Gordon and his garrison were successfully holding out; but news was difficult to get, and the spies of the Intelligence Department showed a certain reluctance in braving the dangers of the desert and the vigilance of the *Mahdi's* followers; the news that they did bring in, too, was somewhat untrustworthy.

Briefly stated, the plan of the approaching campaign was that the greater portion of the mounted troops under Sir Herbert Stewart was to advance across the desert from Korti to Metammeh, establishing fortified posts at the wells along the route. Sir Charles Wilson was to go with Stewart, and at Metammeh was to proceed in Gordon's steamers to Khartoum; and having communicated with Gordon, to return to Metammeh to report the result to Sir Herbert Stewart.

Simultaneously with the despatch of the Desert Column, a force under General Earle was to be sent up the river to punish the murderers of Colonel Stewart and the Consuls, and then to advance to Berber to co-operate with Stewart's force in an attack on the *Mahdi* before Khartoum, under the personal command of Lord Wolseley, who was to have joined Stewart with the remainder of the mounted troops and a force of infantry.

On the 30th of December a messenger, who had been sent to Khartoum on October the 29th, returned, and brought into Korti a piece of paper the size of a postage stamp, on which was written

THE LIGHT CAMEL CORPS

"Khartoum all right." It was signed C. G. Gordon, and dated 14th of Dec. 1884; and the messenger said he was told to deliver a verbal message to the effect that food in Khartoum was running short, and the troops suffering from want of provisions; he went on to say, "We want you to come quickly. Do not scatter your troops, the enemy is numerous; bring plenty of troops if you can;" and the advice was to come only by way of Metammeh or Berber, and to do so without letting rumours of the advance spread abroad.

On the 30th of December, Sir Herbert Stewart started from Korti with part of the Desert Column. The column was preceded by thirty-four scouts of the 19th Hussars, who were followed by the Guards Camel Regiment, and 650 camels belonging to the Heavy and Light regiments. The men of these two divisions of the corps remained behind, their camels, as well as 500 transport camels, being loaded with provisions and stores. The mounted infantry brought up the rear.

The Guards were dismounted at Gakdul, and remained in charge of the stores, while their camels, together with those of the other Camel Corps, returned to Korti, when the "Heavies" and "Lights" were remounted, and the Guards' and transport camels loaded up again with stores and provisions, and, accompanied by the Sussex regiment, returned to Gakdul. On the 12th of January this second column had reached Gakdul.

Leaving 400 men of the Sussex Regiment to garrison Gakdul, Sir Herbert Stewart marched off from Gakdul on the 13th. The numbers of the force which paraded at 2 p. m., outside the hills on the plain were.

Naval Brigade, with one Gardner gun.	about 30 of all ranks.
Heavy Camel Regiment	,, 380 ,, ,,
Three troops of 19th Hussars	,, 90 ,, ,,
Half-battery, Royal Artillery, with three 7-pounder screw guns.	,, 30 ,, ,,
Royal Engineers	,, 25 ,, ,,
Guards' Camel Regiment	,, 367 ,, ,,
Mounted Infantry Camel Regiment	,, 360 ,, ,,
Sussex Regiment	,, 100 ,, ,,
Medical and Commissariat Staff	,, 45 ,, ,,
Native drivers	,, 120 ,, ,,

A total of about 1,500 men, 90 horses, and 2,300 camels; a mere handful of men to be exposed to the savage onslaught of some 12,000 of the *Mahdi's* fanatics. With the exception of the 19th Hussars on their horses, and the natives who walked, the whole of the force was mounted on camels. Three powerful camels carried a screw gun and its ammunition between them; 100 rounds of ammunition were taken per gun. A number of camels were fitted with litters for the sick and wounded. A train of some 500 camels carried stores of all sorts to form a depot at Metammeh.

With the scouts of the 19th in front, the "Heavies" led the way, followed by the Guards, then the baggage and stores, and the Mounted Infantry bringing up the rear.

Soon after starting, a Remington rifle was picked up on the rocks. This, and the marks of recent horse tracks, rather pointed to the fact that the advance was known to the enemy. The first afternoon's march was over a vast gravelly plain, with gentle undulations. After covering about ten miles, during which fifteen camels succumbed, the column halted for the night. Reveille next morning sounded at 3, and before 5 the force was again on the move. This day's march was over a tract of loose sand, and at 10 o'clock a two hours' halt was called, and the stragglers brought up. Recent horse tracks were seen, shewing that the enemy's scouts were about, but no messages had been received from the hussars' scouts.

Many of the camels were falling from want of food and from overwork. If a camel dropped, his load and saddle were taken off him and placed upon another, already loaded, for the spare camels had all been used up. The poor brutes toiled on in an extraordinary way. A camel would be seen going slower and until the tail of the animal in front, to which he was tied, looked like coming off; then he would stop for a second, give a mighty shiver, and drop down stone dead.

After passing Jebel-el-Nus the scenery changed to a broad grassy valley with some trees, and rocky hills all round. At 5 p. m. the column camped for the night at Jebel Sergain, where the camels were tied down and preparations made for a probable attack, so that the wretched beasts could not move to get a meal of the *savas* grass which grew plentifully in the neighbourhood.

Next morning the column again started before daylight, and at daybreak the hills of Abu Klea could be seen in the distance, and the 19th Hussars were ordered to push on and occupy the wells.

Between ten and eleven the force halted, and shortly after Major Barrow of the 19th came in to report that he had found the enemy in force between the main column and the wells. With three or four men he had pursued some of the Arab scouts into the Abu Klea valley, but had been forced to retire. The route from the halting place of the column to the Abu Klea wells was through a pass of the mountain in front; and when this was ascended, detached bodies of the enemy

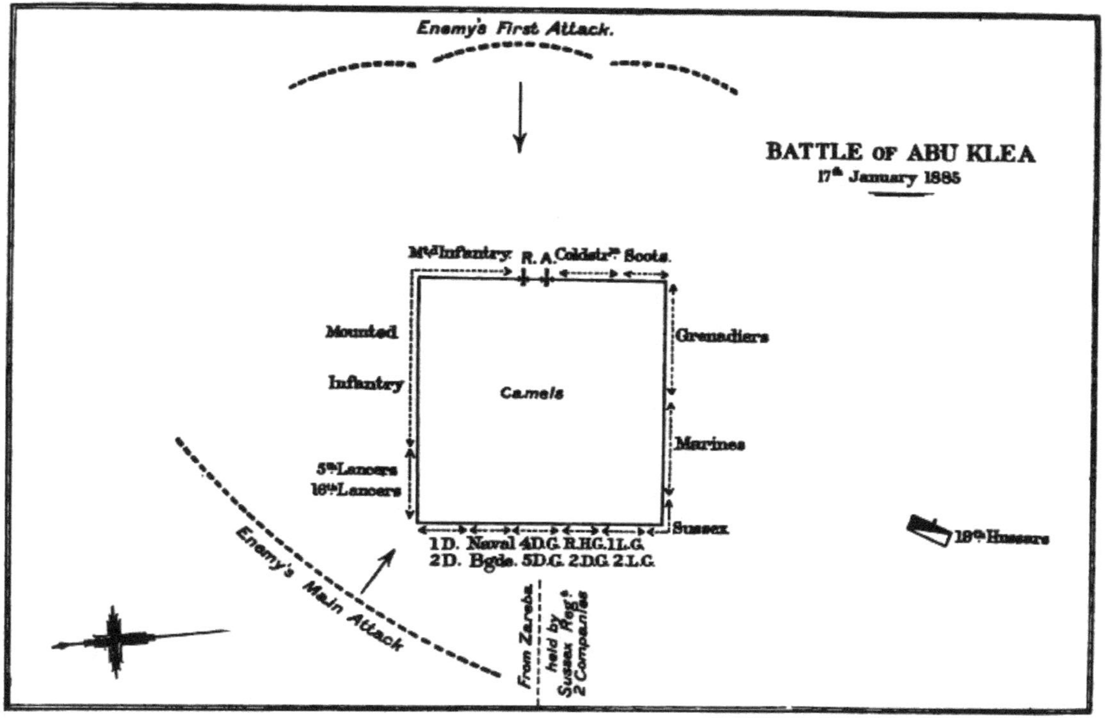
BATTLE OF ABU KLEA
17th January 1885
Enemy's First Attack.
Mtd Infantry.
R. A.
Coldstrm Scots.
Mounted
Infantry
Grenadiers
Camels
Marines
5th Lancers
16th Lancers
Sussex
1 D. Naval 4D.G. R.H.G. 1 L.G.
2 D. Bgde. 5D.G. 2D.G. 2 L.G.
19th Hussars
Enemy's Main Attack
From Zareba
held by
Sussex Regt.
2 Companies

could be seen on the hill tops ahead. Sir Herbert Stewart and Sir Charles Wilson went on to reconnoitre the position of the enemy; the former returning to select a place at which to halt the convoy, while the latter went on and joined the Hussars down the valley, whence could be seen a long line of banners, and puffs of white smoke from the rifles of the enemy being fired at the advanced party of the Hussars, though at too great a distance for the bullets to reach them. Sir Charles Wilson returned to report that there was a large force in front, part of which must belong to the *Mahdi's* army, and that a serious encounter might be looked for. A couple of thousand yards to the right of the British column swarms of the enemy began to wave their spears and to execute a wild dance, after which they commenced firing.

Sir Herbert Stewart had halted the column on a stony plateau, where a *zariba* was quickly built of stone and the thorny branches of the mimosa. Pickets were sent out to occupy two hills on the left, where the mounted infantry built a small fort. It was getting late and the general had decided not to attack until the morning. Emboldened by the growing darkness, the enemy's riflemen were creeping up on the right of the advanced post, and commenced a long-range fire from a hill, which became so heavy that the picket had to be withdrawn; the enemy still creeping round the right, the cavalry vedettes were also withdrawn.

The firing lasted all night, while the men lay in the *zariba* waiting for an attack which was not made; though sometimes the beating of tom-toms sounded quite close. And in the dense darkness, if anyone struck a match to light a pipe, or if, in the hospital, where there were already some wounded, a light was shewn for an instant, it always drew a bullet. However, there was not much damage done, and the morning of the 17th of January broke at last. The enemy's fire became hotter, and a few officers and men were hit. Some of their horsemen rode down to the right of the *zariba*, but were dispersed by a few rounds of shell. Sir Herbert Stewart determined to march out and give battle, leaving a force to hold the *zariba*; and, after having breakfast under a brisk fire from the enemy, the men were delighted to get the order to form square and advance.

The square was formed by the Guards and Mounted Infantry in front; the rear face by four companies of the Heavy Camel Regiment, with its fifth company round the angle, and on the left face of the square; the detachment of the Sussex Regiment on the right face towards the rear; the Naval Brigade and the Gardner gun between the

The 19th Hussars taking Abu Klea Wells

third and fourth companies of the Heavies; and in the centre some thirty camels for carrying water, ammunition, and wounded men, driven by natives. Some of the Sussex, and the baggage guards, were to remain in charge of the *zariba*, and the 19th. Hussars were to operate on the left of the square, the front and flanks of which were covered by skirmishers.

The square was rapidly in order, and the troops marched down the valley towards the row of flags which stretched across it, while the 19th. moved off to the left. Several times the square halted, and returned the fire of the enemy who moved along parallel with it. Men were falling fast, and the whistling of bullets overhead was incessant. Sir Charles Wilson has given a graphic description of the advance, and the sudden appearance of the enemy, in *Egypt and the Soudan*.

> When the skirmishers got within about 200 yards of the flags the square was halted for the rear to close up, and at this moment the enemy rose from the ravine in which they were hidden in the most perfect order They advanced at a quick even pace, as if on parade, and our skirmishers had only just time to get into the square before they were upon us; one poor fellow who lagged behind was caught and speared at once. . . I could not have believed beforehand that men in close formation would have been able to advance for 200 to 400 yards over bare ground in the face of the Martini-Henrys When they got within eighty yards the fire of the Guards and Mounted Infantry began to take good effect, and a huge pile of dead rose in front of them.
>
> Then, to my astonishment, the enemy took ground to the right as if on parade, so as to envelope the rear of the square. I remember thinking 'By Jove, they will be into the square!' and almost the next moment I saw a fine old *sheikh* on horseback plant his banner in the centre of the square behind the camels. He was at once shot down, falling on his banner I had noticed him in the advance with his banner in one hand and a book of prayers in the other, and never saw anything finer. The old man never swerved to the right or left and never ceased chanting his prayers until he had planted his banner in our square directly the *sheikh* fell the Arabs began running in under the camels to the front part of the square. Some of the rear rank now faced about and began firing.

By the fire Herbert Stewart's horse was shot almost immediately afterwards the enemy retired, and loud and long cheering broke from the square. They retired slowly, and for a short time hesitated in the valley before they made their final bolt. During this period of excitement groups of three to five Arabs, who had feigned death, would start up from the slain and rush wildly at the square. They were met by a heavy fire but so badly directed that some of them got right up to the bayonets There was one strange incident. An unwounded Arab armed with a spear, jumped up and charged an officer. The officer grasped the spear with the left hand, and with his right ran his sword through the Arab's body; and there for a few seconds they stood, the officer being unable to withdraw his sword until a man ran up and shot the Arab.

There is little doubt that when the Arabs got into the square, some officers and men fell by the rifles of the ranks who turned about and fired into the square. This, it was surmised, caused the death of Carmichael of the 5th. Lancers, and of Gough of the Royals.

Many of the rifles were rendered useless by the cartridges jamming, and the men had to take to the bayonets. The Gardner gun jammed at the tenth round.

In *The Nineteenth Century*, Lieut.-Colonel the Hon. R. Talbot, commanding the Heavy Camel Regiment, gives an account of the battle.

The total strength of the Heavies was 390.

RIGHT WING.

1st. Company—1st. and 2nd. Life Guards.
2nd.   „   —The Blues and The Queen's Bays.

LEFT WING.

3rd. Company—4th. and 5th. Dragoon Guards.
4th.   „   —Royal Dragoons and Scots Greys.
5th.   „   —5th. and 16th. Lancers.

By the time the attack took place, the company of the Royals and Greys had been partly moved from the rear to the left face, to fill up the gap caused by the gradual lengthening out of the sides of the square, due to the impossibility of keeping up the strings of camels. By this movement the rear of the square was considerably weakened.

The route taken was parallel to, and a few hundred yards from, the *wady*, or shallow ravine, that ran on the left to the wells of Abu Klea,

The Battle of Abu Klea

in which grew stunted trees and thick grass concealing deep water courses, giving admirable cover for the enemy; and the course of the march was commanded by hills to the right and rear occupied by Arab riflemen.

Directly the square started from the *zariba*, many men and some officers were hit; amongst them being Lord St.Vincent and Major Dickson. Skirmishers from the Heavies were sent out to the rear and rear flanks to silence the fire of the enemy. After a slow march of some two miles, a large force of Arabs at about 500 to 700 yards' distance sprang up and advanced as if to attack the left leading corner of the square. The square was halted, and moved to the right on to a slight elevation, a simple movement for men but difficult for camels, some of which were left outside. There was a gap on the left face of the square through which the Gardner gun was taken into action until it jammed.

A solid column of the enemy was seen to be advancing from the *wady* on the left, but the fire of the rear face of the square had to be reserved, being masked by the skirmishers who were still out; the last of whom was overtaken and speared. Close upon the heels of the skirmishers came the great body of Arabs, led by their chiefs on horseback. Until that moment the Heavy Camel Regiment had withheld their fire, which was then delivered at the advancing column. Taking advantage of the opening in the square, the Arabs hurled themselves with terrific rapidity and fury upon it. The company of the 4th. and 5th. Dragoon Guards had a few moments before been wheeled outwards by Colonel Burnaby, with the intention, as Lt.-Colonel Talbot understood, of bringing their fire to bear:—

> But no sooner did he see that not only on the flanks but on the rear, the attack was being developed, than he rode in front of the company and shouted to the men to wheel back. The order was obeyed, the men stepping steadily backwards. Before they had got back into their original place, the Arabs were in through the interval thus created, and through the gap already existing at the left rear corner of the square. Burnaby, whose horse had fallen, was one of the first to be attacked, and as he lay on the ground, he received a mortal wound in the neck from a sword cut.

The Royals, Greys, and 5th. Lancers, upon whose rear the camels pressed, hampering their free movement, were now attacked in rear by those of the enemy who had succeeded in passing the 4th. and 5th.

Dragoon Guards, coming through and under the camels, at the time they were engaged with the enemy in front.

A severe hand-to-hand fight ensued, in which the strength and determination of our men told, and not an Arab escaped alive. The affair was a matter of moments, and from first to last not more than five minutes elapsed. The fire of the Mounted Infantry principally, and of the Guards Camel Regiment (who faced their rear rank about), of the detachment of the Sussex and of the right wing of the Heavy Camel Regiment, prevented the Arabs from reinforcing their attacking column; but the brunt of the fight, the hand-to-hand encounter, was borne by the left wing of the last-named regiment. No men could have fought better, and although two detachments lost their officers, their places were at once assumed by the non-commissioned officers. It was an Inkerman on a small scale—a soldiers' battle; strength, determination, steadiness, and unflinching courage alone could have stemmed the onslaught.

It was at this point that Major Carmichael of the 5th Lancers was killed, and his subaltern. Lieutenant Costello, wounded.

The British losses were:—

	Killed.	*Wounded.*
Officers	9	9
N. C. O. and men	65	85

The brunt of the attack fell upon the left wing of the Heavy Camel Regiment and the Naval Brigade, and it was at that corner of the square that all the officers were killed, and the majority of the casualties occurred. Seven of the officers killed belonged to the Heavies, and the other two to the Naval Brigade.

The following were the losses of the Detachment of the 5th Lancers.

Killed.

Major L. M. Carmichael.
No. 2344 Corporal C. Percival.
  " 2333 Lance Corporal S. Parker
  " 2085 Private C. Peters.
  " 1897 " E. Bell.
  " 2155 " J. McGrath.
  " 2129 " A. Russell.

Wounded.

Lieutenant H. Costello and 2 N. C. O. and men.

For the bravery he displayed during the engagement. No. 2151, Private G. Austin, 5th Lancers, was eventually awarded the medal for "Distinguished Conduct in the Field."

It was now getting on for five o'clock, and the 19th Hussars who had been sent on to look for the Wells, sent back word that they had found and occupied them. The square slowly moved towards the wells, where the troops bivouacked in square for the night. A party of three hundred volunteers from the Heavies, Guards and Mounted Infantry, went back to the *zariba* for the baggage camels, whence they returned at seven o'clock next morning, and the troops were able to get their first meal since noon of the 16th—and this was the 18th.

The enemy's losses must have been very great, for a staff officer counted some eleven hundred bodies on the ground round the place which had been occupied by the square.

A small garrison of the Sussex Regiment, the wounded, and the stores, were left behind in occupation of the Wells, and at 3.30 p. m. on the 18th the column continued its march to the Nile. After a terribly hard night, during which more than once the direction was lost and at one time the confusion amongst the baggage camels was terrible, a halt was called just before daybreak, and the guide, escorted by some hussars, went on to reconnoitre. The officer in charge of the party soon reported that he had seen Metammeh, and that the enemy were moving from it towards the column.

About 7 a.m. Sir Herbert Stewart, seeing that the force would have to fight its way to the river, some five miles distant, decided to breakfast the men, then close up the transport and march for the river bank, with the fighting men going between the transport and the town. A *zariba* was then commenced of boxes, camel saddles, sand etc., and during its construction the enemy's sharpshooters commenced firing with their Remingtons. A great number of camels, which were tied down in the centre, were shot. The attack grew hotter as the parapet in front of the men gradually rose, and a company of guardsmen were extended along a low ridge fifty yards in front of the *zariba* to endeavour to keep down the fire.

Inside the *zariba* men were falling fast, and at a little after 10 a.m. Sir Herbert Stewart was mortally wounded with a bullet in the groin, and Sir Charles Wilson took over the command.

The *zariba* and two small redoubts having at length reached a condition to resist an attack, it was decided to leave in it a garrison consisting of half of the Heavies, the 19th, Naval Brigade, guns, and baggage, and that the remainder should fight their way to the river.

A square was formed with the Guards and Mounted Infantry in front and on its flanks, and with the remaining half of the Heavies and Sussex in the rear. Some camels for wounded, water, etc. were in the centre, and small reserves of dismounted hussars and sappers were at the corners of the square.

The square was formed under a heavy fire, and as the men of each corps forming it came up, they lay down on the ground in proper position. At length, at about half-past two in the afternoon, the advance commenced, and under a continuous and heavy fire the square slowly moved forward. At an occasional halt, volleys were fired wherever the enemy's smoke appeared thickest, while the guns from the *zariba* shelled them when they could get a target. The march was a terrible one and the men were falling quickly. Matters were becoming extremely critical. To go on looked like fighting to the last man; to retreat meant being utterly destroyed.

Suddenly the Arabs began to collect in large bodies in front, and the long wished for moment had arrived. "Thank God! They're going to charge!" and on they came towards the left-hand corner of the square. As our men halted to receive the charge, they gave a wild cheer. "Cease fire" was ordered, and instantly obeyed, and then, with the enemy at 300 yards distance, "commence fire." The soldiers aimed low, and fired their volleys as steadily as on an Aldershot field day. The advancing host of savages seemed to melt away before the continuous roar of musketry. Not an Arab got within eighty yards of the square, and in a few minutes the front ranks were swept away, and the Arabs, brave as they were, wavered, scattered and bolted towards Metammeh. Three ringing cheers arose from the parched throats in the square, and the Battle of Abu Kru was won. No casualties occurred during the charge.

The work, however, was not yet over; the Nile must be reached before nightfall. After a short halt, the square moved on again, and eventually, half an hour after dark, the river was reached.

The wounded were first taken to drink. Perfect discipline was observed, and not a man left his place in the ranks until his company was marched up to take its fill. The front face having drunk its fill was marched back to relieve the rear face, and so on, in order that no flank should be left undefended in case of attack.

A *zariba* of bush was formed, sentries and pickets posted, and in a few minutes the exhausted force was asleep.

Twenty-one officers and men had been killed, and eighty-six wounded.

Before daybreak next morning the force stood to arms in expectation of an attack, which, however, was not delivered. A position was then selected at the deserted village of Abu Kru. It was soon placed in a condition of defence, and garrisoned by a hundred men of the Heavies, and in it were placed the wounded. Leaving a detachment of the Sussex Regiment to keep a watch on Metammeh, the remainder of the force marched back to the camel *zariba*, and brought up the troops and stores which had been left there.

The next morning the Heavies, the Guards, and the Mounted Infantry moved out to the attack of Metammeh, but the place was found too strong, and the force retired. During the advance, Gordon's promised steamers from Khartoum arrived and promptly landed a party of Egyptian soldiers and four guns, which soon came into action. With the steamers came a message from Gordon that Khartoum was all right, though woefully short of provisions.

On the evening of the 23rd a convoy was despatched to Gakdul to fetch provisions, and the next morning Sir Charles Wilson started in Gordon's steamers for Khartoum, taking with him twenty men of the Sussex Regiment and some 150 of Gordon's soldiers. Gordon in his messages had asked for a few red-coats to be sent, as their presence would do wonders in Khartoum; the Sussex men were accordingly rigged out in red serge jumpers.

On the 31st of January the convoy returned from Gakdul with stores and three guns, but with no fresh camels.

An officer with the force at Gubat (Abu Kru) thus describes the morning of the 1st February. Lieutenant Dawson writes in his journal:—

> No member of our small force as long as he lives will ever forget this morning. Just at dawn I was awoke by someone outside our hut calling for Boscawen. I jumped up and went out to see who it was, and then made out, to my surprise, Stuart-Wortley, whom we all thought at Khartoum. I looked towards the river, expecting in the faint light to see the steamers; then seeing nothing, and observing by his face that there was something wrong, I said, 'Why, good heavens, where are the steamers—what is the

news?' He said, 'The very worst.' Then it all came out.

Sir Charles Wilson and his steamers had got close to Khartoum, where they were received with a tremendous fire, and found the place in possession of the enemy. They returned with difficulty, and on going down the Shabluka cataract, his steamers were wrecked. The troops were landed on an island and entrenched themselves, whilst Stuart-Wortley was sent down river in a *nugger* for assistance. To continue quoting from Dawson's journal:

> The first necessity was of course to get Sir Charles Wilson off the island, and also to be ready at any moment for an overwhelming force coming down from Khartoum and cutting us off. The *Mahdi* was now free to move his whole force, numbers impossible to estimate, and besides was largely reinforced by guns and 15,000 stands of rifles.

Sir Charles Beresford and his blue jackets were sent up in a steamer to rescue Wilson, which, under great difficulties, they succeeded in doing; and another convoy, escorted by 300 Heavies, Guards, and Mounted Infantry, started off for Gakdul for stores and ammunition, and took with them some no sick and wounded. On the 6th of February Sir Charles Wilson left Abu Kru for Korti, with an escort of the Guards Camel Regiment, and on the 11th of February the convoy from Gakdul arrived, bringing with them six companies of the Royal Irish Regiment, and General Butler.

It was evident that for the small force at Abu Kru to attempt to take and hold Metammeh, or to hold on to its camp on the Nile bank, would be futile now that Khartoum had fallen, and the *Mahdi's* followers were swarming down. Butler therefore retired from Abu Kru to Abu Klea. The convoy of wounded was sent away previously, and near Abu Klea was attacked by a large force of the enemy, who, however, retired on the arrival of the Light Camel Regiment from Gakdul.

From Abu Klea Butler finally retired to Gakdul, where his force arrived on the 26th of February. Sir Herbert Stewart died of his wound on the 16th of February.

From Gakdul, the force marched to Korti, having lost during the expedition 30 officers and 450 men out of its strength of 2,000.

The River Column, under Major-General Brackenbury, returned to Korti on the 8th of March.

This then was the end of the double expedition which it was

hoped would meet to co-operate for the relief of Khartoum and the rescue of General Gordon, of whose death there was now little doubt on the part of the officers in command, although in England it was not till sometime afterwards that the hope was abandoned that he had escaped to the Equatorial provinces, or had found protection with some friendly tribe, or was even kept in durance by the *Mahdi* himself.

The rebels had entered Khartoum at daylight on the 26th of January, through the treachery of Farag Pasha, who opened the gates in the South wall. Nearly all the native stories agree that Gordon, on learning that he was betrayed, made a rush for the magazine in the Catholic mission building. Finding that the building was in possession of the enemy, Gordon returned to Government House and was killed while trying to re-enter it. Some say that he was shot; others that he was stabbed. Writing of the departure of the troops of the Desert Column from Korti down the Nile, the author of *With the Camel Corps up the Nile* (reprinted by Leonaur 2010) says:

> The first to move were the Heavies, who, after having been in turn Cavalry, Infantry, and Mounted Infantry, now made their debut as boatmen. With about seventeen men and their kits to one boat, they paddled off on the afternoon of the 11th of March. Eight boats took the whole lot, a sadly reduced remnant of the magnificent corps which had started across the Bayuda.

The corps had suffered greater losses than the other camel regiments. Out of a total of 20 officers and 390 men, only 8 officers and 210 men were returning. The Camel Corps returned slowly down the Nile, and eventually embarked at Alexandria on board the P. & O. s.s. *Australia*, and sailed for home on the 4th of July. On the 27th of May, during the journey down the Nile, Lieutenant Costello of the 5th Lancers died of enteric fever at Abu Fatmeh. The lists over the page are the losses of the Camel Corps during the campaign:

Upon arrival in England, the 5th Lancers detachment were present at the inspection of the Camel Corps by Her Majesty the Queen at Osborne.

For their services in the Soudan, the detachment received the Egyptian Medal and two clasps for "Nile 1884-85," and "Abu Klea."

Major A. G. Spencer and Lieutenant Ayrton were sent out to the Nile to take over the command of the 5th Lancers detachment, vice Carmichael and Costello.

HEAVY CAMEL REGIMENT.

	OFFICERS.			MEN			TOTAL LOSS	
	K.	W.	Died.	K.	W.	Died.	Officers	Men.
1st Life Guards	0	0	0	2	0	2	0	4
2nd ,, ,,	0	1	0	2	0	3	0	5
Royal Horse Guards	0	1	0	1	4	4	0	5
2nd Dragoon Guards	0	1	0	5	1	2	0	7
4th ,, ,,	2	0	0	7	5	1	2	8
5th ,, ,,	1	0	0	10	7	1	1	11
1st Dragoons	1	0	0	12	4	3	1	15
2nd ,,	1	0	0	11	5	4	1	15
5th Lancers	1	1	1	5	4	5	2	10
16th ,,	1	0	1	4	1	3	2	7
Total :	7.	4.	2	59.	31.	28	9.	87

GUARDS CAMEL REGIMENT.

	K.	W.	Died.
Officers	0.	3.	0
Men	26.	38.	23

MOUNTED INFANTRY CAMEL REGIMENT.

	K.	W.	Died.
Officers	0.	5.	1
Men	11.	67.	?

The following are the names of the Officers, Non-Commissioned Officers and Men of the 5th Lancers Detachment of the Camel Corps who fell during the Nile Campaign.

Killed.

Major L. M. Carmichael.
No 2344 Corporal C. Percival.
No 2333 Lance Corporal S. Parker
No 2085 Private C. Peters.
No 1897 " E. Bell.
No 2155 " J. McGrath.
No 2129 " A. Russell.

Died.

Lieutenant H. Costello.
No 2425 Private C. Rayman.
No 2445 " J. Harvey.
No 2240 " G. Watson.
No 2207 " E. Marks.

Meanwhile an expedition was being organised for Suakim, to oppose the gathering hordes of savage tribesmen who were being collected by Osman Digna against that place. In February 1885, the regiment was called upon to furnish two squadrons for service with the expedition, which was to be commanded by Lieut.-General Sir Gerald Graham V.C.

The squadrons were under the command of Lieut.-Colonel Chichester, and with him went the following officers,

Major A. B. Harvey.
Captain E. C. Gilborne.
Captain L. H. Jones.
Captain J. Sinclair.
Lieutenant B. Mundy.
Lieutenant W. H. Goodair.
Lieutenant J. H. Rennie,
Lieutenant M. McNeill.
Lieutenant M. B. Doyne.
Lieutenant J. Richardson.
and 249 Non-commissioned officers and men, and 200 horses.

The detachment sailed from Kingstown on board the S.S. *Lydian Monarch* on the 20th of February, and on the 24th the Headquarters of the regiment, under Lt.-Colonel Vandeleur, moved from Dublin to Dundalk.

Upon arrival at Suez, Lieut.-Colonel Chichester was ordered to Cairo, and Major Harvey took command of the service squadrons. The *Lydian Monarch* arrived at Suakim on the 13th of March, and disembarked the squadrons, with whom was Sir Gerald Graham.

On the night of the 11th-12th, a determined attack had been made on the British camp, and successfully driven off. Small parties of the enemy continued nightly to get into camp, and on one or two occasions they succeeded in getting into a tent and stabbing the men.

> The nearly naked Hadendowas, with bare feet and greased skins, as dusky as the night, crept and glided on their faces along every hollow and gully, carefully taking advantage of each bush that could screen their approach, and, if alarmed, lying perfectly still, after casting the sand with a rapid noiseless motion over their prostrate bodies, so that the keenest eye could hardly detect them from a stone. When they wished to make a sign to each other they imitated the cry of the desert birds with marvellous fidelity, and often has this low plaintive cry been the signal for their onslaught.

THE CAMEL CORPS FOR THE NILE OPERATION

Sometimes it was a volley followed by a rush with swords and spears, but more often a dark figure would seem to rise out of the very ground at the sentry's feet and stab him in the back; or if it was impossible to get sufficiently near to him unperceived, they would wait until he moved away on his beat, knowing well his exact position by the crunching of his heavy ammunition boots on the gravel, and, wriggling past like serpents, slip among the tents; then would follow the death scream, the rush of feet, and fierce volleys poured in rapid succession into the night after a few shadowy forms disappearing into the darkness, content at having achieved their work of murder and mutilation.

This would be the signal for a general alarm along the whole line; the Arabs further out in the desert would open fire with their Remingtons, bullets would come whizzing into the camp in all directions, and the force be kept on the alert until the long hours of the night passed away and the sun rose on another day of incessant work at the wharves and trenches for men who had enjoyed no sleep.

And in addition to these trials there were the sandstorm, the great heat and the flies to endure.

On the 16th, the laying of the Suakim-Berber Railway was commenced.

On the 19th of March the Cavalry Brigade made a reconnaissance to Hasheen. Early in the morning the brigade, consisting of the 5th Lancers, 20th Hussars, 9th Bengal Cavalry (a sword regiment, had been armed with lances before leaving India), R.H.A., and Mounted Infantry, was turned out. The English Cavalry were thrown forward, and gradually spread themselves over the plain like a huge fan, while the Indian cavalry, guns, and Mounted Infantry followed in support. An eye-witness writes:

> I do not think I ever witnessed a more imposing spectacle than was presented by the beautiful working of this cavalry force, as they gradually felt their way across the plain towards the mountains in the direction of Hasheen.

The village, however, was practically deserted, and the force returned to camp by one o'clock. Some prisoners were taken, and the British loss was one man killed, and an officer and a man wounded. Before retiring, a letter addressed to Osman Digna was left stuck on a cleft stick near the village. It was a reply to a boastful letter sent by him to our camp a fortnight before, in which he referred to the power and success of the *Mahdi*, and exhorted our generals to submit and become Mahommedans. In reply he was reminded of the inability of the *Mahdi's* troops to withstand the British, and he in turn was exhorted to surrender. This letter was next day found trampled in the dirt.

The advance from Suakim to Hasheen was ordered for the next day, much to the delight of the camp. The men, weary with daily toil, sick of remaining within the limited space of the camp, and under extremely unhealthy conditions, and harassed by night attacks and alarms, were only too glad at the prospect of an active engagement with the enemy. At 5.30 a.m. the whole force moved out, with the exception of the 53rd (Shropshire) which regiment remained behind to guard the camp.

The formation was an open square. The front face was composed of the battalions of the 2nd Brigade under Sir John McNeill, the 49th, 70th, and Royal Marines. On the right face were the Guards Brigade, under General Freemantle; and the left face was formed by the Indian Brigade, consisting of the 15th Sikhs and 17th and 28th Bombay Native Infantry under General Hudson. Inside the square were the artillery, a small battery of six Gardner guns, the ambulance and the transport. The cavalry, consisting of two squadrons of 5th Lancers, two of 20th Hussars, and four of 9th B.C. and the greater part of the Mounted Infantry, were opened out in advance of the square, and scouting every yard of ground.

At 8.30 a.m. the square had reached the first ridge of hills, the enemy retiring before the advance. The 70th (East Surrey) Regiment set to work to construct four sand-bag redoubts, with *zariba*s on the summits, on the left of the line of advance. About 9 a.m. the 49th (Berkshire) Regiment reached the foot of Dihilbat Hill, which rose sheer above them like a wall, the enemy clustering on its summit. Supported by the Marines, the men of the Berkshires, without firing a shot, swarmed up the side of the mountain in attack formation, and under a heavy fire from the enemy. On reaching a ledge halfway up, they opened fire. The enemy returned the fire for a few minutes, until the Marines, advancing to enfilade them, they wavered and ran; whereupon the Berkshire men crossed a ravine in front of their spur, and rushing on, gained the summit.

The Indian infantry deployed and advanced upon the village of Hasheen, the Guards' Brigade, formed in square, covering their rear; while the Mounted Infantry acted on the extreme right; and the artil-

The Royal Marines

lery came into action. Meanwhile a large body of the enemy, driven from the hills on the left by the advance of the Berkshires and Marines, descended into the plain on the other side, and a squadron of the Bengal Cavalry were sent to intercept them. The enemy, however, charged the 9th B.C. who were obliged to fall back, losing four of their men, whose horses were hamstrung by the enemy. When the collision came, the Arabs threw themselves on the ground, slashing at the horses' legs with their swords; and, with surprising agility, they sped over the ground after the retreating horsemen.

The Indian Infantry, formed in two sides of a square, had now reached Hasheen, with the Guards in complete square covering their rear. A party of the enemy of about a hundred and fifty strong suddenly appeared from behind a hill within three hundred yards of the Guards, and actually charged the brigade, but were met with such a withering fire from the square, that they turned and fled.

On the extreme right rear of the British force the 5th Lancers now got their opportunity. A number of the enemy tried to break through in the direction of the redoubts which the 70th were constructing, and Major Harvey charged the Arabs on the flank, going right through them, and then, wheeling about, riding them down a second time. The Arabs practised their usual tactics, and lay flat on the ground when they saw the lancers approaching, doing their best to hamstring the horses as they passed. But on this occasion, they had the Queen of weapons to reckon with, and the lance put an end to many a *Mahdist* before he could put his plan into execution.

The leader of this dashing charge was himself wounded by one of the lances of the Bengal Cavalry, with which an Arab had armed himself. Kneeling on the ground, the fellow kept himself in front of Harvey, who was somewhat perplexed to know what he was going to do, so he went straight at him with his drawn sword. The Arab suddenly jumped on one side, and as Harvey passed him, endeavoured to run him through with the lance. So quick was the Arab, that the sword was too late to parry the point, and the spear was lodged deeply in the rider's thigh, so deeply indeed, as to wrench it from the Arab's grasp.

With the bridle in one hand and his sword in the other, there was no possibility of Harvey withdrawing the lance, which caught in a bush and nearly unhorsed the gallant major. Another officer of the Fifth laid four of the enemy low before he emptied his revolver, and such execution did the lancers do, that only seven of the enemy made their escape. The casualties amongst the Fifth were. Troop Sergeant-

Major Nicholls and four men killed. Major Harvey and seven men wounded.

While this charge was being made, the artillery opened fire upon two large bodies of the enemy. One of these, about 2,000 strong, was retreating in front. The other, quite double that strength, which had come from Tamai, was on the British left rear. About 1 p.m., the second, and the Indian brigades were ordered to fall back upon the Guards, and at 2 p.m. the whole force began their march back to the hill occupied by the 70th Regiment. The Indians led, followed by the 46th and Marines, while the Guards' brigade, still in square, with the artillery, transport etc. in the centre, brought up the rear. The Guards were under a heavy fire, and halted every two hundred yards or so to fire volleys into the scrub.

The ridge where the 70th had now completed the redoubts and *zariba*, was reached at 3 p.m. and a halt was called. Leaving the 70th with two guns and four Gardners, and five days provisions and water, to hold the redoubts and *zariba*, the remainder of the force set off on their return march to Suakim, reaching camp about seven in the evening. The action of Hasheen cost the British force some 22 officers and men killed and 43 wounded. The enemy must have lost very heavily. On the 25th March, the 70th were withdrawn to Suakim, and the *zariba* and redoubts they had built destroyed. Major Harvey was soon after invalided home, and Captain Gilborne assumed command of the two squadrons.

It was now determined to march on Tamai without further delay, and as the distance from Suakim was too great for troops to make the journey and return to Suakim in one day, it was decided to establish two *zariba*s on the line of advance, one four miles, and the other eight miles from Suakim. At 7 a. m. on Sunday the 22nd of March, the advance on Tamai began. One squadron of 5th Lancers scouted in front, followed by the British square consisting of 30 of the Naval Brigade with four Gardner guns, a detachment of Royal Engineers with Field Telegraph, the telegraph uncoiling its wire as they went, a battalion of the Berkshire Regiment, and another of the Royal Marine Light Infantry.

The second square followed on the right rear, and consisted of the Indian infantry brigade. In its centre was a vast and unwieldy column of transport, consisting of 580 camels with 11,500 gallons of water, 500 camels with supplies, and about 400 pack-mules, draft-horses, and baggage camels with commissariat, water tanks, ammunition, and am-

Charge of the 5th Lancers

bulance: a total of 1,500 baggage animals. The force was under command of Sir John McNeill, with General Hudson in charge of Indian contingent.

It was terrible work getting the vast convoy of animals along in the midst of the thorn bushes, and it soon became evident that the original plan of forming a *zariba* eight miles out could not be carried out in time for the Indian brigade to return. As the force advanced, the Lancers began to report that parties of the enemy were hovering about. Sir John McNeill therefore determined to halt at six miles and there to form one *zariba*.

At 10.30 a.m. the force emerged on a fairly open space of sandy and gravelly ground, some 300 to 400 yards across, dotted with thorn bushes and surrounded by thick bush and scrub, from which material was cut to form a *zariba*, consisting, as usual, of a hedge about four feet high, with a two foot ditch behind. It was a triple *zariba*, three enclosures of diamond shape standing corner to corner. That nearest Suakim was for the Royal Marines and half the Naval Brigade; the centre one was for the camels; and that nearer Tamai for the Berkshires, two Gardner guns, and the other half of the sailors.

The work of building the *zariba* began. Infantry pickets were thrown out 150 yards to the front. A quarter of a mile or so further, in front of these pickets, the squadron of 5th Lancers, under Captain L. H. Jones, covered some three miles of frontage, with Cossack posts and a support nearer the *zariba*. Every precaution was adopted which the small numbers at his disposal would admit of. In proportion to the ground to be covered, it must be admitted that the exterior line was very weak. Owing to the scarcity of mounted men, it is evident that it was impossible to extend the radius of observation, as by so doing the distances between the posts would have been increased; while to patrol the bush, or to scout two or three miles from the main force was practically impossible to such a handful of troopers.

About 2.30 p.m. when the *zariba* was nearing completion, a lancer rode in and reported to Sir John McNeill that the enemy was gathering in front and advancing rapidly, and was almost immediately followed by another lancer, with similar intelligence. Orders were at once given for the working and covering parties to be called in, and while these instructions were being carried into effect, the Cavalry and Infantry pickets were to be seen coming in on every side, with the Arabs close on their heels.

The Arabs were now surging onwards, chiefly South and West, in

GORDON HIGHLANDERS AT TAMAI

one vast impetuous mass, enveloped in clouds of dust, filling the air with a pandemonium of shouts and yells, and making frantic efforts to storm the position. The infantry faced the fierce rush with undaunted bravery, one battalion of natives only quailing before the shock, and these had been thrown into partial disorder by the stampede of the transport animals.

The Arabs now crowded in by the uncompleted salient, killing some of the sailors who were gallantly defending their charge. The rear-rank of the Berkshire half-battalion, then engaged in defending the western face of the redoubt, were now ordered to face about and occupy the vacated position through which the Arabs were pouring. This they at once did, and meeting the enemy half-way, quickly despatched every Arab who had entered, one hundred and twelve dead bodies being afterwards counted as having fallen within the limits of this redoubt alone.

The first wild rush of the enemy checked, the position was safe, and the Arabs were being repelled at every point. No sound could now be heard save that of the steady and sustained roar of musketry. With unflinching firmness, the British and Indian troops settled to their work, and volley after volley was repeated, with all the rapidity and precision of clockwork. The fire was too terrible to be withstood, and the enemy fell back and disappeared among the bushes. The whole affair lasted but twenty minutes.

Colonel Way, an eye-witness, thus describes the battle:

> Everything seemed to come at once, camels, transport of all kinds, including water carts, ammunition, mules, native infantry, Madras sappers, sick bearers, transport corps, Cavalry, and Arabs fighting in the midst. All these passed close by me and went out at the other side of the *zariba*.... The dust raised by this crowd was so great that I could not see anything beyond our *zariba* for a minute or two, and it was impossible to see who was standing or what was likely to happen. The men behaved splendidly, and stood quite still. It was about the highest test of discipline I shall ever see, as in my opinion nothing could beat it.

At the moment of the Arab onslaught, the camels and transport were being marshalled outside the *zariba* preparatory to returning to Suakim, and had stampeded.

About 3.30 p.m. a large force of the enemy appeared to the southeast of the *zariba*s, but these were dispersed by a counterattack delivered by the Marines, led by Sir John McNeill in person.

A squadron of the 20th Hussars and another of the 9th B. C. patrolling from Suakim, reached the *zariba* about 4 p.m. On the way they had had a skirmish with the enemy, and on being joined by Lieutenant Goodair's troop of 5th Lancers, had pursued the Arabs, and prevented an attempt of the enemy to creep round by the sea-coast and turn their flank, and were able to push the Arabs back towards the *zariba*, where, being enfiladed by the fire of our men, they dispersed towards the sea.

The *zariba* was now completed and strengthened, and every preparation made for the possibility of a night attack.

When darkness came on the men were ranged all round the defences two deep, as if on parade. One rank lay down and slept, while the other, with bayonets fixed, kept two hours watch, fully armed and ready. Absolute silence reigned, a profound but watchful silence, not a light was shown, and nothing was permitted that might attract attention.

A sufficient garrison was left to defend the *zariba*, and the squadron of the 5th Lancers returned to Suakim with the remainder of the force.

In a telegraphic despatch on the battle dated Suakim, March 23rd, 1885, Lt.-General Graham stated:

> The cavalry, 5th Lancers, did their best to give information, but the ground being covered with bush, it was impossible to see any distance."

The British Losses were:—

	K.	W.	M.
Officers	4	8	1
N. O. C. & Men	66	125	35
Followers	14	18	122

A large number of camels and other transport animals were killed.

The casualties in the 5th Lancers squadron were Lieut. Richardson and 4 N.C.O. and men missing (killed); and 1 man killed.

Early in the day during the advance from Suakim, Lieutenant Richardson of the 5th Lancers, with four of his men, had been sent on an officer's patrol to the left of the line of advance. His horse getting knocked up after being out some hours, Richardson rode into Suakim about midday, and, on a fresh horse, returned to his patrol duties. Neither he nor his men were ever heard of again.

They were no doubt cut off and slain by the Arabs during the course of the afternoon. Richardson's silver whistle was found some time afterwards at a spot in the bush, some six miles from Suakim and a couple of miles south of the *zariba*. The whistle was distinctly marked with a spear thrust, and encrusted with blood; and it is only too evident that the patrol had been caught in the great Arab wave sweeping down from Tamai on the British force, and killed to a man. The only other traces found of the patrol were at the capture of Tamai, on the 3rd of April, when a lancer's scabbard and saddle were discovered.

The next few days the regiment was employed on convoy duty, and on the 2nd of April was part of the force which marched for Tamai, where, on the next day, the enemy made some slight opposition. The British losses amounted to 1 man killed; and 1 officer, 14 men and 1 follower wounded. Tamai was destroyed, and on the 4th the force returned to Suakim.

The Australian contingent—which arrived at Suakim on the 29th of March—took part in this advance. There is no need to follow the campaign further. The regiment was employed on convoy duty, patrolling etc. with some small fighting, until by the 16th of May the campaign was at an end and the "construction of the railway to any considerable distance, postponed."

On the 20th of May the 5th Lancer squadrons embarked at Suakim on board the S,S, *Lydian Monarch* for home. At Suez Captain Sinclair's squadron, with Lieutenants Rennie and McNeill, was landed to take over the horses of the 20th Hussars, for the purpose of bringing them to England.

The first squadron disembarked at Portsmouth on the 12th of June, and joined Regimental Headquarters now quartered at Brighton.

The second squadron, after staying at Suez a fortnight, was railed with the 20th Hussars to Alexandria, where they embarked on board the S.S. *Oregon*, and landed at Portsmouth on the 27th of June. They went to Aldershot, where the 20th Hussars horses were handed over to various regiments, and then rejoined Head Quarters at Brighton.

In recognition of their services during the campaign. Major Harvey was promoted to Brevet Lieutenant-Colonel, and Captains Gilborne and Little, (the latter had been employed on the staff) each received a Brevet Majority; and in addition to these officers, Captain Jones was mentioned in despatches. For their services the two squadrons received the Egyptian Medal with clasps for "Suakim 1885" and "Tofrek."

The following Officers, N.C.O. and men fell in the campaign.

Killed.

Lieut. J. Richardson.
No. 1486 Troop Sergeant Major C. Nicholls.
" 2294 Corporal G. Pell.
" 2388 Lance Corporal J. Blood.
" 2621 Private J. Edwards.
" 1993 " J. Rose.
" 1999 " J. Shaughnessy.
" 2366 " J. Wilson.
" 1770 " J. Howard.

Died.

" 1500 Sergeant C. Yorke.
" 2079 Private F. Turner.
" 2629 " M. Ryan.

In 1886, the Past and Present Regiment erected a memorial in St Martin's Church, Brighton, to the memory of the officers, non-commissioned officers, and men of the regiment who fell in the Nile and Suakim Expeditions.

Lieut.-Col. Vandeleur had resigned the command of the regiment on the 25th of May and was succeded by Lieut.-Colonel Ward Bennitt, who was promoted from the 6th Inniskilling Dragoons on the 29th of July, Lt.-Col. Harvey having in the meantime been temporarily in command.

ALSO FROM LEONAUR
AVAILABLE IN SOFTCOVER OR HARDCOVER WITH DUST JACKET

THE FALL OF THE MOGHUL EMPIRE OF HINDUSTAN by H. G. Keene—By the beginning of the nineteenth century, as British and Indian armies under Lake and Wellesley dominated the scene, a little over half a century of conflict brought the Moghul Empire to its knees.

LADY SALE'S AFGHANISTAN by Florentia Sale—An Indomitable Victorian Lady's Account of the Retreat from Kabul During the First Afghan War.

THE CAMPAIGN OF MAGENTA AND SOLFERINO 1859 by Harold Carmichael Wylly—The Decisive Conflict for the Unification of Italy.

FRENCH'S CAVALRY CAMPAIGN by J. G. Maydon—A Special Correspondent's View of British Army Mounted Troops During the Boer War.

CAVALRY AT WATERLOO by Sir Evelyn Wood—British Mounted Troops During the Campaign of 1815.

THE SUBALTERN by George Robert Gleig—The Experiences of an Officer of the 85th Light Infantry During the Peninsular War.

NAPOLEON AT BAY, 1814 by F. Loraine Petre—The Campaigns to the Fall of the First Empire.

NAPOLEON AND THE CAMPAIGN OF 1806 by Colonel Vachée—The Napoleonic Method of Organisation and Command to the Battles of Jena & Auerstädt.

THE COMPLETE ADVENTURES IN THE CONNAUGHT RANGERS by William Grattan—The 88th Regiment during the Napoleonic Wars by a Serving Officer.

BUGLER AND OFFICER OF THE RIFLES by William Green & Harry Smith—With the 95th (Rifles) during the Peninsular & Waterloo Campaigns of the Napoleonic Wars.

NAPOLEONIC WAR STORIES by Sir Arthur Quiller-Couch—Tales of soldiers, spies, battles & sieges from the Peninsular & Waterloo campaingns.

CAPTAIN OF THE 95TH (RIFLES) by Jonathan Leach—An officer of Wellington's sharpshooters during the Peninsular, South of France and Waterloo campaigns of the Napoleonic wars.

RIFLEMAN COSTELLO by Edward Costello—The adventures of a soldier of the 95th (Rifles) in the Peninsular & Waterloo Campaigns of the Napoleonic wars.

AVAILABLE ONLINE AT www.leonaur.com
AND FROM ALL GOOD BOOK STORES

ALSO FROM LEONAUR
AVAILABLE IN SOFTCOVER OR HARDCOVER WITH DUST JACKET

AFGHANISTAN: THE BELEAGUERED BRIGADE *by G. R. Gleig*—An Account of Sale's Brigade During the First Afghan War.

IN THE RANKS OF THE C. I. V *by Erskine Childers*—With the City Imperial Volunteer Battery (Honourable Artillery Company) in the Second Boer War.

THE BENGAL NATIVE ARMY *by F. G. Cardew*—An Invaluable Reference Resource.

THE 7TH (QUEEN'S OWN) HUSSARS: Volume 4—1688-1914 *by C. R. B. Barrett*—Uniforms, Equipment, Weapons, Traditions, the Services of Notable Officers and Men & the Appendices to All Volumes—Volume 4: 1688-1914.

THE SWORD OF THE CROWN *by Eric W. Sheppard*—A History of the British Army to 1914.

THE 7TH (QUEEN'S OWN) HUSSARS: Volume 3—1818-1914 *by C. R. B. Barrett*—On Campaign During the Canadian Rebellion, the Indian Mutiny, the Sudan, Matabeleland, Mashonaland and the Boer War Volume 3: 1818-1914.

THE KHARTOUM CAMPAIGN *by Bennet Burleigh*—A Special Correspondent's View of the Reconquest of the Sudan by British and Egyptian Forces under Kitchener—1898.

EL PUCHERO *by Richard McSherry*—The Letters of a Surgeon of Volunteers During Scott's Campaign of the American-Mexican War 1847-1848.

RIFLEMAN SAHIB *by E. Maude*—The Recollections of an Officer of the Bombay Rifles During the Southern Mahratta Campaign, Second Sikh War, Persian Campaign and Indian Mutiny.

THE KING'S HUSSAR *by Edwin Mole*—The Recollections of a 14th (King's) Hussar During the Victorian Era.

JOHN COMPANY'S CAVALRYMAN *by William Johnson*—The Experiences of a British Soldier in the Crimea, the Persian Campaign and the Indian Mutiny.

COLENSO & DURNFORD'S ZULU WAR *by Frances E. Colenso & Edward Durnford*—The first and possibly the most important history of the Zulu War.

U. S. DRAGOON *by Samuel E. Chamberlain*—Experiences in the Mexican War 1846-48 and on the South Western Frontier.

AVAILABLE ONLINE AT **www.leonaur.com**
AND FROM ALL GOOD BOOK STORES

Printed in Australia
AUHW020850200922
369222AU00002B/17